THIS IS YOUR **PASSBOOK**® FOR ...

COMPUTER SPECIALIST (SOFTWARE)

NATIONAL LEARNING CORPORATION®
passbooks.com

PASSBOOK® SERIES

THE *PASSBOOK® SERIES* has been created to prepare applicants and candidates for the ultimate academic battlefield – the examination room.

At some time in our lives, each and every one of us may be required to take an examination – for validation, matriculation, admission, qualification, registration, certification, or licensure.

Based on the assumption that every applicant or candidate has met the basic formal educational standards, has taken the required number of courses, and read the necessary texts, the *PASSBOOK® SERIES* furnishes the one special preparation which may assure passing with confidence, instead of failing with insecurity. Examination questions – together with answers – are furnished as the basic vehicle for study so that the mysteries of the examination and its compounding difficulties may be eliminated or diminished by a sure method.

This book is meant to help you pass your examination provided that you qualify and are serious in your objective.

The entire field is reviewed through the huge store of content information which is succinctly presented through a provocative and challenging approach – the question-and-answer method.

A climate of success is established by furnishing the correct answers at the end of each test.

You soon learn to recognize types of questions, forms of questions, and patterns of questioning. You may even begin to anticipate expected outcomes.

You perceive that many questions are repeated or adapted so that you can gain acute insights, which may enable you to score many sure points.

You learn how to confront new questions, or types of questions, and to attack them confidently and work out the correct answers.

You note objectives and emphases, and recognize pitfalls and dangers, so that you may make positive educational adjustments.

Moreover, you are kept fully informed in relation to new concepts, methods, practices, and directions in the field.

You discover that you arre actually taking the examination all the time: you are preparing for the examination by "taking" an examination, not by reading extraneous and/or supererogatory textbooks.

In short, this PASSBOOK®, used directedly, should be an important factor in helping you to pass your test.

COMPUTER SPECIALIST (SOFTWARE)

DUTIES

Computer Specialists (Software), under supervision, with considerable latitude for independent action or the exercise of independent judgment, are responsible for the analysis, design, development, implementation, enhancement, maintenance and security of database management systems, operating systems, data communications systems, applications, mobile applications, websites, and/or related software functions; may supervise a unit engaged in work related to these areas or may independently perform related work of a highly complex, technical nature. All Computer Specialists (Software) perform related work.

SCOPE OF THE EXAMINATION

The multiple-choice test is designed to assess the extent to which candidates have certain knowledge and abilities determined to be important to the performance of the tasks of a Computer Specialist (Software). Task areas to be tested are as follows: database management systems, operating systems and user roles, data communication systems, system applications, mobile applications, web based environments, and project leader capacity.

The test may include questions on: knowledge of software principles including applications and operating systems; knowledge of the systems development life cycle (SDLC) including flow creation, data mapping, system analysis, database structures and data entities; knowledge of coding principles; knowledge of diagnosing software issues (e.g., system abends, debugging, missing files, etc.); standards of proper employee ethical conduct; and other related areas. The test may also include questions requiring the use of any of the following abilities: written expression, problem sensitivity, number facility, deductive reasoning, critical thinking, and principles and techniques of project leadership.

HOW TO TAKE A TEST

I. YOU MUST PASS AN EXAMINATION

A. WHAT EVERY CANDIDATE SHOULD KNOW

Examination applicants often ask us for help in preparing for the written test. What can I study in advance? What kinds of questions will be asked? How will the test be given? How will the papers be graded?

As an applicant for a civil service examination, you may be wondering about some of these things. Our purpose here is to suggest effective methods of advance study and to describe civil service examinations.

Your chances for success on this examination can be increased if you know how to prepare. Those "pre-examination jitters" can be reduced if you know what to expect. You can even experience an adventure in good citizenship if you know why civil service exams are given.

B. WHY ARE CIVIL SERVICE EXAMINATIONS GIVEN?

Civil service examinations are important to you in two ways. As a citizen, you want public jobs filled by employees who know how to do their work. As a job seeker, you want a fair chance to compete for that job on an equal footing with other candidates. The best-known means of accomplishing this two-fold goal is the competitive examination.

Exams are widely publicized throughout the nation. They may be administered for jobs in federal, state, city, municipal, town or village governments or agencies.

Any citizen may apply, with some limitations, such as the age or residence of applicants. Your experience and education may be reviewed to see whether you meet the requirements for the particular examination. When these requirements exist, they are reasonable and applied consistently to all applicants. Thus, a competitive examination may cause you some uneasiness now, but it is your privilege and safeguard.

C. HOW ARE CIVIL SERVICE EXAMS DEVELOPED?

Examinations are carefully written by trained technicians who are specialists in the field known as "psychological measurement," in consultation with recognized authorities in the field of work that the test will cover. These experts recommend the subject matter areas or skills to be tested; only those knowledges or skills important to your success on the job are included. The most reliable books and source materials available are used as references. Together, the experts and technicians judge the difficulty level of the questions.

Test technicians know how to phrase questions so that the problem is clearly stated. Their ethics do not permit "trick" or "catch" questions. Questions may have been tried out on sample groups, or subjected to statistical analysis, to determine their usefulness.

Written tests are often used in combination with performance tests, ratings of training and experience, and oral interviews. All of these measures combine to form the best-known means of finding the right person for the right job.

II. HOW TO PASS THE WRITTEN TEST

A. *NATURE OF THE EXAMINATION*

To prepare intelligently for civil service examinations, you should know how they differ from school examinations you have taken. In school you were assigned certain definite pages to read or subjects to cover. The examination questions were quite detailed and usually emphasized memory. Civil service exams, on the other hand, try to discover your present ability to perform the duties of a position, plus your potentiality to learn these duties. In other words, a civil service exam attempts to predict how successful you will be. Questions cover such a broad area that they cannot be as minute and detailed as school exam questions.

In the public service similar kinds of work, or positions, are grouped together in one "class." This process is known as *position-classification*. All the positions in a class are paid according to the salary range for that class. One class title covers all of these positions, and they are all tested by the same examination.

B. *FOUR BASIC STEPS*

1) Study the announcement

How, then, can you know what subjects to study? Our best answer is: "Learn as much as possible about the class of positions for which you've applied." The exam will test the knowledge, skills and abilities needed to do the work.

Your most valuable source of information about the position you want is the official exam announcement. This announcement lists the training and experience qualifications. Check these standards and apply only if you come reasonably close to meeting them.

The brief description of the position in the examination announcement offers some clues to the subjects which will be tested. Think about the job itself. Review the duties in your mind. Can you perform them, or are there some in which you are rusty? Fill in the blank spots in your preparation.

Many jurisdictions preview the written test in the exam announcement by including a section called "Knowledge and Abilities Required," "Scope of the Examination," or some similar heading. Here you will find out specifically what fields will be tested.

2) Review your own background

Once you learn in general what the position is all about, and what you need to know to do the work, ask yourself which subjects you already know fairly well and which need improvement. You may wonder whether to concentrate on improving your strong areas or on building some background in your fields of weakness. When the announcement has specified "some knowledge" or "considerable knowledge," or has used adjectives like "beginning principles of…" or "advanced … methods," you can get a clue as to the number and difficulty of questions to be asked in any given field. More questions, and hence broader coverage, would be included for those subjects which are more important in the work. Now weigh your strengths and weaknesses against the job requirements and prepare accordingly.

3) Determine the level of the position

Another way to tell how intensively you should prepare is to understand the level of the job for which you are applying. Is it the entering level? In other words, is this the position in which beginners in a field of work are hired? Or is it an intermediate or advanced level? Sometimes this is indicated by such words as "Junior" or "Senior" in the class title. Other jurisdictions use Roman numerals to designate the level – Clerk I, Clerk II, for example. The word "Supervisor" sometimes appears in the title. If the level is not indicated by the title, check the description of duties. Will you be working under very close supervision, or will you have responsibility for independent decisions in this work?

4) Choose appropriate study materials

Now that you know the subjects to be examined and the relative amount of each subject to be covered, you can choose suitable study materials. For beginning level jobs, or even advanced ones, if you have a pronounced weakness in some aspect of your training, read a modern, standard textbook in that field. Be sure it is up to date and has general coverage. Such books are normally available at your library, and the librarian will be glad to help you locate one. For entry-level positions, questions of appropriate difficulty are chosen – neither highly advanced questions, nor those too simple. Such questions require careful thought but not advanced training.

If the position for which you are applying is technical or advanced, you will read more advanced, specialized material. If you are already familiar with the basic principles of your field, elementary textbooks would waste your time. Concentrate on advanced textbooks and technical periodicals. Think through the concepts and review difficult problems in your field.

These are all general sources. You can get more ideas on your own initiative, following these leads. For example, training manuals and publications of the government agency which employs workers in your field can be useful, particularly for technical and professional positions. A letter or visit to the government department involved may result in more specific study suggestions, and certainly will provide you with a more definite idea of the exact nature of the position you are seeking.

III. KINDS OF TESTS

Tests are used for purposes other than measuring knowledge and ability to perform specified duties. For some positions, it is equally important to test ability to make adjustments to new situations or to profit from training. In others, basic mental abilities not dependent on information are essential. Questions which test these things may not appear as pertinent to the duties of the position as those which test for knowledge and information. Yet they are often highly important parts of a fair examination. For very general questions, it is almost impossible to help you direct your study efforts. What we can do is to point out some of the more common of these general abilities needed in public service positions and describe some typical questions.

1) General information

Broad, general information has been found useful for predicting job success in some kinds of work. This is tested in a variety of ways, from vocabulary lists to questions about current events. Basic background in some field of work, such as sociology or economics, may be sampled in a group of questions. Often these are principles which have become familiar to most persons through exposure rather than through formal training. It is difficult to advise you how to study for these questions; being alert to the world around you is our best suggestion.

2) Verbal ability

An example of an ability needed in many positions is verbal or language ability. Verbal ability is, in brief, the ability to use and understand words. Vocabulary and grammar tests are typical measures of this ability. Reading comprehension or paragraph interpretation questions are common in many kinds of civil service tests. You are given a paragraph of written material and asked to find its central meaning.

3) Numerical ability

Number skills can be tested by the familiar arithmetic problem, by checking paired lists of numbers to see which are alike and which are different, or by interpreting charts and graphs. In the latter test, a graph may be printed in the test booklet which you are asked to use as the basis for answering questions.

4) Observation

A popular test for law-enforcement positions is the observation test. A picture is shown to you for several minutes, then taken away. Questions about the picture test your ability to observe both details and larger elements.

5) Following directions

In many positions in the public service, the employee must be able to carry out written instructions dependably and accurately. You may be given a chart with several columns, each column listing a variety of information. The questions require you to carry out directions involving the information given in the chart.

6) Skills and aptitudes

Performance tests effectively measure some manual skills and aptitudes. When the skill is one in which you are trained, such as typing or shorthand, you can practice. These tests are often very much like those given in business school or high school courses. For many of the other skills and aptitudes, however, no short-time preparation can be made. Skills and abilities natural to you or that you have developed throughout your lifetime are being tested.

Many of the general questions just described provide all the data needed to answer the questions and ask you to use your reasoning ability to find the answers. Your best preparation for these tests, as well as for tests of facts and ideas, is to be at your physical and mental best. You, no doubt, have your own methods of getting into an exam-taking mood and keeping "in shape." The next section lists some ideas on this subject.

IV. KINDS OF QUESTIONS

Only rarely is the "essay" question, which you answer in narrative form, used in civil service tests. Civil service tests are usually of the short-answer type. Full instructions for answering these questions will be given to you at the examination. But in case this is your first experience with short-answer questions and separate answer sheets, here is what you need to know:

1) Multiple-choice Questions

Most popular of the short-answer questions is the "multiple choice" or "best answer" question. It can be used, for example, to test for factual knowledge, ability to solve problems or judgment in meeting situations found at work.

A multiple-choice question is normally one of three types—

- It can begin with an incomplete statement followed by several possible endings. You are to find the one ending which *best* completes the statement, although some of the others may not be entirely wrong.
- It can also be a complete statement in the form of a question which is answered by choosing one of the statements listed.
- It can be in the form of a problem – again you select the best answer.

Here is an example of a multiple-choice question with a discussion which should give you some clues as to the method for choosing the right answer:

When an employee has a complaint about his assignment, the action which will *best* help him overcome his difficulty is to
- A. discuss his difficulty with his coworkers
- B. take the problem to the head of the organization
- C. take the problem to the person who gave him the assignment
- D. say nothing to anyone about his complaint

In answering this question, you should study each of the choices to find which is best. Consider choice "A" – Certainly an employee may discuss his complaint with fellow employees, but no change or improvement can result, and the complaint remains unresolved. Choice "B" is a poor choice since the head of the organization probably does not know what assignment you have been given, and taking your problem to him is known as "going over the head" of the supervisor. The supervisor, or person who made the assignment, is the person who can clarify it or correct any injustice. Choice "C" is, therefore, correct. To say nothing, as in choice "D," is unwise. Supervisors have and interest in knowing the problems employees are facing, and the employee is seeking a solution to his problem.

2) True/False Questions

The "true/false" or "right/wrong" form of question is sometimes used. Here a complete statement is given. Your job is to decide whether the statement is right or wrong.

SAMPLE: A roaming cell-phone call to a nearby city costs less than a non-roaming call to a distant city.

This statement is wrong, or false, since roaming calls are more expensive.

This is not a complete list of all possible question forms, although most of the others are variations of these common types. You will always get complete directions for answering questions. Be sure you understand *how* to mark your answers – ask questions until you do.

V. RECORDING YOUR ANSWERS

Computer terminals are used more and more today for many different kinds of exams.

For an examination with very few applicants, you may be told to record your answers in the test booklet itself. Separate answer sheets are much more common. If this separate answer sheet is to be scored by machine – and this is often the case – it is highly important that you mark your answers correctly in order to get credit.

An electronic scoring machine is often used in civil service offices because of the speed with which papers can be scored. Machine-scored answer sheets must be marked with a pencil, which will be given to you. This pencil has a high graphite content which responds to the electronic scoring machine. As a matter of fact, stray dots may register as answers, so do not let your pencil rest on the answer sheet while you are pondering the correct answer. Also, if your pencil lead breaks or is otherwise defective, ask for another.

Since the answer sheet will be dropped in a slot in the scoring machine, be careful not to bend the corners or get the paper crumpled.

The answer sheet normally has five vertical columns of numbers, with 30 numbers to a column. These numbers correspond to the question numbers in your test booklet. After each number, going across the page are four or five pairs of dotted lines. These short dotted lines have small letters or numbers above them. The first two pairs may also have a "T" or "F" above the letters. This indicates that the first two pairs only are to be used if the questions are of the true-false type. If the questions are multiple choice, disregard the "T" and "F" and pay attention only to the small letters or numbers.

Answer your questions in the manner of the sample that follows:

32. The largest city in the United States is
    A. Washington, D.C.
    B. New York City
    C. Chicago
    D. Detroit
    E. San Francisco

1) Choose the answer you think is best. (New York City is the largest, so "B" is correct.)
2) Find the row of dotted lines numbered the same as the question you are answering. (Find row number 32)
3) Find the pair of dotted lines corresponding to the answer. (Find the pair of lines under the mark "B.")
4) Make a solid black mark between the dotted lines.

VI. BEFORE THE TEST

Common sense will help you find procedures to follow to get ready for an examination. Too many of us, however, overlook these sensible measures. Indeed, nervousness and fatigue have been found to be the most serious reasons why applicants fail to do their best on civil service tests. Here is a list of reminders:

- Begin your preparation early – Don't wait until the last minute to go scurrying around for books and materials or to find out what the position is all about.
- Prepare continuously – An hour a night for a week is better than an all-night cram session. This has been definitely established. What is more, a night a week for a month will return better dividends than crowding your study into a shorter period of time.
- Locate the place of the exam – You have been sent a notice telling you when and where to report for the examination. If the location is in a different town or otherwise unfamiliar to you, it would be well to inquire the best route and learn something about the building.
- Relax the night before the test – Allow your mind to rest. Do not study at all that night. Plan some mild recreation or diversion; then go to bed early and get a good night's sleep.
- Get up early enough to make a leisurely trip to the place for the test – This way unforeseen events, traffic snarls, unfamiliar buildings, etc. will not upset you.
- Dress comfortably – A written test is not a fashion show. You will be known by number and not by name, so wear something comfortable.
- Leave excess paraphernalia at home – Shopping bags and odd bundles will get in your way. You need bring only the items mentioned in the official notice you received; usually everything you need is provided. Do not bring reference books to the exam. They will only confuse those last minutes and be taken away from you when in the test room.
- Arrive somewhat ahead of time – If because of transportation schedules you must get there very early, bring a newspaper or magazine to take your mind off yourself while waiting.
- Locate the examination room – When you have found the proper room, you will be directed to the seat or part of the room where you will sit. Sometimes you are given a sheet of instructions to read while you are waiting. Do not fill out any forms until you are told to do so; just read them and be prepared.
- Relax and prepare to listen to the instructions
- If you have any physical problem that may keep you from doing your best, be sure to tell the test administrator. If you are sick or in poor health, you really cannot do your best on the exam. You can come back and take the test some other time.

VII. AT THE TEST

The day of the test is here and you have the test booklet in your hand. The temptation to get going is very strong. Caution! There is more to success than knowing the right answers. You must know how to identify your papers and understand variations in the type of short-answer question used in this particular examination. Follow these suggestions for maximum results from your efforts:

1) Cooperate with the monitor

The test administrator has a duty to create a situation in which you can be as much at ease as possible. He will give instructions, tell you when to begin, check to see that you are marking your answer sheet correctly, and so on. He is not there to guard you, although he will see that your competitors do not take unfair advantage. He wants to help you do your best.

2) Listen to all instructions

Don't jump the gun! Wait until you understand all directions. In most civil service tests you get more time than you need to answer the questions. So don't be in a hurry. Read each word of instructions until you clearly understand the meaning. Study the examples, listen to all announcements and follow directions. Ask questions if you do not understand what to do.

3) Identify your papers

Civil service exams are usually identified by number only. You will be assigned a number; you must not put your name on your test papers. Be sure to copy your number correctly. Since more than one exam may be given, copy your exact examination title.

4) Plan your time

Unless you are told that a test is a "speed" or "rate of work" test, speed itself is usually not important. Time enough to answer all the questions will be provided, but this does not mean that you have all day. An overall time limit has been set. Divide the total time (in minutes) by the number of questions to determine the approximate time you have for each question.

5) Do not linger over difficult questions

If you come across a difficult question, mark it with a paper clip (useful to have along) and come back to it when you have been through the booklet. One caution if you do this – be sure to skip a number on your answer sheet as well. Check often to be sure that you have not lost your place and that you are marking in the row numbered the same as the question you are answering.

6) Read the questions

Be sure you know what the question asks! Many capable people are unsuccessful because they failed to *read* the questions correctly.

7) Answer all questions

Unless you have been instructed that a penalty will be deducted for incorrect answers, it is better to guess than to omit a question.

8) Speed tests

It is often better NOT to guess on speed tests. It has been found that on timed tests people are tempted to spend the last few seconds before time is called in marking answers at random – without even reading them – in the hope of picking up a few extra points. To discourage this practice, the instructions may warn you that your score will be "corrected" for guessing. That is, a penalty will be applied. The incorrect answers will be deducted from the correct ones, or some other penalty formula will be used.

9) Review your answers

If you finish before time is called, go back to the questions you guessed or omitted to give them further thought. Review other answers if you have time.

10) Return your test materials

If you are ready to leave before others have finished or time is called, take ALL your materials to the monitor and leave quietly. Never take any test material with you. The monitor can discover whose papers are not complete, and taking a test booklet may be grounds for disqualification.

VIII. EXAMINATION TECHNIQUES

1) Read the general instructions carefully. These are usually printed on the first page of the exam booklet. As a rule, these instructions refer to the timing of the examination; the fact that you should not start work until the signal and must stop work at a signal, etc. If there are any *special* instructions, such as a choice of questions to be answered, make sure that you note this instruction carefully.

2) When you are ready to start work on the examination, that is as soon as the signal has been given, read the instructions to each question booklet, underline any key words or phrases, such as *least, best, outline, describe* and the like. In this way you will tend to answer as requested rather than discover on reviewing your paper that you *listed without describing*, that you selected the *worst* choice rather than the *best* choice, etc.

3) If the examination is of the objective or multiple-choice type – that is, each question will also give a series of possible answers: A, B, C or D, and you are called upon to select the best answer and write the letter next to that answer on your answer paper – it is advisable to start answering each question in turn. There may be anywhere from 50 to 100 such questions in the three or four hours allotted and you can see how much time would be taken if you read through all the questions before beginning to answer any. Furthermore, if you come across a question or group of questions which you know would be difficult to answer, it would undoubtedly affect your handling of all the other questions.

4) If the examination is of the essay type and contains but a few questions, it is a moot point as to whether you should read all the questions before starting to answer any one. Of course, if you are given a choice – say five out of seven and the like – then it is essential to read all the questions so you can eliminate the two that are most difficult. If, however, you are asked to answer all the questions, there may be danger in trying to answer the easiest one first because you may find that you will spend too much time on it. The best technique is to answer the first question, then proceed to the second, etc.

5) Time your answers. Before the exam begins, write down the time it started, then add the time allowed for the examination and write down the time it must be completed, then divide the time available somewhat as follows:

- If 3-1/2 hours are allowed, that would be 210 minutes. If you have 80 objective-type questions, that would be an average of 2-1/2 minutes per question. Allow yourself no more than 2 minutes per question, or a total of 160 minutes, which will permit about 50 minutes to review.
- If for the time allotment of 210 minutes there are 7 essay questions to answer, that would average about 30 minutes a question. Give yourself only 25 minutes per question so that you have about 35 minutes to review.

6) The most important instruction is to *read each question* and make sure you know what is wanted. The second most important instruction is to *time yourself properly* so that you answer every question. The third most important instruction is to *answer every question*. Guess if you have to but include something for each question. Remember that you will receive no credit for a blank and will probably receive some credit if you write something in answer to an essay question. If you guess a letter – say "B" for a multiple-choice question – you may have guessed right. If you leave a blank as an answer to a multiple-choice question, the examiners may respect your feelings but it will not add a point to your score. Some exams may penalize you for wrong answers, so in such cases *only*, you may not want to guess unless you have some basis for your answer.

7) Suggestions
   a. Objective-type questions
      1. Examine the question booklet for proper sequence of pages and questions
      2. Read all instructions carefully
      3. Skip any question which seems too difficult; return to it after all other questions have been answered
      4. Apportion your time properly; do not spend too much time on any single question or group of questions
      5. Note and underline key words – *all, most, fewest, least, best, worst, same, opposite*, etc.
      6. Pay particular attention to negatives
      7. Note unusual option, e.g., unduly long, short, complex, different or similar in content to the body of the question
      8. Observe the use of "hedging" words – *probably, may, most likely*, etc.
      9. Make sure that your answer is put next to the same number as the question
      10. Do not second-guess unless you have good reason to believe the second answer is definitely more correct
      11. Cross out original answer if you decide another answer is more accurate; do not erase until you are ready to hand your paper in
      12. Answer all questions; guess unless instructed otherwise
      13. Leave time for review

   b. Essay questions
      1. Read each question carefully
      2. Determine exactly what is wanted. Underline key words or phrases.
      3. Decide on outline or paragraph answer

4. Include many different points and elements unless asked to develop any one or two points or elements
5. Show impartiality by giving pros and cons unless directed to select one side only
6. Make and write down any assumptions you find necessary to answer the questions
7. Watch your English, grammar, punctuation and choice of words
8. Time your answers; don't crowd material

8) Answering the essay question

Most essay questions can be answered by framing the specific response around several key words or ideas. Here are a few such key words or ideas:

M's: manpower, materials, methods, money, management
P's: purpose, program, policy, plan, procedure, practice, problems, pitfalls, personnel, public relations
   a. Six basic steps in handling problems:
      1. Preliminary plan and background development
      2. Collect information, data and facts
      3. Analyze and interpret information, data and facts
      4. Analyze and develop solutions as well as make recommendations
      5. Prepare report and sell recommendations
      6. Install recommendations and follow up effectiveness

   b. Pitfalls to avoid
      1. *Taking things for granted* – A statement of the situation does not necessarily imply that each of the elements is necessarily true; for example, a complaint may be invalid and biased so that all that can be taken for granted is that a complaint has been registered
      2. *Considering only one side of a situation* – Wherever possible, indicate several alternatives and then point out the reasons you selected the best one
      3. *Failing to indicate follow up* – Whenever your answer indicates action on your part, make certain that you will take proper follow-up action to see how successful your recommendations, procedures or actions turn out to be
      4. *Taking too long in answering any single question* – Remember to time your answers properly

IX. AFTER THE TEST

Scoring procedures differ in detail among civil service jurisdictions although the general principles are the same. Whether the papers are hand-scored or graded by machine we have described, they are nearly always graded by number. That is, the person who marks the paper knows only the number – never the name – of the applicant. Not until all the papers have been graded will they be matched with names. If other tests, such as training and experience or oral interview ratings have been given, scores will be combined. Different parts of the examination usually have different weights. For example, the written test might count 60 percent of the final grade, and a rating of training and experience 40 percent. In many jurisdictions, veterans will have a certain number of points added to their grades.

After the final grade has been determined, the names are placed in grade order and an eligible list is established. There are various methods for resolving ties between those who get the same final grade – probably the most common is to place first the name of the person whose application was received first. Job offers are made from the eligible list in the order the names appear on it. You will be notified of your grade and your rank as soon as all these computations have been made. This will be done as rapidly as possible.

People who are found to meet the requirements in the announcement are called "eligibles." Their names are put on a list of eligible candidates. An eligible's chances of getting a job depend on how high he stands on this list and how fast agencies are filling jobs from the list.

When a job is to be filled from a list of eligibles, the agency asks for the names of people on the list of eligibles for that job. When the civil service commission receives this request, it sends to the agency the names of the three people highest on this list. Or, if the job to be filled has specialized requirements, the office sends the agency the names of the top three persons who meet these requirements from the general list.

The appointing officer makes a choice from among the three people whose names were sent to him. If the selected person accepts the appointment, the names of the others are put back on the list to be considered for future openings.

That is the rule in hiring from all kinds of eligible lists, whether they are for typist, carpenter, chemist, or something else. For every vacancy, the appointing officer has his choice of any one of the top three eligibles on the list. This explains why the person whose name is on top of the list sometimes does not get an appointment when some of the persons lower on the list do. If the appointing officer chooses the second or third eligible, the No. 1 eligible does not get a job at once, but stays on the list until he is appointed or the list is terminated.

X. HOW TO PASS THE INTERVIEW TEST

The examination for which you applied requires an oral interview test. You have already taken the written test and you are now being called for the interview test – the final part of the formal examination.

You may think that it is not possible to prepare for an interview test and that there are no procedures to follow during an interview. Our purpose is to point out some things you can do in advance that will help you and some good rules to follow and pitfalls to avoid while you are being interviewed.

What is an interview supposed to test?

The written examination is designed to test the technical knowledge and competence of the candidate; the oral is designed to evaluate intangible qualities, not readily measured otherwise, and to establish a list showing the relative fitness of each candidate – as measured against his competitors – for the position sought. Scoring is not on the basis of "right" and "wrong," but on a sliding scale of values ranging from "not passable" to "outstanding." As a matter of fact, it is possible to achieve a relatively low score without a single "incorrect" answer because of evident weakness in the qualities being measured.

Occasionally, an examination may consist entirely of an oral test – either an individual or a group oral. In such cases, information is sought concerning the technical knowledges and abilities of the candidate, since there has been no written examination for this purpose. More commonly, however, an oral test is used to supplement a written examination.

Who conducts interviews?

The composition of oral boards varies among different jurisdictions. In nearly all, a representative of the personnel department serves as chairman. One of the members of the board may be a representative of the department in which the candidate would work. In some cases, "outside experts" are used, and, frequently, a businessman or some other representative of the general public is asked to serve. Labor and management or other special groups may be represented. The aim is to secure the services of experts in the appropriate field.

However the board is composed, it is a good idea (and not at all improper or unethical) to ascertain in advance of the interview who the members are and what groups they represent. When you are introduced to them, you will have some idea of their backgrounds and interests, and at least you will not stutter and stammer over their names.

What should be done before the interview?

While knowledge about the board members is useful and takes some of the surprise element out of the interview, there is other preparation which is more substantive. It *is* possible to prepare for an oral interview – in several ways:

1) Keep a copy of your application and review it carefully before the interview

This may be the only document before the oral board, and the starting point of the interview. Know what education and experience you have listed there, and the sequence and dates of all of it. Sometimes the board will ask you to review the highlights of your experience for them; you should not have to hem and haw doing it.

2) Study the class specification and the examination announcement

Usually, the oral board has one or both of these to guide them. The qualities, characteristics or knowledges required by the position sought are stated in these documents. They offer valuable clues as to the nature of the oral interview. For example, if the job involves supervisory responsibilities, the announcement will usually indicate that knowledge of modern supervisory methods and the qualifications of the candidate as a supervisor will be tested. If so, you can expect such questions, frequently in the form of a hypothetical situation which you are expected to solve. NEVER go into an oral without knowledge of the duties and responsibilities of the job you seek.

3) Think through each qualification required

Try to visualize the kind of questions you would ask if you were a board member. How well could you answer them? Try especially to appraise your own knowledge and background in each area, *measured against the job sought*, and identify any areas in which you are weak. Be critical and realistic – do not flatter yourself.

4) Do some general reading in areas in which you feel you may be weak

For example, if the job involves supervision and your past experience has NOT, some general reading in supervisory methods and practices, particularly in the field of human relations, might be useful. Do NOT study agency procedures or detailed manuals. The oral board will be testing your understanding and capacity, not your memory.

5) Get a good night's sleep and watch your general health and mental attitude

You will want a clear head at the interview. Take care of a cold or any other minor ailment, and of course, no hangovers.

What should be done on the day of the interview?

Now comes the day of the interview itself. Give yourself plenty of time to get there. Plan to arrive somewhat ahead of the scheduled time, particularly if your appointment is in the fore part of the day. If a previous candidate fails to appear, the board might be ready for you a bit early. By early afternoon an oral board is almost invariably behind schedule if there are many candidates, and you may have to wait. Take along a book or magazine to read, or your application to review, but leave any extraneous material in the waiting room when you go in for your interview. In any event, relax and compose yourself.

The matter of dress is important. The board is forming impressions about you – from your experience, your manners, your attitude, and your appearance. Give your personal appearance careful attention. Dress your best, but not your flashiest. Choose conservative, appropriate clothing, and be sure it is immaculate. This is a business interview, and your appearance should indicate that you regard it as such. Besides, being well groomed and properly dressed will help boost your confidence.

Sooner or later, someone will call your name and escort you into the interview room. *This is it.* From here on you are on your own. It is too late for any more preparation. But remember, you asked for this opportunity to prove your fitness, and you are here because your request was granted.

What happens when you go in?

The usual sequence of events will be as follows: The clerk (who is often the board stenographer) will introduce you to the chairman of the oral board, who will introduce you to the other members of the board. Acknowledge the introductions before you sit down. Do not be surprised if you find a microphone facing you or a stenotypist sitting by. Oral interviews are usually recorded in the event of an appeal or other review.

Usually the chairman of the board will open the interview by reviewing the highlights of your education and work experience from your application – primarily for the benefit of the other members of the board, as well as to get the material into the record. Do not interrupt or comment unless there is an error or significant misinterpretation; if that is the case, do not hesitate. But do not quibble about insignificant matters. Also, he will usually ask you some question about your education, experience or your present job – partly to get you to start talking and to establish the interviewing "rapport." He may start the actual questioning, or turn it over to one of the other members. Frequently, each member undertakes the questioning on a particular area, one in which he is perhaps most competent, so you can expect each member to participate in the examination. Because time is limited, you may also expect some rather abrupt switches in the direction the questioning takes, so do not be upset by it. Normally, a board member will not pursue a single line of questioning unless he discovers a particular strength or weakness.

After each member has participated, the chairman will usually ask whether any member has any further questions, then will ask you if you have anything you wish to add. Unless you are expecting this question, it may floor you. Worse, it may start you off on an extended, extemporaneous speech. The board is not usually seeking more information. The question is principally to offer you a last opportunity to present further qualifications or to indicate that you have nothing to add. So, if you feel that a significant qualification or characteristic has been overlooked, it is proper to point it out in a sentence or so. Do not compliment the board on the thoroughness of their examination – they have been sketchy, and you know it. If you wish, merely say, "No thank you, I have nothing further to add." This is a point where you can "talk yourself out" of a good impression or fail to present an important bit of information. Remember, *you close the interview yourself.*

The chairman will then say, "That is all, Mr. _____, thank you." Do not be startled; the interview is over, and quicker than you think. Thank him, gather your belongings and take your leave. Save your sigh of relief for the other side of the door.

How to put your best foot forward

Throughout this entire process, you may feel that the board individually and collectively is trying to pierce your defenses, seek out your hidden weaknesses and embarrass and confuse you. Actually, this is not true. They are obliged to make an appraisal of your qualifications for the job you are seeking, and they want to see you in your best light. Remember, they must interview all candidates and a non-cooperative candidate may become a failure in spite of their best efforts to bring out his qualifications. Here are 15 suggestions that will help you:

1) Be natural – Keep your attitude confident, not cocky

If you are not confident that you can do the job, do not expect the board to be. Do not apologize for your weaknesses, try to bring out your strong points. The board is interested in a positive, not negative, presentation. Cockiness will antagonize any board member and make him wonder if you are covering up a weakness by a false show of strength.

2) Get comfortable, but don't lounge or sprawl

Sit erectly but not stiffly. A careless posture may lead the board to conclude that you are careless in other things, or at least that you are not impressed by the importance of the occasion. Either conclusion is natural, even if incorrect. Do not fuss with your clothing, a pencil or an ashtray. Your hands may occasionally be useful to emphasize a point; do not let them become a point of distraction.

3) Do not wisecrack or make small talk

This is a serious situation, and your attitude should show that you consider it as such. Further, the time of the board is limited – they do not want to waste it, and neither should you.

4) Do not exaggerate your experience or abilities

In the first place, from information in the application or other interviews and sources, the board may know more about you than you think. Secondly, you probably will not get away with it. An experienced board is rather adept at spotting such a situation, so do not take the chance.

5) If you know a board member, do not make a point of it, yet do not hide it

Certainly you are not fooling him, and probably not the other members of the board. Do not try to take advantage of your acquaintanceship – it will probably do you little good.

6) Do not dominate the interview

Let the board do that. They will give you the clues – do not assume that you have to do all the talking. Realize that the board has a number of questions to ask you, and do not try to take up all the interview time by showing off your extensive knowledge of the answer to the first one.

7) Be attentive

You only have 20 minutes or so, and you should keep your attention at its sharpest throughout. When a member is addressing a problem or question to you, give him your undivided attention. Address your reply principally to him, but do not exclude the other board members.

8) Do not interrupt

A board member may be stating a problem for you to analyze. He will ask you a question when the time comes. Let him state the problem, and wait for the question.

9) Make sure you understand the question

Do not try to answer until you are sure what the question is. If it is not clear, restate it in your own words or ask the board member to clarify it for you. However, do not haggle about minor elements.

10) Reply promptly but not hastily

A common entry on oral board rating sheets is "candidate responded readily," or "candidate hesitated in replies." Respond as promptly and quickly as you can, but do not jump to a hasty, ill-considered answer.

11) Do not be peremptory in your answers

A brief answer is proper – but do not fire your answer back. That is a losing game from your point of view. The board member can probably ask questions much faster than you can answer them.

12) Do not try to create the answer you think the board member wants

He is interested in what kind of mind you have and how it works – not in playing games. Furthermore, he can usually spot this practice and will actually grade you down on it.

13) Do not switch sides in your reply merely to agree with a board member

Frequently, a member will take a contrary position merely to draw you out and to see if you are willing and able to defend your point of view. Do not start a debate, yet do not surrender a good position. If a position is worth taking, it is worth defending.

14) Do not be afraid to admit an error in judgment if you are shown to be wrong

The board knows that you are forced to reply without any opportunity for careful consideration. Your answer may be demonstrably wrong. If so, admit it and get on with the interview.

15) Do not dwell at length on your present job

The opening question may relate to your present assignment. Answer the question but do not go into an extended discussion. You are being examined for a *new* job, not your present one. As a matter of fact, try to phrase ALL your answers in terms of the job for which you are being examined.

Basis of Rating

Probably you will forget most of these "do's" and "don'ts" when you walk into the oral interview room. Even remembering them all will not ensure you a passing grade. Perhaps you did not have the qualifications in the first place. But remembering them will help you to put your best foot forward, without treading on the toes of the board members.

Rumor and popular opinion to the contrary notwithstanding, an oral board wants you to make the best appearance possible. They know you are under pressure – but they also want to see how you respond to it as a guide to what your reaction would be under the pressures of the job you seek. They will be influenced by the degree of poise you display, the personal traits you show and the manner in which you respond.

ABOUT THIS BOOK

This book contains tests divided into Examination Sections. Go through each test, answering every question in the margin. At the end of each test look at the answer key and check your answers. On the ones you got wrong, look at the right answer choice and learn. Do not fill in the answers first. Do not memorize the questions and answers, but understand the answer and principles involved. On your test, the questions will likely be different from the samples. Questions are changed and new ones added. If you understand these past questions you should have success with any changes that arise. Tests may consist of several types of questions. We have additional books on each subject should more study be advisable or necessary for you. Finally, the more you study, the better prepared you will be. This book is intended to be the last thing you study before you walk into the examination room. Prior study of relevant texts is also recommended. NLC publishes some of these in our Fundamental Series. Knowledge and good sense are important factors in passing your exam. Good luck also helps. So now study this Passbook, absorb the material contained within and take that knowledge into the examination. Then do your best to pass that exam.

———

EXAMINATION SECTION

EXAMINATION SECTION

TEST 1

DIRECTIONS: Each question or incomplete statement is followed by several suggested answers or completions. Select the one that BEST answers the question or completes the statement. *PRINT THE LETTER OF THE CORRECT ANSWER IN THE SPACE AT THE RIGHT.*

1. Which of the following is the BEST fact-finding technique that is most helpful in collecting quantitative data?   1.____
   A. Interviews
   B. Record reviews and comparisons
   C. Questionnaires
   D. Workshops

2. _____ data is a type of data collected from open-ended questions.   2.____
   A. Quantitative
   B. Qualitative
   C. Experimental
   D. Non-official

3. Usually a feasibility study is carried out   3.____
   A. after completion of final requirement specification
   B. before the start of the project
   C. before the completion of final requirements specifications
   D. at any time

4. In the analysis phase, which diagram is used to present declaration of the goals and objectives of the project.   4.____
   A. Data flow diagram
   B. Entity relationship diagram
   C. Flowchart
   D. Documentation

5. In SDLC, _____ is used to ensure that no alternative is ignored during data analysis.   5.____
   A. data flow diagram
   B. organizational chart
   C. Gantt chart
   D. decision table

6. Which of the following software is used to measure hardware and software alternatives?   6.____
   A. Automated design tools
   B. DFD
   C. Report generators
   D. Project management

7. _____ is responsible to write Software Requirement Specifications Document (SRS).   7.____
   A. Project manager
   B. System analyst
   C. Programmer
   D. User

8. An entity which relates to itself in an ERD model is referred to as _____ relationship.   8.____
   A. recursive
   B. one-to-many
   C. many-to-many
   D. one-to-one

9. The goal of normalization is   9._____
   A. to increase the number of relations
   B. to increase redundancy
   C. independence of any other relation
   D. to get stable data structure

10. CMM stands for   10._____
   A. Capability Maturity Model   B. Configuration Maturity Model
   C. Capacity Building Manager   D. Company Management Method

11. Data _____ is terminology used for data accuracy and completeness in any   11._____
    database.
    A. constraint   B. redundancy   C. model   D. integrity

12. A candidate key is defined as   12._____
    A. a primary key
    B. the primary key selected to be the key of a relation
    C. an attribute or group of attributes that can be a primary key
    D. both A and B

13. The ability of a class to derive the properties from previously defined class   13._____
    is
    A. encapsulation   B. polymorphism
    C. information hiding   D. inheritance

14. A queue data structure stores and retrieves items in a _____ manner.   14._____
    A. last in, first out   B. first in, last out
    C. first in, first out   D. last in, last out

15. The process of writing a program from an algorithm is called   15._____
    A. coding   B. decoding   C. encoding   D. encrypting

16. The CORRECT sequence for creating and executing C++ program is: 16._____
    A. Compiling-Editing-Saving-Executing-Linking
    B. Editing-Executing-Compiling-Linking
    C. Editing-Saving-Compiling-Linking-Executing
    D. Linking-Executing-Saving-Compiling

17. As an instructor, you have given your class a programming problem.   17._____
    Every student comes up with a different instruction code for the same problem.
    Suppose one student has a code of 50 lines, while another has a code of 100
    instructions for the same problem.
    Which of the following statements is TRUE?
    A. The greater execution time is required for more instructions than that of
       less instructions.
    B. Execution time of all programs are the same.
    C. The number of instruction codes does not affect the solution.
    D. Compilation time is greater with more numbers of instruction.

18. In programming languages, a counter can be defined as
    A. the final value of a loop
    B. a variable that counts loop iterations
    C. the initial value of a loop
    D. the stop value of loop

18.____

19. Which reserve word is used in programming languages to move the control back to the start of the loop body?
    A. Break   B. Go to   C. Continue   D. Switch

19.____

20. The FIRST line in switch block contains the
    A. value of first criterion
    B. statement to be executed if the first criteria is true
    C. expression to be evaluated
    D. statement to be executed if none of the criteria is true

20.____

21. What is the output of the following code?
```
int main ()
{
    int a = 19;
    {
        cout << "value of a: "<<a<<endl;
        a = a + 1;
    }while(a<20);
    return 0;
}
```

    A. 19   B. 20   C. 11   D. 100

21.____

22. A computer dedicated to screening access to a network from outside the network is known as
    A. hot site   B. cold site   C. firewall   D. vaccine

22.____

23. In anticipation of physical destruction, every organization should have a
    A. biometric scheme   B. disaster recovery plan
    C. DES   D. set of active plan

23.____

24. Debug is a term denoting
    A. error correction process
    B. writing of instructions in developing a new program
    C. fault detection in equipment
    D. determine useful life

24.____

25. A feature of word processing software to link the name and addresses with a standard document is called
    A. mail merge   B. database management
    C. references   D. review/comment

25.____

KEY (CORRECT ANSWERS)

1.	C		11.	D
2.	B		12.	C
3.	A		13.	D
4.	C		14.	C
5.	D		15.	A
6.	A		16.	C
7.	A		17.	A
8.	A		18.	B
9.	D		19.	C
10.	A		20.	B

21.	A
22.	C
23.	B
24.	A
25.	A

TEST 2

DIRECTIONS: Each question or incomplete statement is followed by several suggested answers or completions. Select the one that BEST answers the question or completes the statement. *PRINT THE LETTER OF THE CORRECT ANSWER IN THE SPACE AT THE RIGHT.*

1. The SDLC is defined as a process consisting of _____ phases.　　　　1.____
   A. two　　　　　　B. four　　　　　C. three　　　　D. five

2. A framework that describes the set of activities performed at each stage of　　2.____
   a software development project is
   A. SDLC　　　　　　　　　　　B. deployment
   C. waterfall model　　　　　　　D. SDLC model

3. How is noise defined in terms of software development?　　　　3.____
   A. Writing irrelevant statement to the software development in the SRS
      document
   B. Adding clashing requirements in the SRS document
   C. Writing over-specific requirements
   D. Writing information about employees

4. Basically, a SWOT analysis is said to be a strategic　　　　4.____
   A. analysis　　　　B. measure　　　C. goal　　　D. alignment

5. In the system design phase of the SDLC, ____ is not part of the system's　　5.____
   design phase.
   A. design of alternative systems
   B. writing a systems design report
   C. suggestions of alternative solutions
   D. selection of best system

6. In the system development life cycle, which of the following studies is conducted　　6.____
   to determine the possible organizational resistance for a new system?
   _____ feasibility.
   A. Organizational　　B. Operational　　C. Economic　　D. Employee

7. The _____ model is BEST suited when organization is very keen and　　7.____
   motivated to identify the risk on early stages.
   A. waterfall　　　　B. RAD　　　　C. spiral　　　D. incremental

8. Scope of problem is defined with a　　　　8.____
   A. critical path method (CPM) chart
   B. project evaluation and review technique (PERT) chart
   C. data flow diagram (DFD)
   D. context diagram

9. _____ is referred to as a method of database distribution in which different portions of the database reside at different nodes in the network.

    A. Splitting   B. Partitioning   C. Replication   D. Dividing

9.____

10. As a computer specialist (software), your client needs an information system that must communicate with existing systems. For that purpose, you need to adopt a design method and accurate linking with the existing system. Your designed system will be

    A. database   B. system interface

    C. help desks   D, design interface

10.____

11. In entity relation, when primary keys are linked with a foreign key, it forms a _____ relationship between the tables that connect them.

    A. many-to-many   B. one-to-one

    C. parent-child   D. server-and-client

11.____

12. In normalization, a relation is in a third normal form when no _____ attribute is determining another non-key attribute.

    A. dependent   B. non-key

    C. key   D. none of the above

12.____

13. In library management databases, which terminology is used to refer to a specific record in your database?

    A. Relation   B. Instance   C. Table   D. Column

13.____

14. In database, a rule which describes that foreign key value must match with the primary key value in the other relationship is called

    A. referential integrity constraint   B. key match rule

    C. entity key group rule   D. foreign/primary match rule

14.____

15. The attribute on the left-hand side of the arrow in a functional dependency is known as

    A. candidate key   B. determinant

    C. foreign key   D. primary key

15.____

16. A report may be based on a

    A. table   B. query

    C. relations   D. both A and B

16.____

17. A software program which is used to build reports that summarize data from a database is known as

    A. report writer   B. reporter

    C. report builder   D. report generator

17.____

18. Which one of the following database objects is created FIRST?

    A. Table   B. Form   C. Report   D. Query

18.____

19. In data structures, a _____-linked list does not contain a null pointer at the end of the list.

    A. circular   B. doubly   C. null   D. stacked

    19.____

20. Polymorphism is described as the
    A. process of returning data from functions by reference
    B. specialization of classes through inheritance
    C. use of classes to represent objects
    D. packaging of data defining an object as a private member variable of class

    20.____

21. In C++, dynamic binding is useful for the functions that are
    A. overridden   B. defined once
    C. undefined   D. bounded

    21.____

22. In programming language, a function template is required when
    A. implementation details of function are independent of parameter data types
    B. all functions should be function templates
    C. two different functions have different implementation details
    D. two functions have the same type of parameters

    22.____

23. _____ are used to group classes for ease of use, maintainability and reusability.

    A. Use cases   B. States   C. Objects   D. Packages

    23.____

24. The description of structure and organization of data in database is contained in
    A. data dictionary   B. data mine
    C. structured query language   D. data mapping

    24.____

25. What is the output of the following programming code?

    ```
    Int p, q, r;
    P=10, q=3, r=2,
    If (p+q)<14&&(r<q-3)
    Cout <<r;
    Else
    Cout << p;
    ```

    A. -2   B. 4   C. 10   D. -4

    25.____

KEY (CORRECT ANSWERS)

1.	D		11.	C
2.	D		12.	B
3.	A		13.	B
4.	A		14.	A
5.	C		15.	B
6.	B		16.	D
7.	C		17.	B
8.	D		18.	A
9.	C		19.	A
10.	B		20.	B

21.	A
22.	D
23.	C
24.	A
25.	C

TEST 3

DIRECTIONS: Each question or incomplete statement is followed by several suggested answers or completions. Select the one that BEST answers the question or completes the statement. *PRINT THE LETTER OF THE CORRECT ANSWER IN THE SPACE AT THE RIGHT.*

1. The parallelogram symbol in a flow chart indicates a
   A. process   B. progress   C. condition   D. input/output

   1.____

2. A feasibility study in SDLC performs
   A. cost/benefit analysis
   B. designing technique analysis
   C. debugging selection
   D. programming language selection

   2.____

3. Who is responsible for performing the feasibility study?
   A. Organizational managers
   B. Both organizational manager and system analyst
   C. Users of the proposed system
   D. Both perspective user and systems designers

   3.____

4. A study of employees' working habits, phobias and obsessions during implementation of a new system is called _____ analysis.
   A. personality   B. cultural feasibility
   C. economic feasibility   D. technological feasibility

   4.____

5. As a computer specialist (software), a(n) _____ model is based on a regression testing technique.
   A. waterfall   B. RAD   C. V   D. iterative

   5.____

6. The adaptable model which describes features of the proposed system and is implemented before the installation of the actual system is known as
   A. JAD   B. template   C. RAD   D. prototype

   6.____

7. Milestones in system development life cycle represent
   A. cost of project   B. status of project
   C. user expectation   D. final product of project

   7.____

8. Scheduling deadlines and milestones can be shown on a
   A. system survey   B. decision table
   C. prototype   D. Gantt chart

   8.____

9. Suppose your current organization wants to expand its business into different cities. For that purpose, it needs to distribute business applications across multiple locations. For example, computer systems, storing the data center for Web server, database and telecommunication functions. This is an example of
    A. applications architecture planning
    B. technology architecture planning
    C. enterprise resource planning (ERP)
    D. strategic planning

9.____

10. All of the following are components of a physical database EXCEPT
    A. file organization
    B. data volume
    C. data distribution
    D. normalize the relations

10.____

11. Suppose working as a computer specialist (software) your organization has assigned you a task to develop a database for an academic institution. Which one is the MOST appropriate association in the database for a class that might have multiple prerequisites?
    A. Generalization association
    B. N-ary association
    C. Aggregation association
    D. Reflexive association

11.____

12. While working on an academic institute database, according to you, which one is the MOST suitable special association to model a course that has an instructor, teaching assistants, a classroom, meeting time slot and class schedule?
    A. Generalization association
    B. N-ary association
    C. Aggregation association
    D. Reflexive association

12.____

13. Which one of the following is the MOST suitable association that shows that multiple textbooks for a course are required to make a reading list?
    A. Aggregation association
    B. Generalization association
    C. N-ary association
    D. Reflexive association

13.____

14. In parameters, passing by value
    A. actual parameters and formal parameters must be similar types
    B. actual parameters and formal parameters can be different types
    C. parameters passing by value can be used both for input and output purpose
    D. both A and B

14.____

15. In data structures, which of the following can be used to facilitate adding nodes to the end of the linear linked list?
    A. Head pointer
    B. Zero head node
    C. Tail pointer
    D. Precede pointer

15.____

16. A full binary tree with n leaves consist of _____ nodes.
    A. n   B. 2^{n-1} C. n-1   D. log n

16.____

17. Linear model and prototyping model are combined to form a _____ model.
    A. waterfall
    B. incremental
    C. build & fix
    D. spiral

    17.____

18. An example of query is
    A. selection of all records that match a set of criteria
    B. importing spreadsheet file into the database
    C. search for specific record
    D. both A and C are correct

    18.____

19. The database development process involves mapping of conceptual data model into a(n) _____ model.
    A. object-oriented
    B. network data
    C. implementation
    D. hierarchical data

    19.____

20. In database, one field or combination of fields for which more than one record may have the same combination of values is called the
    A. secondary key
    B. index
    C. composite key
    D. linked key

    20.____

21. Customers, cars and parts are examples of
    A. entities   B. attributes   C. cardinals   D. relationships

    21.____

22. A ping program used to send a multiple packet to a server to check its ability to handle a quantity of traffic maliciously is called
    A. pagejacking
    B. jam sync
    C. ping storm
    D. ping strangeness

    22.____

23. Which one of the following is the key factor to develop a new system to manage a disaster?
    A. Equipment replacement
    B. Unfavorable weather
    C. Lack of insurance coverage
    D. Loss of processing ability

    23.____

24. As a computer specialist (software), you ask 100 client organization employees to fill out a survey that includes questions about educational background, their job type, salary and amount spent on purchases of a widget annually. After you enter the data in a spreadsheet program, you decide to look for a relationship between income and the amount spent on widgets. The BEST way to display the data for this kind of assumption is a _____ chart.
    A. bullet   B. line   C. pic   D. scatter

    24.____

25. Suppose it is your very first day of your job. When you turn on your computer, the system unit is visibly on but the monitor is dark. What is the exact issue?
    A. The monitor model is too old to work
    B. The operating system is not working
    C. The monitor is not connected to the PC
    D. Call the help desk officer

    25.____

KEY (CORRECT ANSWERS)

1.	D	11.	D
2.	A	12.	B
3.	A	13.	C
4.	B	14.	A
5.	D	15.	C
6.	D	16.	B
7.	B	17.	B
8.	D	18.	D
9.	B	19.	C
10.	D	20.	A

21.	A
22.	C
23.	D
24.	D
25.	C

TEST 4

DIRECTIONS: Each question or incomplete statement is followed by several suggested answers or completions. Select the one that BEST answers the question or completes the statement. *PRINT THE LETTER OF THE CORRECT ANSWER IN THE SPACE AT THE RIGHT.*

1. A collection of logically related data elements that can be used for multiple processing needs is called
   A. files   B. a register   C. a database   D. organization

   1.____

2. For the purpose of data gathering, your organization and client have secretly engaged you in the client group that is being studied. You are considered a(n)
   A. observer-as-participant   B. observer
   C. complete participant   D. part-time employee

   2.____

3. For data gathering, interviews in which the topics are pre-decided but the sequence and phrasing can be adapted during the interview is called a(n)
   A. informal conversational interview
   B. closed quantitative interview
   C. standardized open-ended interview
   D. interview-guided approach

   3.____

4. In SDLC, which of the following analysis methods is adopted to start with the "intricate image" and then breaks it down into smaller sections?
   A. Financial   B. Bottom up   C. Reverse
   D. Top-down   E. Executive

   4.____

5. As a computer specialist (software), which one of the following is the biggest reason for the failure of system development projects?
   A. Lack of JAD sessions
   B. Purchasing COTS
   C. Imprecise or missing business requirements
   D. Hurdles from employees

   5.____

6. The _____ model is the BEST suited model to create client/server applications.
   A. waterfall   B. spiral   C. incremental   D. concurrent

   6.____

7. Which hardware component is essential for function of a database management system?
   A. Larger capacity, high speed disk
   B. Mouse
   C. High resolution monitors
   D. Printer

   7.____

8. _____ refers to a method of database distribution in which one database contains data that are included in another database.
   A. Splitting   B. Partitioning
   C. Replication   D. Dividing

   8.____

9. In the database design process, which one of the following is referred to modality?
    A. Optional
    B. Mandatory
    C. Unidirectional
    D. Both A and B

9._____

10. According to the research conducted by an international professional organization, out of 100 most occupied jobs that they researched, the top job classification was a
    A. database administrator
    B. cryptographer
    C. programmer
    D. computer engineer

10._____

11. In the database, different attributes in two different tables having the same name are referred to as
    A. a synonym
    B. a homonym
    C. an acronym
    D. mutually exclusive

11._____

12. Consider two tables: Class and Student are related by a "one-to-many" relationship. In which table should the corresponding foreign key be placed?
    A. Only Class table requires foreign key.
    B. Only Student table requires foreign key.
    C. Both tables require foreign key.
    D. Composite entity must be added so foreign keys will be required in both Class and Student tables.

12._____

13.

Using the above E-R diagram, which one of the following statements is TRUE?
    A. Both tables should have the same number of (primary) key attributes.
    B. Table A should have a larger number of key attributes.
    C. Table B should have a larger number of key attributes.
    D. The diagram does not propose which table might have more attributes in its primary key.

13._____

14. Which form of functional dependency is the set of attributes that is neither a subset or any of the keys nor the candidate key?
    A. Full functional dependency
    B. Partial dependency
    C. Primary functional dependency
    D. Transitive dependency

14._____

15. The true dependencies are formed by the _____ rule.
    A. reflexive
    B. referential
    C. inferential
    D. termination

15._____

16. Which facility helps DBMS to synchronize its files and journals while occasionally suspending all processing?
    A. Checkpoint facility
    B. Backup recovery
    C. Recovery manager
    D. Database change log

16._____

17. In data structures, which one of the following operations is used to retrieve and then remove the top of the stack?
    A. Create Stack
    B. Push
    C. Pop
    D. Pull

17.____

18. Class definition
    A. must have a constructor specified
    B. must end with a semicolon
    C. provides the class interface
    D. both B and C

18.____

19. Which operator is used in compound condition to join two conditions?
    A. Relational operator
    B. Logical operator
    C. Relational result
    D. Logical result

19.____

20. The conditional portion of IF statements can contain any
    A. valid expression
    B. expression that can be evaluated to Boolean value
    C. valid variable
    D. valid constant or variable

20.____

21. System analysts suggest that telecommuting will become more popular with managers and client teams when
    A. workers are forced to telecommute
    B. the manager finally gives up the idea of controlling the worker
    C. multimedia teleconferencing system becomes affordable
    D. automobiles become outdated

21.____

22. Error reports are an example of _____ reports.
    A. scheduled   B. exception   C. on-demand   D. external

22.____

23. Word processing, electronic filling, and electronic mails are part of
    A. help desk
    B. electronic industry
    C. office automation
    D. official tasks

23.____

24. In a word processor, the block that appears at the top and bottom of every page which display deals is called the
    A. top and bottom margin
    B. headline and end note
    C. title and page number
    D. header and footer

24.____

25. In word processing software, _____ are inserted as a cross-reference.
    A. placeholders   B. bookmarks   C. objects   D. word fields

25.____

KEY (CORRECT ANSWERS)

1.	C		11.	C
2.	C		12.	B
3.	D		13.	D
4.	B		14.	D
5.	C		15.	A
6.	D		16.	A
7.	A		17.	C
8.	C		18.	A
9.	D		19.	D
10.	D		20.	A

21.	C
22.	B
23.	C
24.	D
25.	D

EXAMINATION SECTION

TEST 1

DIRECTIONS: Each question or incomplete statement is followed by several suggested answers or completions. Select the one that BEST answers the question or completes the statement. *PRINT THE LETTER OF THE CORRECT ANSWER IN THE SPACE AT THE RIGHT.*

1. A disk error is caused by
   A. slow processor
   B. faulty RAM
   C. settings issue of CMOS
   D. all of the above

   1.____

2. 10/100 in network interface means
   A. protocol speed
   B. mega bit per second
   C. fiber speed
   D. server speed

   2.____

3. The tracks of hardware is subdivided as
   A. vectors   B. disks   C. sectors   D. clusters

   3.____

4. ESD damages the
   A. power supply
   B. expansion board
   C. keyboard
   D. monitor

   4.____

5. On the I/O card, the _____ drive has the 34 pin.
   A. floppy   B. SCSI   C. IDE   D. all of the above

   5.____

6. In case of a failure of power supply, what kind of beep will you hear?
   A. Short beep
   B. One long beep
   C. Continuous long beeps
   D. All of the above

   6.____

7. Which of the following adapters will you set before you install a SCSI CD-ROM?
   A. An unused SCSI address
   B. B0007
   C. SCSI ID-1
   D. None of the above

   7.____

8. What would you use to evaluate the serial and parallel ports?
   A. High volt probe
   B. Cable scanner
   C. Loop backs
   D. Sniffer

   8.____

9. An error message of 17xx means a problem with
   A. CMOS
   B. ROM BIOS
   C. DMA control
   D. hard drive

   9.____

10. The bi-directional bus is called a _____ bus.
    A. data   B. control   C. address   D. multiplexed

    10.____

11. _____ defines the quality of the printer output.
    A. Dot per inch   B. Dot per square inch
    C. Dots printed per unit time   D. Dots pixel

11._____

12. What would you do if APM stops functioning?
    A. Uncheck "enable advanced printing feature"
    B. Check "print spooled documents first"
    C. Check "start printing after last page"
    D. All of the above

12._____

13. What would you do to import XML incorporating GUID to a tally?
    A. Transfer data into MS Excel sheet and import to tally account
    B. Import Export Menu
    C. Both A and B
    D. None of the above

13._____

14. The writing device of Palm is called a
    A. stylus   B. pointer
    C. cursor   D. none of the above

14._____

15. A USB port of a computer has the ability to connect _____ number of devices.
    A. 12   B. 154   C. 127   D. 8

15._____

16. A _____ problem causes a system to not boot and beep.
    A. motherboard   B. RAM   C. BIOS   D. hard disk

16._____

17. What would you do if the computer cannot access the website in the corporate setting?
    A. Take a look at the proxy server   B. Check user authentication
    C. Ping Hosts   D. Check firewall

17._____

18. Which of the following is used to measure the database size?
    A. The total disk space
    B. Select sum (bytes)/1024/1024 from dba_data_files
    C. Both A and B
    D. None of the above

18._____

19. RAID defines
    A. fault tolerance   B. data transfer rate
    C. random access memory   D. read AID

19._____

20. The hard disk is measured in
    A. GHz   B. GB   C. Gwatts   D. MB

20._____

21. _____ cannot be shared over a network.
    A. Floppy   B. Keyword   C. Printer   D. CPU

21._____

22. Access does not support
    A. number   B. picture   C. memo   D. text

22.____

23. A network map shows
    A. devices and computers on network
    B. the location of your computer on the network
    C. information about the network
    D. none of the above

23.____

24. While making a chart in MS Word, the categories are shown on
    A. X axis   B. Y axis
    C. none of the above   D. both A and B

24.____

25. What would you do if Google Chrome does not open on a corporate computer?
    A. Turn off the antivirus temporarily   B. Check date settings of computer
    C. Check settings of antivirus   D. All of the above

25.____

KEY (CORRECT ANSWERS)

1.	D		11.	B
2.	B		12.	D
3.	C		13.	C
4.	B		14.	A
5.	A		15.	C
6.	D		16.	B
7.	A		17.	A
8.	C		18.	C
9.	D		19.	A
10.	A		20.	B

21.	D
22.	B
23.	A
24.	D
25.	D

TEST 2

DIRECTIONS: Each question or incomplete statement is followed by several suggested answers or completions. Select the one that BEST answers the question or completes the statement. *PRINT THE LETTER OF THE CORRECT ANSWER IN THE SPACE AT THE RIGHT.*

1. _____ is the computer's default IP address.
   A. 192.168.1.1
   B. 255.000.1
   C. 01010101
   D. None of the above

   1._____

2. Which of the following is a scheduling algorithm?
   A. FCFS
   B. SJF
   C. RR
   D. All of the above

   2._____

3. The trouble with the Shortest Job First algorithm is
   A. too long to be an effective algorithm
   B. to evaluate the next CPU request
   C. too complex
   D. all of the above

   3._____

4. ADSL contains _____ as the largest bandwidth.
   A. voice communication
   B. upstream data
   C. downstream data
   D. control data

   4._____

5. A Toshiba satellite ST1313 running Windows XP has trouble playing sounds. What would you do?
   A. Download sound driver for Realtek
   B. Install default Windows Vista
   C. Change sound card
   D. Change the speaker

   5._____

6. What would you do if your Wi-Fi keeps disconnecting?
   A. Check to see if computer is in the range of Wi-Fi
   B. Install the latest PC wireless card
   C. Click troubleshoot problems
   D. All of the above

   6._____

7. If your attachment in an e-mail is not opening, what is the problem?
   A. You don't have the software to open the file
   B. Your computer clock is at fault
   C. Your software is not compatible with the OS
   D. All of the above

   7._____

8. A DIMM has _____ number of pins.
   A. 72
   B. 32
   C. 32 to 72
   D. 71

   8._____

9. What is the frequency of the SDRAM clock?
    A. 122 Mhz   B. 133 Mhz   C. 82 Mhz   D. 122 Ghz

9.____

10. IRQ6 is connected to
    A. sound card   B. Com1   C. floppy   D. LPT1

10.____

11. You can check the availability of the IRQ while installing PCI NICS through
    A. dip switches   B. CONFIG.SYS
    C. jumper setting   D. BIOS

11.____

12. What would you use if you have a smudged keyboard?
    A. TMC solvent   B. Silicone spray
    C. Alcohol   D. All-purpose cleaner

12.____

13. Which port would you switch to if the laser printer is working slow?
    A. RS232   B. SCSI   C. Serial   D. Parallel

13.____

14. If a mouse is moving erratically, the problem is
    A. dirty ball   B. faulty connection
    C. faulty driver   D. faulty IRQ setting

14.____

15. If a dot matrix printer quality is light, it is an issue of
    A. paper quality   B. faulty ribbon advancement
    C. head position   D. low cartridge

15.____

16. When configuring the hard drive, what would you do after low-level format?
    A. Formatting the DOS partition   B. Install OS
    C. Hard disk partition   D. None of the above

16.____

17. Which of the following errors means a change in two or more bits of data?
    A. Burst   B. Double bit
    C. Single bit   D. All of the above

17.____

18. Pentium system voltage is _____ volts.
    A. +12   B. +5   C. +8   D. +3.3

18.____

19. What would you do if the IDE hard drive is not recognized by the system after installation?
    A. Install drivers   B. Check the jumpers on hard disk
    C. Check information of hard disk   D. All of the above

19.____

20. What would you do to abort a deadlock?
    A. Terminate deadlock process
    B. Terminate the programs one by one
    C. Terminate programs at once
    D. All of the above

20.____

21. What would you do if you cannot share files over the network?   21.____
    A. Check network discovery   B. Check Share files
    C. Check password protection   D. All of the above

22. How would you protect a corporate computer from losing data due to a utility power   22.____
    blackout?
    A. Install a surge protector
    B. Install uninterrupted power supply
    C. Reduce power consumption
    D. All of the above

23. What would you do if the network key is lost?   23.____
    A. Install the latest network   B. Clear cache
    C. Set up the router again   D. None of the above

24. What settings prevent issues if you forget the password to log into Windows?   24.____
    A. Check use account and family safety
    B. Boot in to install disk and rest password
    C. Both A and B
    D. None of the above

25. What would you do to troubleshoot a computer monitor?   25.____
    A. Turn off the power supply   B. Hold down the power button
    C. Check settings of the monitor   D. All of the above

KEY (CORRECT ANSWERS)

1.	A		11.	D
2.	D		12.	D
3.	B		13.	D
4.	A		14.	A
5.	A		15.	B
6.	D		16.	A
7.	A		17.	A
8.	A		18.	D
9.	B		19.	B
10.	C		20.	C

21.	D
22.	D
23.	C
24.	A
25.	B

TEST 3

Each question or incomplete statement is followed by several suggested answers or completions. Select the one that BEST answers the question or completes the statement. *PRINT THE LETTER OF THE CORRECT ANSWER IN THE SPACE AT THE RIGHT.*

1. What would you do if your monitor has no display while it is getting power?
   A. Check picture settings
   C. Check video card
   B. Switch to a functional monitor
   D. All of the above

   1._____

2. How would you troubleshoot DirectX?
   A. Install DirectX diagnostic tool
   C. Re-install DirectX
   B. Run troubleshoot
   D. All of the above

   2._____

3. What would you do if there is a conflict of network IP address?
   A. Convert Static IP address to DHCP
   B. Exclude Static IP address from DHCP server
   C. Both A and B
   D. None of the above

   3._____

4. _____ defines the time interval between process submission and completion.
   A. Waiting time
   C. Response time
   B. Turnaround time
   D. Throughput

   4._____

5. Mutual exclusion _____ for a non-sharable device including printers.
   A. must exist
   C. may exist
   B. must not exist
   D. may not exist

   5._____

6. A kernel cannot schedule
   A. kernel level thread
   C. process
   B. user level thread
   D. all of the above

   6._____

7. What would you do if the computer is not able to find the C: drive when you boot?
   A. Swap hard drives to identify the issue
   B. Reboot
   C. Put your hard drive in a bag and place it in a freezer for the night
   D. All of the above

   7._____

8. Data security does not need a
   A. big RAM
   C. audit log
   B. strong password
   D. scan

   8._____

9. What would you do if you get an error message that prompts, "Cannot obtain IP"?
    A. Open command prompt
    B. Type "ipconfig/renew" in the command prompt
    C. Click the troubleshoot network
    D. All of the above

9.____

10. _____ should be used to transfer large data.
    A. DMA
    B. Programmed I/O
    C. Controller register
    D. LPT1

10.____

11. What would you do after recovery from a system failure?
    A. Repair ingeneration of the system
    B. Notify the parties at both ends
    C. Adjust the recovery system
    D. Systematically log failures

11.____

12. _____ is not present in a computer.
    A. USB port
    B. Parallel port
    C. ROM
    D. Com1/Com2

12.____

13. _____ produces a print with pins of grid.
    A. Inkjet
    B. Laser
    C. Daisy wheel
    D. Dot matrix

13.____

14. What would you do if Windows Vista/7/XP does not sleep?
    A. Check settings of the device manager
    B. Uncheck all the options that wakes up the computer
    C. Look for advanced power management
    D. All of the above

14.____

15. What is the use of the System File Checker tool?
    A. Replace missing files
    B. Replace corrupt files
    C. Scan drive
    D. All of the above

15.____

16. What would you do if the PC reboots between the processes of updating?
    A. Undo updates by System Restore
    B. Go to recovery options
    C. Press F8 and select "repair your computer"
    D. All of the above

16.____

17. What would you do if there is no sound in a PC?
    A. Verify the settings
    B. Select default in Playback
    C. Check speaker cables
    D. All of the above

17.____

18. _____ keeps a record of the major events such as warning and errors.
    A. Event viewer
    B. Windows
    C. Windows Vista
    D. ALU

18.____

19. A run time error "DLL is not supported" means
    A. bad installation
    B. corrupt MS Word
    C. low memory
    D. all of the above

20. What would you do if the system gives error MSGSRV32 after recovering from power?
    A. Disable all programs using SETI
    B. Disable power management
    C. Reboot computer
    D. All of the above

21. While encrypting Windows XP files, you see "Encrypt contents to secure data" as grey. What is the possible reason?
    A. Using Windows XP home edition
    B. The hard drive is not NTFS formatted
    C. The hard drive is FAT32 file system
    D. All of the above

22. You get _____ error message if you are installing a program from a CD that is not clean.
    A. Win 32 application
    B. Is not a valid Win 32 application
    C. Missing File Win 32
    D. None of the above

23. What does it mean when the printer is blinking?
    A. Printer error
    B. Printer ready
    C. Printer is processing
    D. Printer is working

24. If MCI CD audio driver is not installed, the computer will
    A. not play audio CDs
    B. mute DVD
    C. both A and B
    D. none of the above

25. What would you do if the computer plug is emitting sparks?
    A. Disconnect all peripheral devices from the computer
    B. Change the power cord
    C. Check the power supply
    D. All of the above

KEY (CORRECT ANSWERS)

1.	D		11.	A
2.	A		12.	D
3.	C		13.	D
4.	B		14.	D
5.	A		15.	D
6.	B		16.	D
7.	D		17.	D
8.	A		18.	A
9.	B		19.	A
10.	A		20.	A

21.	D
22.	B
23.	A
24.	A
25.	D

TEST 4

Each question or incomplete statement is followed by several suggested answers or completions. Select the one that BEST answers the question or completes the statement. *PRINT THE LETTER OF THE CORRECT ANSWER IN THE SPACE AT THE RIGHT.*

1. How would you find out the APM version of Windows?   1._____
   A. Device Manager tab in the systems
   B. Install Advanced Power Management
   C. Check settings of control panel
   D. All of the above

2. How would you find the AMI POST beep codes?   2._____
   A. On the beep code page   B. On the CPU
   C. Settings   D. All of the above

3. MemTest86 is a _____ diagnostic tool.   3._____
   A. USB   B. bootable
   C. ineffective   D. all of the above

4. If you experience slow performance of your computer, the problem is   4._____
   A. RAM   B. processor   C. ROM   D. Throughput

5. How do you remove a RAM module?   5._____
   A. Pressing the small levers at both ends of the module
   B. Click safely remove hardware
   C. You cannot remove a RAM
   D. By uninstalling the RAM

6. How do you connect the computer clock with the Internet?   6._____
   A. By installing an Internet clock
   B. By setting the date in Time option in the control panel
   C. Processing the clock
   D. All of the above

7. To remove and re-install the real-time clock, you have to run the system on   7._____
   A. power   B. safe mode
   C. normal mode   D. all of the above

8. To keep track of the time, a computer has a battery called   8._____
   A. CMOS   B. CMAS   C. CMSC   D. CDMA

9. What is the problem if the graphic card is heating?   9._____
   A. Faulty motherboard   B. Driver issues
   C. Outdated BIOS   D. Faulty fan

10. What should you know or do before removing a failed PC power supply?   10._____
    A. ESD procedures   B. Disconnect all connectors
    C. Both A and B   D. None of the above

11. _____ drive has the faster data transfer rate.   11._____
    A. IDE   B. SSD   C. SATA   D. Flash

12. SATA and IDE are two different types of ports used to connect   12._____
    A. storage devices   B. RAM
    C. ROM   D. graphic memory

13. Which of the following mediums cannot be used to install OS?   13._____
    A. CD/DVD ROM   B. USB flash drive
    C. Floppy disk   D. RAM

14. Which Windows is touch optimized?   14._____
    A. Windows ME   B. Windows 8
    C. Windows Vista   D. Windows 98

15. What is the other name used for a USB flash drive?   15._____
    A. Pen Drive   B. Thumb Drive
    C. Flash Disk   D. All of the above

16. RATS is defined as   16._____
    A. Regression Analysis Time Series   B. Regression Analysis Time Sharing
    C. Real Analysis Series   D. Real Analysis Time Series

17. _____ keeps a record of the major events such as warning and errors.   17._____
    A. Event viewer   B. Windows
    C. Windows Vista   D. ALU

18. You must use a _____ to notify Windows that you are about to uninstall   18._____
Plug and Play devices.
    A. Device Manager   B. Device Driver
    C. Control Panel   D. Both A and B

19. _____ is used for data entry storage but not for processing.   19._____
    A. Mouse   B. Dumb Terminal
    C. Micro computer   D. Dedicated data entry system

20. Which of the following is NOT a PnP device?   20._____
    A. Mouse   B. Printer   C. Keyboard   D. Joystick

21. WindowsKey + R takes you to   21._____
    A. Run   B. Device Manager
    C. Hardware components   D. None of the above

22. Which of the following has no dipswitches?
    A. Zorro Device
    B. Micro channel
    C. NuBus
    D. All of the above

    22.____

23. Use _____ to ensure security holes are patched.
    A. automatic updates
    B. password
    C. both A and B
    D. none of the above

    23.____

24. What would you do if the speaker is not working?
    A. Check connectors
    B. Check power supply
    C. Check sound card
    D. All of the above

    24.____

25. You get a message abclink.xyz when starting your computer. What would you do?
    A. Press any key to continue
    B. Check settings
    C. Uninstall a program
    D. All of the above

    25.____

_____

KEY (CORRECT ANSWERS)

1.	A		11.	B
2.	A		12.	A
3.	B		13.	D
4.	A		14.	B
5.	A		15.	D
6.	B		16.	A
7.	C		17.	A
8.	A		18.	A
9.	D		19.	B
10.	C		20.	B

21.	A
22.	A
23.	A
24.	D
25.	D

_____

EXAMINATION SECTION
TEST 1

DIRECTIONS: Each question or incomplete statement is followed by several suggested answers or completions. Select the one that BEST answers the question or completes the statement. *PRINT THE LETTER OF THE CORRECT ANSWER IN THE SPACE AT THE RIGHT.*

1. Which of the following ASCII codes corresponds to the character *1*?　　1._____

    A. 061   B. 100   C. 101   D. 361

2. Generally, the FIRST step in designing a data processing system is to　　2._____

    A. draft a HIPO diagram
    B. select input/output and file descriptors
    C. draft a flowchart
    D. select the processing method

3. A(n) _____ is the term for any signal or message that indicates the receipt of data or commands.　　3._____

    A. indicator   B. concession
    C. address   D. acknowledgement

4. Which of the following aspects of data handling are MOST expensive?　　4._____

    A. Validation and protection
    B. Storage and retrieval
    C. Collection and transcription
    D. Organization and aggregation

5. The flowchart drawing shown at the right represents a _____ symbol.　　5._____

    A. display
    B. document
    C. off-line storage
    D. connector

6. What is the term for the reduction of a mass of data to a manageable form?　　6._____

    A. Compression   B. File restructuring
    C. Summarizing   D. Aggregation

7. In _____ processing, data is handled as soon as it is available.　　7._____

    A. simultaneous   B. batch
    C. distributed   D. transaction

8. Which of the following is a linear data list in which elements are added and removed only from one end of the list?　　8._____

    A. Stack   B. String   C. Queue   D. B-tree

9. When four binary digits are read as a single number, the _____ numbering system is being used.

9.____

    A. shorthand
    C. decimal
    B. quaternary
    D. hexadecimal

10. A company uses its data processing system to prepare a reminder notice for a customer whose payment deadline has passed.
This is an example of

10.____

    A. summarization
    C. issuance
    B. control-break reporting
    D. selection

11. In an array with columns numbered from 4 through 13 and rows from 6 through 12, the MAXIMUM number of elements that can be stored is

11.____

    A. 56   B. 63   C. 70   D. 144

12. The symbol shown at the right represents a(n)

12.____

    A. *OR* gate
    B. inverter
    C. *NOR* gate
    D. *NAND* gate

13. When data is accessed from a database in response to an application program request, which of the following occurs FIRST?

13.____

    A. Data element is accessed and stored in a buffer of the database management system (DBMS).
    B. DBMS issues command to access data from secondary storage.
    C. Control unit transfers control to the DBMS.
    D. DBMS transfers data element to application program storage area.

14. An *interrupt* is

14.____

    A. a notation to the control unit that a condition has arisen that requires attention
    B. the arrest of data processing due to bit error
    C. the primary means by which a technician isolates computer failures
    D. an internal command which causes the computer to cease operation

15. In certain internal sort algorithms, the next logically sequential key in an unsorted list is chosen and placed in the next position in a growing sorted list.
What is the term for this type of sort?

15.____

    A. Stable
    C. Sequential
    B. Selection
    D. Partition-exchange sort

16. A(n) _____ is NOT classified as a *simple* logical data structure.

16.____

    A. array   B. record   C. graph   D. string

17. Each of the following is a component of a control unit EXCEPT a

17.____

    A. compiler
    C. decoder
    B. register
    D. program counter

18. A data report shows information on the sales of a single product, with three subtotals and a grand total.
This is an example of

    A. information retrieval   B. control-break reporting
    C. updating   D. summarizing

18._____

19. Which of the following rules applies to a computer's *AND* gate?
The output is

    A. inactive only if all inputs are active
    B. active if any one of the inputs is active
    C. active only if all inputs are active
    D. inactive if any one of the inputs is active

19._____

20. A _____ is a data collision resolution technique in which a search for an empty location proceeds serially from the record's home address.

    A. collating sequence   B. double hashing
    C. multigraphing   D. linear probing

20._____

21. When a unit needs further information to define the required operation, that information is typically held in the

    A. register   B. control word
    C. instructions   D. memory

21._____

22. Each of the following is a typical application of stacks EXCEPT

    A. identifying windows in a screen management system
    B. inventory lists
    C. selecting the next packet to be processed from a communications line
    D. menu picks in a hierarchical menu system

22._____

23. Which of the following is represented by the flowchart symbol shown at the right?

    A. Connector symbol
    B. Manual action symbol
    C. Flow lines
    D. Communications-link symbol

23._____

24. The MAIN advantage associated with having a head node on a data list is

    A. conservation of space
    B. help in finding the end of a circular list
    C. improved performance when finding a node prior to any node on the list
    D. improved performance when deleting nodes from the list

24._____

25. In octal code, the binary number 101 111 011 would appear as

    A. 243   B. 7F   C. 573   D. DR

25._____

KEY (CORRECT ANSWERS)

1.	A		11.	C
2.	B		12.	D
3.	D		13.	C
4.	C		14.	A
5.	A		15.	B
6.	C		16.	C
7.	D		17.	A
8.	A		18.	B
9.	D		19.	C
10.	C		20.	D

21.	B
22.	C
23.	D
24.	B
25.	C

———

TEST 2

DIRECTIONS: Each question or incomplete statement is followed by several suggested answers or completions. Select the one that BEST answers the question or completes the statement. *PRINT THE LETTER OF THE CORRECT ANSWER IN THE SPACE AT THE RIGHT.*

1. A customer withdraws $200 from her checking account at an automated teller machine, and that amount is immediately deducted from her account balance. This is an example of

    A. multi-key processing   B. control-break reporting
    C. real-time processing   D. data packing

    1.____

2. The quantity of characters in a data numbering system are denoted by the system's

    A. radix   B. code   C. array   D. digits

    2.____

3. Each of the following is an example of *linear* logical data structure EXCEPT

    A. linked list   B. queue
    C. general tree   D. stack

    3.____

4. Which basic computer element is represented by the symbol shown at the right?

    A. NOR gate
    B. Inverter
    C. Exclusive OR gate
    D. AND gate

    4.____

5. _____ is a technique for managing records on storage where a record's key value is mapped to an area of space that can hold multiple records.

    A. Cylinder addressing   B. Bucket addressing
    C. Multi-key processing   D. Sector addressing

    5.____

6. When a computer receives a halt instruction, each of the following is true EXCEPT the

    A. instruction-address counter holds the address of the next instruction to be exe-
        cuted
    B. results of the instruction executed prior to the halt instruction are left undisturbed
        by the halt instruction
    C. computer will not resume operation without manual intervention
    D. memory automatically stores the results of the instruction executed prior to the halt
        instruction

    6.____

7. When a binary operator appears between its operands, it is said to be using the _____ notation method of representing an arithmetic expression.

    A. prefix   B. postfix
    C. insertion sort   D. infix

    7.____

8. When data can be accessed without reference to previous data, the _____ access method is in effect.

    A. direct   B. sequential
    C. cross-keyed   D. indexed

    8.____

9. The purpose of a HIPO diagram is to 9.___

    A. organize the instructions within a routine or subroutine
    B. map out the physical components of a data processing system
    C. prioritize the instructions involved in storage and retrieval of data items
    D. list the steps involved in taking identified inputs and creating required files or outputs

10. A librarian keys in the title of a book on a display terminal to see whether it has been checked out. 10.___
This is an example of

    A. sorting   B. information retrieval
    C. issuance   D. distributed processing

11. What is the term for unselective copying of memory contents to another storage medium? 11.___

    A. Dump   B. Rush   C. Scratch   D. Filigree

12. What is the term for the data structure that is a finite sequence of symbols taken from a character set? 12.___

    A. List   B. Queue   C. String   D. Stack

13. Which of the following types of numbering systems is a shorthand method for replacing a group of three binary digits with a single digit? 13.___

    A. Tertiary   B. Octal
    C. Hexadecimal   D. Triplex

14. When two unequal key values map to the same data address, _____ occurs. 14.___

    A. bubble sorting   B. concatenation
    C. a collision   D. inversion

15. A bank records all deposits made to customer accounts at the end of each work day. 15.___
This is an example of

    A. batch processing   B. hashing
    C. distributed processing   D. control-break reporting

16. Each of the following is held in a computer's primary memory EXCEPT 16.___

    A. programs and data that have been passed to the computer for processing
    B. machine-language instructions
    C. output that is ready to be transmitted to an output device
    D. intermediate processing results

17. *Pushing* and *popping* data are terms used in reference to which data structure? 17.___

    A. Strings   B. Queues   C. B-trees   D. Stacks

18. Which of the following methods for file access makes use of fields which are used to identify each record in the file? 18.___

    A. Keyed   B. Distributed
    C. Sequential   D. Direct

19. Each of the following is an example of a *primitive* logical data structure EXCEPT   19._____

     A. character   B. list   C. boolean   D. integer

20. In hexadecimal code, the number 1110 1111 would appear as   20._____

     A. 6A   B. 116   C. EF   D. 192

21. Which of the following is a data collision resolution stragegy in which synonyms for a record are all stored in the file's primary address space?   21._____

     A. Separate-overflow addressing
     B. Linear probing
     C. Open addressing
     D. Double hashing

22. Typically, the jobs to be performed by a system, as well as the programs that will perform them, are controlled and selected by the   22._____

     A. subroutine   B. executive program
     C. compiler   D. directory

23. In a computer's *NOR* gate, the output is inactive   23._____

     A. *only* if all inputs are inactive
     B. if any one input is inactive
     C. *only* if all inputs are active
     D. if any one input is active

24. A company uses its data processing system to compose an employee phone book with names in alphabetical order.
This is an example of   24._____

     A. sorting   B. b-tree hierarchy
     C. selection   D. issuance

25. Which of the following components of the arithmetic unit is capable of performing logical operations?   25._____

     A. Compiler   B. Carry-in   C. Counter   D. Adder

KEY (CORRECT ANSWERS)

1.	C		11.	A
2.	A		12.	C
3.	C		13.	B
4.	C		14.	C
5.	B		15.	A
6.	D		16.	B
7.	D		17.	D
8.	A		18.	A
9.	D		19.	B
10.	B		20.	C

21.	C
22.	B
23.	D
24.	A
25.	D

———

EXAMINATION SECTION

TEST 1

DIRECTIONS: Each question or incomplete statement is followed by several suggested answers or completions. Select the one that BEST answers the question or completes the statement. *PRINT THE LETTER OF THE CORRECT ANSWER IN THE SPACE AT THE RIGHT.*

1. The term that is used to refer to the storage and retrieval of data is
   A. website   B. database   C. software   D. application

   1.____

2. If you need to store employee data with all the information about the employees, you will store it in a
   A. relation   B. tuple   C. attribute   D. entity

   2.____

3. The term used to describe a specific property of a record is
   A. tuple   B. attribute   C. column   D. row

   3.____

4. Which of the following is used to reflect that records are unique?
   A. Foreign key   B. Candidate key
   C. Primary key   D. Index

   4.____

5. Database can be represented by _____ diagram.
   A. database   B. entity relationship
   C. data flow   D. all of the above

   5.____

6. You can create a table with the statement of _____ table.
   A. create   B. make   C. add   D. define

   6.____

7. A hierarchy representing super type/sub type may have which of the following properties?
   A. One super type may only have one sub type
   B. One sub type may have only one super type
   C. Each sub type may only have one attribute
   D. All of the above

   7.____

8. In the first normal form, the data must be represented by
   A. a primary key
   B. a single value in each cell of the table
   C. more than one table
   D. all of the above

   8.____

9. The purpose of partitioning is to
   A. manage complexity   B. ensure security
   C. use space efficiently   D. none of the above

   9.____

10. Blocking factor is used to represent   10._____
    A. storage of data in the adjacent memory locations
    B. per page physical records
    C. grouped attributes
    D. blocks of data

11. Which of the following is the best description of a secondary key?   11._____
    A. A key that represents a table
    B. Primary key
    C. A key alternate to the primary key
    D. A key that can hold duplicate values

12. Which of the following is used to describe the multi-dimensional databases?   12._____
    A. Relational database   B. Hierarchical database
    C. Data warehouse   D. Network model

13. Client server architecture does not reflect the following: 13._____
    A. It is necessary to have a file server
    B. Needs someone to forward the request
    C. Needs someone to respond to the forwarded request
    D. All of the above

14. Stored procedures have the advantage of   14._____
    A. efficiency with respect to data integrity, as different applications can have
       access to the same stored procedure
    B. faster traffic communication
    C. easier to write
    D. specially designed for client server mode

15. Which of the following is important for data warehouse architecture?   15._____
    A. Data mart
    B. Data may come from a number of sources that may either be internal or
       external
    C. Data is historical
    D. All of the above

16. A transactional system means which of the following?   16._____
    A. This is a system that is used for the purpose of carrying out daily
       transactions based on the live data
    B. This is a system used for the purpose of decision making based on live
       data
    C. This is a system that is used for decision making based on historical data
    D. This is a system that is used to carry out daily transactions based on
       historical data

17. All of the following are correct for a data warehouse EXCEPT

    A. it is utilized by the end users

    B. it is organized with respect to different subject areas

    C. historical data is held

    D. it is used for the purpose of decision making

17.____

18. What are fact tables?

    A. De-normalized structure in the data warehouse

    B. Data structure is partially normalized

    C. Completely normalized structure

    D. None of the above

18.____

19. What type of relationship exists in the dimension and fact table in the star schema?

    A. One to one   B. One to many

    C. Many to many   D. None of the above

19.____

20. A transactional manager is responsible for

    A. the maintenance of transactional logs

    B. holding and keeping track of the database images

    C. maintenance of concurrency control

    D. all of the above

20.____

21. A distributed system has the characteristic of

    A. cost efficiency   B. system complexity

    C. modular expansion   D. faster response

21.____

22. Em Friends();

In the above statement, what represents the name of the class?

    A. Friends   B. Em

    C. Friends()   D. None of the above

23. Object definition language is used as a

    A. language for the object-oriented databases

    B. structured query language

    C. language to interpret the objects of an application

    D. all of the above

23.____

24. The advantage of ODBMS is

    A. it handles complex data on web

    B. it serves as an alternate of RDBMS for all types of applications

    C. its usability for the storage of historical data

    D. all of the above

24.____

25. The object query language has the structure that is much like SQL utilizing the structure of

    A. select-where   B. select-from-where

    C. where-select   D. none of the above

25.____

KEY (CORRECT ANSWERS)

1.	B		11.	C
2.	A		12.	C
3.	B		13.	A
4.	C		14.	A
5.	B		15.	D
6.	A		16.	A
7.	B		17.	A
8.	B		18.	C
9.	B		19.	B
10.	B		20.	D

21.	C
22.	B
23.	A
24.	A
25.	B

TEST 2

DIRECTIONS: Each question or incomplete statement is followed by several suggested answers or completions. Select the one that BEST answers the question or completes the statement. *PRINT THE LETTER OF THE CORRECT ANSWER IN THE SPACE AT THE RIGHT.*

1. What are the basic operations of a record management system?
    A. Adding records   B. Updating records
    C. Deleting records   D. All of the above

    1.____

2. A database management system is intended for
    A. program dependent data
    B. increase in data redundancy
    C. being accessible at many different places at a time
    D. all of the above

    2.____

3. Data dictionary is composed of
    A. database fields
    B. data types of database fields
    C. range and scope of database fields
    D. all of the above

    3.____

4. What is relational algebra?
    A. A language that defines data
    B. A meta definition language
    C. A procedural query language
    D. None of the above

    4.____

5. How is a weak entity represented in an E-R model?
    A. Diamond shape   B. Solid rectangle
    C. Double outlined rectangle   D. Circle

    5.____

6. Which of the following is FALSE about views?
    A. Results of views are based on the data of other tables
    B. View is considered as a virtual table
    C. Definition of view is part of the database
    D. Views are written in the form of a query

    6.____

7. With the use of data types,
    A. proper usage of data storage is performed
    B. data cannot be stored in non-relevant data types
    C. data integrity is enhanced
    D. all of the above

    7.____

8. If an entity does not contain an attribute which can uniquely determine the whole relation, then this entity is called _____ entity.
    A. child   B. strong   C. loose   D. weak

    8.____

9. A join in which a table has a join with itself is termed as _____ join.　9.____
    A. self　　　　　　　　　　　　B. inner
    C. outer　　　　　　　　　　　　D. none of the above

10. What is logical schema?　10.____
    A. A database
    B. Information organization mechanism
    C. Data storage mechanism
    D. None of the above

11. Database anomalies are removed with the help of　11.____
    A. integrity constraints　　　　　B. normal forms
    C. dependencies　　　　　　　　　D. locking

12. Which of the following is the purpose of a trigger?　12.____
    A. Used to initiate different types of functions of DBMS
    B. A program statement used for the debugging purpose
    C. A function that validates a user
    D. A program code that is automatically run on the basis of some action on
       the database

13. Who is responsible for database supervision?　13.____
    A. Database administrator　　　　B. Database manager
    C. DP manager　　　　　　　　　　D. None of the above

14. Which of the following is TRUE about distributed database systems?　14.____
    A. Centralized and accessible at different locations
    B. Replication either partially or completely
    C. Segmentation at different places
    D. All of the above

15. Periodical change of data is termed as　15.____
    A. data update　　　　　　　　　B. data upgrade
    C. restructuring　　　　　　　　　D. none of the above

16. You can change the values of records using the command　16.____
    A. change　　　　　　　　　　　　B. modify
    C. update　　　　　　　　　　　　D. none of the above

17. The SQL comparison operators include　17.____
    A. =　　　　　　　　　　　　　　　B. >
    C. LIKE　　　　　　　　　　　　　D. all of the above

18. For two tables T1 and T2, the union operation will result in the retrieval of　18.____
    A. all rows of T1
    B. all rows of T2
    C. all rows of T1 and T2
    D. rows where all the rows in the two tables which have common columns

19. The word *enum* is used for which of the following?
    A. It establishes the range of values of an attribute
    B. It defines class range
    C. It represents a numeric value
    D. None of the above

19.____

20. _____ associations is a type of association supported with ODL.
    A. Unary   B. Binary
    C. Ternary   D. Unary and binary

20.____

21. Which of the following describes load and index in the BEST way?
    A. This process enhances the quality of data after it is moved to the data warehouse
    B. This is a process that creates data warehouse data and any required indexes are created
    C. This process enhances the quality of data before it is moved to the data warehouse
    D. This process rejects the inappropriate data from the data warehouse

21.____

22. Which of the following is TRUE with respect to two level data warehouse architecture?
    A. At minimum, one data mart is required
    B. Data coming from internal and external sources
    C. Real time updatable data
    D. None of the above

22.____

23. An index file master list
    A. is a sorted file
    B. is based on a list of keys and records
    C. contains each record with a specific number
    D. all of the above

23.____

24. If different columns of a table are located in different places, then it is called
    A. vertical portioning   B. replication
    C. horizontal portioning   D. none of the above

24.____

25. If we store different copies of a database at different locations, then it is called
    A. vertical portioning   B. replication
    C. horizontal portioning   D. none of the above

25.____

KEY (CORRECT ANSWERS)

1.	D		11.	A
2.	C		12.	D
3.	D		13.	A
4.	C		14.	D
5.	C		15.	A
6.	C		16.	C
7.	C		17.	D
8.	D		18.	D
9.	A		19.	A
10.	B		20.	D

21.	B
22.	B
23.	C
24.	A
25.	B

———————

TEST 3

DIRECTIONS: Each question or incomplete statement is followed by several suggested answers or completions. Select the one that BEST answers the question or completes the statement. *PRINT THE LETTER OF THE CORRECT ANSWER IN THE SPACE AT THE RIGHT.*

1. Which of the following is the motive behind the development of database systems?
   A. More information reporting needs
   B. More information management needs
   C. Faster processing of real-time transactions
   D. All of the above

   1.____

2. Which of the following is the term used to refer to a set of data values?
   A. Attribute   B. Domain   C. Row   D. Degree

   2.____

3. The approach used to physically sort the records in a specific order is called
   A. hashing   B. sequential
   C. direct   D. none of the above

   3.____

4. What does cardinality mean?
   A. Number of tuples   B. Attributes count in a table
   C. Number of tables in the database   D. None of the above

   4.____

5. Which of the following refers to the cardinality?
   A. Properties   B. Degree   C. Relations   D. Cartesian

   5.____

6. If each cell of a relation contains an atomic value, then the relation scheme is in the _____ normal form.
   A. complete   B. first
   C. second   D. none of the above

   6.____

7. Sequence is saved in the
   A. database   B. relation
   C. data dictionary   D. database logs

   7.____

8. Which of the following symbols is used to represent attributes in an ER model?
   A. Ellipse   B. Rectangle
   C. Triangle   D. None of the above

   8.____

9. What type of key is used to reflect the relationship among different tables?
   A. Primary   B. Foreign   C. Secondary   D. Hash

   9.____

10. Extraction of some specific records from the database is termed
    A. join   B. selection   C. projection   D. grouping

    10.____

11. Benefits of sequential retrieval against primary key include   11.____
    A. fast processing   B. somewhat faster processing
    C. less resource utilization   D. none of the above

12. Changes of any type are visible from the cursor type of   12.____
    A. forward only   B. dynamic   C. keyset   D. static

13. The data in the DBMS is requested with the help of   13.____
    A. DDL   B. DML   C. VDL   D. SDL

14. The language which has become a standard for database interaction is   14.____
    A. DBASE   B. OQL   C. Oracle   D. SQL

15. What does SQL Count function do?   15.____
    A. Counts values   B. Counts distinct values
    C. Groups values   D. None of the above

16. DBMS helps achieve   16.____
    A. the independence of data
    B. a centralized control over the data
    C. data consistency
    D. all of the above

17. If you need to select on certain columns in your select query, which approach   17.____
will be used?
    A. Selection   B. Projection   C. Outer Join   D. Union

18. Which of the following commands is used for the deletion of a column in a   18.____
table?
    A. Alter   B. Update   C. Drop   D. Delete

19. Which of the following is TRUE concerning the following statement: 19.____
class Cat extends Animal?
    A. Cat is an abstract super class   B. Cat is an abstract sub class
    C. Cat is a concrete sub class   D. Cat is a concrete super class

20. Which of the following can be defined with ODL?   20.____
    A. Properties   B. Structure
    C. Functions   D. All of the above

21. What is the extract process?   21.____
    A. All the data from different operational systems is captured by this process
    B. This process captures a specific portion of data from different operational
       systems
    C. Data available with different decision support systems is captured by this
       process
    D. It captures specific data from a data warehouse

22. What is data transformation?
    A. This is a process that transforms the detailed level data into summary data
    B. Summary data is transformed into detailed data
    C. Data from one source is separated into different categories
    D. Data coming from different sources is combined at one place

22.____

23. What is data scrubbing?
    A. A mechanism that changes data into its appropriate form before moving to a data warehouse
    B. A mechanism that rejects the data out of a data warehouse
    C. This is a mechanism that enhances the quality of data warehouse data
    D. A data loading process

23.____

24. Which of the following is TRUE about lock files?
    A. Only one user can access the file
    B. Authenticated users can modify the file
    C. Its purpose is to secure the critical information
    D. All of the above

24.____

25. What is distributed database?
    A. One logical database that is distributed to multiple places
    B. A set of files distributed at different locations
    C. A database that is placed in one location in the logical form
    D. Database data distributed in different files at one place

25.____

KEY (CORRECT ANSWERS)

1.	D		11.	A
2.	B		12.	B
3.	A		13.	B
4.	A		14.	D
5.	D		15.	A
6.	B		16.	D
7.	C		17.	B
8.	A		18.	A
9.	B		19.	C
10.	B		20.	D

21.	B
22.	A
23.	A
24.	A
25.	A

TEST 4

DIRECTIONS: Each question or incomplete statement is followed by several suggested answers or completions. Select the one that BEST answers the question or completes the statement. *PRINT THE LETTER OF THE CORRECT ANSWER IN THE SPACE AT THE RIGHT.*

1. A DBMS may carry on information processing with _____ systems.   1._____
     A. word processing   B. spreadsheet processing
     C. graphical   D. all of the above

2. A combination of which of the following makes up a database record?   2._____
     A. Attributes   B. Tuples
     C. Entities   D. None of the above

3. Strong keys refer to the entities having _____ keys.   3._____
     A. primary   B. candidate
     C. unique   D. none of the above

4. The purpose of report generator is to _____ data.   4._____
     A. update   B. add   C. delete   D. view and print

5. What is conceptual design?   5._____
     A. Used for the purpose of documentation
     B. Graphical view of the database
     C. Database modeling irrespective of DBMS
     D. Relational model design

6. Which of the following determines the physical location of a record?   6._____
     A. Binary tree   B. Sequence
     C. Hashing   D. Indexing

7. In which model are records organized in the form of a tree?   7._____
     A. Network   B. Hierarchical   C. Network   D. Relational

8. Which type of dependency is NOT allowed in the second normal form?   8._____
     A. Full   B. Loose
     C. Partial   D. None of the above

9. Fifth normal form refers to   9._____
     A. data atomicity   B. fully functional dependency
     C. join dependency   D. none of the above

10. Entity integrity with respect to primary keys infers that it must be   10._____
     A. not null   B. unique
     C. both A and B   D. none of the above

11. During the DBMS operations, which of the following are used?   11._____
    A. Data dictionary   B. Transaction log
    C. Both A and B   D. None of the above

12. Entities properties are also termed as   12._____
    A. relations   B. rows
    C. attributes   D. none of the above

13. How is natural join performed?   13._____
    A. It is based on Cartesian product
    B. Union and Cartesian products are both performed
    C. Projection and Cartesian products are both performed
    D. None of the above

14. Which type of lock can enforce an item to be read but not modified?   14._____
    A. Shared   B. Exclusive   C. Explicit   D. Implicit

15. For a relation,   15._____
    A. data can be stored in any sequence
    B. there is no duplication of data
    C. both A and B are true
    D. none of the above

16. What is NULL?   16._____
    A. Equivalent to 0
    B. Equivalent to space
    C. 0 for numeric value and space for character value
    D. No value

17. The relationship among two entities is referred to as   17._____
    A. unary   B. quaternary   C. ternary   D. binary

18. If there are two relations named R1 and R2 with x number of tuples for   18._____
R1 and y tuples for R2, then the maximum number of join results is
    A. (x+y)/2   B. (x+y)*2   C. x+y   D. xy

19. Committed changes become permanent with the transaction of   19._____
    A. atomic   B. durable
    C. consistent   D. none of the above

20. Which of the following functions may be performed with ODL?   20._____
    A. A complete data set including the duplicates may be returned
    B. A complete data set without the duplicates may be returned
    C. A specific data subset may be returned
    D. All of the above

21. Which of the following is an atomic literal?   21._____
    A. Boolean   B. Strings
    C. Character   D. All of the above

22. What is transient data?
    A. Data that is not available in case any changes to the existing data is made
    B. Data that is not eliminated in case any changes to the data are made
    C. Unchangeable data
    D. Permanent undeletable data

23. Which of the following is reconciled data?
    A. Transactional data of the organization
    B. One source of data to support all the decision-making processes
    C. Selected pieces of data
    D. None of the above

24. What is the objective of a data-mining process?
    A. Extract vital patterns and trends hidden in the data
    B. Composed of a set of algorithms that help find patterns of data
    C. It is best suited with historical data stored in the data warehouse
    D. All of the above

25. Which of the following is TRUE about replication?
    A. Network traffic is reduced
    B. On the failure of database at one site, the database at the other site may be utilized
    C. Storage capacity at each site must be the same
    D. None of the above

KEY (CORRECT ANSWERS)

1.	D		11.	C
2.	A		12.	C
3.	A		13.	C
4.	D		14.	A
5.	C		15.	C
6.	C		16.	D
7.	B		17.	D
8.	C		18.	D
9.	D		19.	B
10.	C		20.	D

21.	D
22.	A
23.	B
24.	D
25.	C

EXAMINATION SECTION
TEST 1

DIRECTIONS: Each question or incomplete statement is followed by several suggested answers or completions. Select the one that BEST answers the question or completes the statement. *PRINT THE LETTER OF THE CORRECT ANSWER IN THE SPACE AT THE RIGHT.*

1. Which of the following is NOT a characteristic of a relational database

    A. It is a two-dimensional table.
    B. Each row is distinct.
    C. The key fields are created by a programmer.
    D. Each column has a distinct name.
    E. The order of columns is immaterial.

1.____

2. Each row of a relational database is called a

    A. table   B. row   C. column
    D. tuple   E. none of the above

2.____

3. Each column of a relational database is called a

    A. table   B. row   C. column
    D. tuple   E. attribute

3.____

4. The _____ is NOT a component of a database application system.

    A. hardware   B. programs
    C. data   D. procedures
    E. decision support system

4.____

5. The structure of the entire database is called a

    A. DBMS   B. schema
    C. application mechanism   D. DBA
    E. hierarchy

5.____

6. Which of the following is the national query language?

    A. IDMS   B. dBase III Plus
    C. SQL   D. DB2
    E. none of the above

6.____

7. Metadata is a term MOST closely associated with the _____ of a data base management system.

    A. forms generator
    B. data dictionary
    C. database programming language
    D. query languages
    E. data models

7.____

8. The _____ is responsible for the development, operation, maintenance, and administration of the database.

    A. DDL   B. DBM   C. DBA   D. DL/1   E. DBTG

8.____

9. In a local area network, the common database is located in the microcomputer   9.____

    A. subdirectory
    B. LAN
    C. file server
    D. Distributed Transaction Manager (DTM)
    E. Device Media Control Locator (DMCL)

10. The _____ data model is also called the *tree* model.   10.____

    A. hierarchical   B. relational   C. network
    D. inverted   E. none of the above

11. A group of one or more attributes (columns in a relation) that uniquely identifies a record   11.____
    in a file is called a

    A. descriptor   B. indicator   C. key
    D. field   E. pointer

12. The *lock manager* is responsible for   12.____

    A. securing the DBMS from unauthorized users
    B. securing the DBMS from disasters such as fire or flood
    C. preventing undesirable results from occurring during concurrent processing
    D. rollback and recovery procedures
    E. all of the above

13. The MOST common computer programming language used with database management   13.____
    systems is

    A. PL/1   B. Fortran   C. Basic
    D. QBE   E. COBOL

14. Which of the following is NOT a microcomputer database management system?   14.____

    A. Rbase   B. dBase   C. Oracle
    D. DB2   E. None of the above

15. Which of the following symbols is NOT used with data flow diagrams?   15.____

A. ◯   B. ▢   C. ↷

D. ◇   E. ▭

16. The *father* of the relational database model is
    16.____

    A. Codd
    B. Martin
    C. Djikstra
    D. Kroenke
    E. Boyce

17. The process of grouping together fields in a database to form a well-structured relation is called
    17.____

    A. dependency
    B. data modeling
    C. normalization
    D. logical database design
    E. relational design

18. A relationship between fields in a database is called
    18.____

    A. relational dependency
    B. functional dependency
    C. first normal form
    D. logical database design
    E. domain/key normal form

19. The notation used for describing a one-to-many relationship between data is
    19.____

    A. 1:M
    B. 1:!
    C. M:1
    D. 1:N
    E. none of the above

20. The data in a database is the property of the
    20.____

    A. users
    B. database administrator
    C. manufacturer of the database software
    D. government
    E. none of the above

21. The data dictionary lists the
    21.____

    A. standard names for data items in the database
    B. files in a database system
    C. relationships between data in a database
    D. all of the above
    E. none of the above

22. The process of recreating a database system from start is called
    22.____

    A. recovery
    B. rollback
    C. rebuilding
    D. back-up
    E. reduplication

23. The process of correcting an error or group of errors is called
    23.____

    A. recovery
    B. rollback
    C. data validation
    D. back-up
    E. re-initiation

24. *Deadlock* occurs when

    A. multiple users *log on* with identical passwords
    B. users cannot decide on who owns the data in the database system
    C. one group of users will not let other users have access to data
    D. two users are waiting for data that each other has locked
    E. database software does not operate properly on certain hardware

24.___

25. The PRIMARY responsibility of the database administrator (DBA) is to

    A. maintain the data dictionary
    B. meet with end users to determine their needs from the database management system
    C. safeguard the database and optimize the benefits users derive from it
    D. develop database applications
    E. specify the software to be used for the database management system

25.___

KEY (CORRECT ANSWERS)

1.	C		11.	C
2.	D		12.	C
3.	E		13.	E
4.	E		14.	E
5.	B		15.	D
6.	C		16.	A
7.	B		17.	C
8.	C		18.	B
9.	C		19.	D
10.	A		20.	A

21.	D
22.	A
23.	B
24.	D
25.	C

TEST 2

DIRECTIONS: Each question or incomplete statement is followed by several suggested answers or completions. Select the one that BEST answers the question or completes the statement. *PRINT THE LETTER OF THE CORRECT ANSWER IN THE SPACE AT THE RIGHT.*

1.   The database administrator (DBA) must TYPICALLY address _____ problems.

   A.   technical
   B.   psychological
   C.   organizational political
   D.   managerial
   E.   all of the above

1._____

2.   The PRIMARY goal of normalization in a database is to

   A.   reduce data redundancy
   B.   maintain database security
   C.   reduce data integrity
   D.   reduce storage requirements
   E.   reduce data entry volume

2._____

3.   Which of the following is NOT typical of a microcomputer database management system?
They

   A.   use simpler administration than of mainframe database systems
   B.   are primarily single-user systems
   C.   are developed by end users
   D.   handle up to five different applications
   E.   use the hierarchial or network data model

3._____

4.   The _____ data model requires the MOST maintenance by a professional database staff.

   A.   relational   B.   network   C.   hierarchial
   D.   tree   E.   none of the above

4._____

5.   Concatenation is

   A.   the joining of two fields (attributes) to uniquely identify a record in a field
   B.   the splitting of one field into two separate parts
   C.   a method of changing the definition of a field
   D.   a type of relationship between two files
   E.   a type of random access

5._____

6.   A general language used to communicate with the database management system is

   A.   DDL   B.   CODASYL   C.   DBTG   D.   DAD   E.   QBE

6._____

7. A mathematical formula for calculating a disk address for a key field is called   7.___

    A. linear projection
    B. location numeration
    C. hierarchial sequential access method
    D. indexing
    E. hashing

8. The transferring of data from a personal computer to a mainframe computer is called   8.___

    A. downloading   B. uploading   C. modeming
    D. handshaking   E. none of the above

9. The initial one-time cost of starting up a database management system is called   9.___

    A. software maintenance
    B. software development
    C. computer system overhead
    D. DBMS installation
    E. training

10. Which of the following is NOT a benefit that is derived from having a well-designed data-base management system?   10.___

    A. Improved security of data
    B. Better information provided to users
    C. Reduced administration resources
    D. More accurate information
    E. Reduced maintenance and program development costs

11. In many companies, user departments are charged for using the database management system.   11.___
Resource utilization billing charges the area user based upon

    A. a fixed amount per period
    B. a fixed amount, dependent on the type of application being used
    C. time, transactions processed, computer resources
    D. a fixed amount per user
    E. the number of transactions processed

12. _____ is NOT a function of the database administrator(DBA).   12.___

    A. Training
    B. Data dictionary management
    C. Database loading
    D. Entering data and querying database for users
    E. Database security

13. The process of evaluating the proper hardware environment for the database manage-ment system is called   13.___

    A. tuning   B. performance monitoring
    C. sizing   D. feature evaluation
    E. feature implementation

14. A data model is the

    A. method for organizing a database
    B. physical structure of the database
    C. language used to query the database
    D. database management system software
    E. conceptual view of the database

14._____

15. The data model which is GENERALLY considered to be the *slowest* in performance is the _____ model.

    A. network   B. hierarchial   C. inverted
    D. relational   E. all of the above

15._____

16. Which data model provides the link in which data is related together within the data itself?

    A. Network   B. Hierarchial   C. Plex
    D. Tree   E. Relational

16._____

Questions 17-20.

DIRECTIONS: Use the following relational database to answer Questions 17 through 20.

23	SIMMONS	1B	.324
31	WILSON	OF	.309
19	FARMER	P	.144

17. How many *tuples* are depicted?

    A. One   B. Two   C. Three
    D. Four   E. None of the above

17._____

18. How many *tables* are depicted?

    A. One   B. Two   C. Three
    D. Four   E. None of the above

18._____

19. How many *data elements* are depicted?

    A. One   B. Two   C. Three
    D. Four   E. None of the above

19._____

20. How many *attributes* are depicted?

    A. One   B. Two   C. Three
    D. Four   E. None of the above

20._____

21. A database administrator (DBA) is analogous to a

    A. salesperson   B. accountant   C. vice president
    D. auditor   E. controller

21._____

22. _____ is the preferred method of recovering a database system from a system failure.   22._____

    A. Reprocessing
    B. Rollback
    C. Rollforward
    D. Rollback/rollforward
    E. Restoring from backup tapes or disks

23. A set of possible values for a data field that defines a range of valid data entries for that field is called a   23._____

    A. derived range   B. validation check
    C. domain   D. enumerated range
    E. condition name

24. The _____ database operation produces a new relationship by combining two existing relations.   24._____

    A. extract   B. join   C. combine
    D. selection   E. all of the above

25. Which of the following is a selection criteria for a data model?   25._____

    A. Vendor support   B. Security
    C. Performance   D. User interface
    E. All of the above

KEY (CORRECT ANSWERS)

1.	E	11.	C
2.	A	12.	D
3.	E	13.	C
4.	B	14.	A
5.	A	15.	D
6.	A	16.	E
7.	E	17.	C
8.	B	18.	A
9.	D	19.	E
10.	C	20.	D

21.	E
22.	D
23.	C
24.	B
25.	E

EXAMINATION SECTION
TEST 1

DIRECTIONS: Each question or incomplete statement is followed by several suggested answers or completions. Select the one that BEST answers the question or completes the statement. *PRINT THE LETTER OF THE CORRECT ANSWER IN THE SPACE AT THE RIGHT.*

1. A database uses _____ to identify information.

    A. record numbers   B. register addresses
    C. field names   D. directories

1.____

2. _____ could be added to a database in order to increase the number of search and access points available to a user.

    A. Subject discriptors   B. Partitions
    C. Term authority lists   D. Call programs

2.____

3. The central idea behind the management of a database is

    A. procedural and nonprocedural interfaces
    B. minimal redundancy and minimal storage space
    C. physical data independence
    D. the separation of data description and data manipulation

3.____

4. Which of the following is NOT a type of query language operator used in database searches?

    A. Object-oriented   B. Logical
    C. Relational   D. Mathematical

4.____

5. When accessing a record in an indexed file, which of the following steps would be performed FIRST?

    A. Accessing the index
    B. Disk access to the record or bucket
    C. Data transfer from disk to main program memory
    D. Relative address conversion to absolute address

5.____

6. A database management system (DBMS) that employs a hierarchy, but may relate each lower-level data element to more than one parent element, is classified specifically as a(n) _____ DBMS.

    A. object-oriented   B. network
    C. relational   D. aggregational

6.____

7. A value-added field might be added to a database in order to

    A. standardize field formats
    B. estimate the disk capacity for a full database
    C. provide indexing consistency
    D. improve retrieval

7.____

8. Each of the following disks is a type of direct-access disk-storage system EXCEPT   8.____

    A. magnetic disk   B. floppy
    C. moving-capstan   D. fixed-head

9. In determining an appropriate file organization, three principal factors must be consid-   9.____
ered.
Which of the following is NOT one of these factors?

    A. Volatility   B. Conversion
    C. Activity   D. Size

10. A _____ file is used to update or modify data in a master file.   10.____

    A. descriptor   B. transaction
    C. secondary   D. conversion

11. Which of the following steps in designing and using a database would be performed   11.____
FIRST?

    A. Selecting a name for the file
    B. Deciding the form into which information should be stored
    C. Data definition
    D. Defining the type of data to be stored in each field

12. Each of the following is an advantage associated with the use of a DBMS over a flat-file   12.____
system EXCEPT

    A. fewer storage requirements
    B. better data integrity
    C. lower software costs
    D. lower operating costs

13. Memory storage space that is not directly addressable by processor instructions, but by   13.____
specialized I/O instructions, is called

    A. allocated memory   B. secondary storage
    C. internal storage   D. main memory

14. Which of the following is NOT a disadvantage associated with sequential file processing?   14.____

    A. Master files must be sorted into key field sequence.
    B. Files are only current immediately after an update.
    C. Files are difficult to design.
    D. Transaction files must be stored in the same key.

15. When data is updated in some, but not all, of the files in which it appears, _____ has   15.____
occurred.

    A. data confusion   B. data dependence
    C. cross-keying   D. data redundancy

16. The MOST common medium for direct-access storage is   16.____

    A. optical disk   B. magnetic tape
    C. hard card   D. magnetic disk

17. The purpose of *hashing* is to

    A. discover an unpartitioned sector onto which data may be written
    B. determine a schedule by which batch-processed data may be submitted to the computer
    C. create a buffer delay between data entry and output during interactive processing
    D. convert the key field value for a record to the address of the record on a file

17.____

18. What is the term for the description of a specific set of data corresponding to a model of an enterprise, which is obtained by using a particular data description language?

    A. Schema
    C. Object instance
    B. Descriptor
    D. Conceptualization

18.____

19. In a sequential file, records are arranged in sequence according to one or more

    A. query languages
    C. key fields
    B. column numbers
    D. hash marks

19.____

20. Which of the following is NOT a mathematical query language operator used in database searches?

    A. +
    B. >=
    C. ^
    D. /

20.____

21. In _____ file organization, the cost per each transaction processed remains about the same as the percent of records accessed on a file increases.

    A. sequential
    C. indexed sequential
    B. hashed
    D. random

21.____

22. For more complex data types, such as those used in multimedia applications, what type of DBMS would be MOST useful?

    A. Hierarchical
    C. Object-oriented
    B. Relational
    D. Network

22.____

23. When determining how many generations of a file to retain in a database, the PRIMARY factor is usually

    A. hardware capabilities
    B. storage space
    C. whether files are keyed or indexed
    D. probability of need to access old data for recovery purposes

23.____

24. When data is transferred from a user program to secondary storage, it first passes through

    A. program private memory
    C. I/O buffers
    B. file system buffers
    D. program code

24.____

25. In order to maintain files in a database, each of the following operations is typically required EXCEPT

    A. balancing index trees
    B. altering the file system's directory
    C. changing field widths
    D. adding fields to records

25.____

KEY (CORRECT ANSWERS)

1.	C		11.	B
2.	A		12.	C
3.	D		13.	B
4.	A		14.	C
5.	A		15.	A
6.	B		16.	D
7.	D		17.	D
8.	C		18.	A
9.	B		19.	C
10.	B		20.	B

21.	D
22.	C
23.	D
24.	D
25.	B

TEST 2

1. An installation has two tape drives and one disk drive. An application program requires access to three sequential files: an old master file, a transaction file, and an updated master file.
   Typically, the _____ file should be stored on the disk.   1._____

   A. old master
   B. transaction
   C. updated master
   D. both versions of the master

2. The purpose of *record blocking* is to   2._____

   A. allow multiple records to be brought into main memory in a single access to secondary storage
   B. create the illusion of a *virtual device* for the program until the spooler copies a record to the real device
   C. allocate more free buffer space to a file prior to run-unit determination
   D. offload responsibilities for building data paths from the CPU

3. Entries in a database's secondary key tables (index files), which tell the computer where a data is stored on the disk, are   3._____

   A. logical records
   C. physical records
   B. data addresses
   D. secondary keys

4. Of the types of file organization below, which involves the LOWEST volatility?   4._____

   A. Direct
   C. Master-keyed
   B. Sequential
   D. Indexed

5. Typically each of the following elements is defined during the *data definition* process EXCEPT   5._____

   A. field types
   C. number of columns
   B. field names
   D. width of fields

6. A database's master index contains   6._____

   A. the key values for an indexed sequential file
   B. the machine code for every field in a given set of records
   C. the logical record for every randomly-accessed file
   D. each field's physical location on a disk pack

7. Which of the following types of information would MOST likely be stored in a logic field?   7._____

   A. Calendar month/day/year
   B. A patient or customer's mailing address
   C. Numbers that may later be involved in some mathematical calculations
   D. The designation of an employee's status is hourly or salaried

8. When determining how frequently a sequential master file should be updated, each of the following factors should be considered EXCEPT

    A. activity ratio   B. rate of data change
    C. storage space   D. urgency for current data

8._____

9. Which of the following programs is a file manager, rather than a DBMS?

    A. Q&A   B. FoxPro   C. Approach   D. Paradox

9._____

10. Which of the following is NOT an advantage associated with the use of indexed file processing?

    A. No need for hashing algorithm
    B. Random access is faster than direct processing
    C. Can function with applications required for both sequential and direct processing
    D. Access to specific records faster than sequential processing

10._____

11. Of the query language operators listed below, which is mathematical?

    A. AND   B. SUB   C. <   D. SQRT(N)

11._____

12. A collection of records may sometimes be structured as a file on secondary storage, rather than as a data structure in main memory.
Which of the following is NOT a possible reason for this?

    A. Permanence of storage
    B. Security concerns
    C. Size of collection
    D. Selective access requirements

12._____

13. What is the term for the disk rotation time needed for the physical record to pass under read/write heads?

    A. Transaction time   B. Latency time
    C. Head displacement time   D. Transfer time

13._____

14. The subset of a database schema required by a particular application program is referred to as a(n)

    A. root   B. user's view
    C. logical structure   D. node

14._____

15. Which of the following steps in designing and using a database would be performed LAST?

    A. Defining the type of data that will be stored in each field
    B. Assigning field names
    C. Data definition
    D. Defining the width of alphanumeric and numeric fields

15._____

16. What type of database structure organizes data in the form of two-dimensional tables?

    A. Relational   B. Network
    C. Logical   D. Hierarchical

16._____

17. What is the term for the specific modules that are capable of reading and writing buffer contents on devices?   17._____

    A. Spoolers   B. Device handlers
    C. I/O managers   D. Memory allocators

18. Each of the following is a disadvantage associated with the use of a DBMS EXCEPT   18._____

    A. extensive conversion costs
    B. possible wide distribution of data losses and damage
    C. reduced data security
    D. start-up costs

19. _____ decisions about a database begin after a feasibility study and continue to be refined throughout the design and creation process.   19._____

    A. Procedural   B. Structural
    C. Conversion   D. Content

20. Each of the following is an advantage associated with direct file processing EXCEPT   20._____

    A. ability to update several files at the same time
    B. no need for separate transaction files
    C. files do not have to be sorted into key field sequence
    D. fewer storage space required than for sequential processing

21. The core of any file management system accesses secondary storage through   21._____

    A. the I/O manager   B. file system buffers
    C. relative addressing   D. key access

22. Each of the following is a responsibility typically belonging to a file system EXCEPT   22._____

    A. maintaining directories
    B. interfacing the CPU with a secondary storage device
    C. establishing paths for data flow between main memory and secondary storage
    D. buffering data for delivery to the CPU or secondary devices

23. In a hierarchical database, there are several phone numbers belonging to a single address.   23._____
This is an example of

    A. vector data aggregate   B. data dependence
    C. data confusion   D. data redundancy

24. A DBMS might access the data dictionary for each of the following purposes EXCEPT   24._____

    A. change the description of a data field
    B. to determine if a data element already exists before adding
    C. request and deliver information from the database to the user
    D. determine what application programs can access what data elements

25. _____ would MOST likely be stored in a memo field.   25.____

    A. A revisable listing of symptoms specific to a particular ailment
    B. The designation of a patient's gender (male/female)
    C. A patient's billing number
    D. The date of a patient's last visit

KEY (CORRECT ANSWERS)

1.	B	11.	D
2.	A	12.	B
3.	A	13.	B
4.	B	14.	B
5.	C	15.	D
6.	A	16.	A
7.	D	17.	B
8.	C	18.	C
9.	A	19.	B
10.	B	20.	D

21.	A
22.	B
23.	A
24.	C
25.	A

EXAMINATION SECTION
TEST 1

1. The stage in a system's life cycle in which logical and physical specifications are produced is called

    A. implementation   B. design
    C. conception   D. documentation

1._____

2. Which of the following is a network topology that links a number of computers by a single circuit with all messages broadcast to the entire network?

    A. Daisy–chain   B. Broadband
    C. Bus   D. Ring

2._____

3. Of the following statements about information as a resource, which is generally FALSE?

    A. It has value and lends itself to the process of management.
    B. It can be overabundant and overused.
    C. Its usefulness tends to decrease with time.
    D. It can be consumed and expended in the same way as many capital resources.

3._____

4. What is the term for the extra bit built into EBCDIC and ASCII codes that is used as a check bit to insure accuracy?

    A. Parity   B. Auditor   C. Damper   D. Buffer

4._____

5. In the systems development process, which of the following is typically performed FIRST?

    A. Conversion   B. Programming
    C. Production   D. Testing

5._____

6. Which of the following is a term for a device used to store and retrieve large numbers of optical disks?

    A. Warehouse   B. Vault   C. Clearing   D. Jukebox

6._____

7. Each of the following can generally be said to be an element of the changing contemporary business environment EXCEPT

    A. global work groups   B. stable environment
    C. location independence   D. time–based competition

7._____

8. Of the following methods of changing from one information system to another, which is generally considered to be the safest?

    A. Pilot study   B. Direct cutover
    C. Phased approach   D. Parallel strategy

8._____

9. Which of the following is NOT typically a characteristic of a management information sys-   9.____
   tem?

    A. Extensive analytical capability
    B. Known and stable information requirements
    C. Internal rather than external orientation
    D. Generally reporting–and control–oriented

10. In information systems terminology, a person, place, or thing about which information   10.____
    must be kept is referred to as a(n)

    A. element   B. entity
    C. assemblage   D. pixel

11. Which of the following are considered to be moral dimensions that are emblematic of the   11.____
    information age?
        I. Accountability and control
        II. Property rights
        III. Quality of life
        IV. Information rights and obligations
  The CORRECT answer is:

    A. I, II   B. I, II, III
    C. I, III, IV   D. I, II, III, IV

12. In order to be classified as a *mainframe,* a computer must typically have at LEAST   12.____

    A. 1 remote access server
    B. 50 megabytes of RAM
    C. 1 gigabyte of RAM
    D. 5 gigabytes of secondary storage space

13. For most organizations, the FIRST step in developing a telecommunications plan should   13.____
    be to

    A. identify critical areas where telecommunications currently has an impact
    B. identify the organization's long–range business plan
    C. identify critical areas where telecommunications may have a future impact
    D. audit existing telecommunications functions

14. What is the term for a change in a data signal, from positive to negative or vice–versa,   14.____
    that is used as a measure of transmission speed?

    A. Baud   B. Switch   C. Byte   D. Bit

15. Currently, in service industries such as finance, insurance, and real estate, information   15.____
    technology generally constitutes about _____% of invested capital.

    A. 10   B. 30   C. 50   D. 70

16. Which of the following signifies the emerging standard language for relational database   16.____
    management systems?

    A. SGML   B. HTML   C. Perl   D. SQL

17. Over time, organizations have developed an ethical framework for handling system–related issues. Generally, the first step in any organization's ethical analysis should be to identify

    A. the higher–order values involved
    B. the potential consequences of any decision
    C. reasonable options
    D. the stakeholders

17._____

18. Telephone lines that are continously available for transmission by a lessee are described as

    A. validated
    C. formalized
                         B. denuded
                         D. dedicated

18._____

19. In a typical telecommunications system, a message that originates from the host computer will then pass through a

    A. front–end processor
    C. controller
                          B. modem
                         D. multiplexer

19._____

20. The table or list that relates record keys to physical locations on direct access files is called the

    A. key   B. index   C. card file   D. criterion

20._____

21. Which of the following offers the best definition of *data* as it applies to information systems?

    A. Things that are known to have occurred, to exist, or to be true
    B. Productions of exact copies of documents by electronic scanning and transmission
    C. Information not previously known to people within an organization
    D. Raw facts that have not been organized and arranged into understandable and usable form

21._____

22. A logical unit of a program that performs one or a small number of functions is known as a(n)

    A. module   B. element   C. loop   D. packet

22._____

23. Which of the following is a fourth–generation computer language?

    A. FORTRAN   B. dBASE   C. C   D. Ada

23._____

24. The logical description of an entire database, listing all the data elements and the relationships among them, is known as the

    A. value chain
    C. matrix
                          B. schema
                         D. shell

24._____

25. Systems theory defines a system as an entity that is generally greater than the sum of its parts. Which of the following terms describes this condition?

    A. Synchronicity
    C. Interdependence
                           B. Collectivism
                         D. Synergy

25._____

KEY (CORRECT ANSWERS)

1.	B		11.	D
2.	C		12.	B
3.	D		13.	D
4.	A		14.	A
5.	D		15.	D
6.	D		16.	D
7.	B		17.	A
8.	D		18.	D
9.	A		19.	A
10.	B		20.	B

21.	D
22.	A
23.	B
24.	B
25.	D

TEST 2

DIRECTIONS: Each question or incomplete statement is followed by several suggested answers or completions. Select the one that BEST answers the question or completes the statement. *PRINT THE LETTER OF THE CORRECT ANSWER IN THE SPACE AT THE RIGHT.*

1. Of the types of organizational change that are enabled by information technology, which involves the highest levels of risk and reward?

    A. Paradigm shift
    B. Automation
    C. Business reengineering
    D. Rationalization of procedures

1.____

2. Most local–area networks (LANS) are _____ networks.

    A. token ring   B. ring   C. star   D. bus

2.____

3. Which of the following is an input device which translates images into digital form for processing?

    A. Surveyor   B. Pen   C. Compiler   D. Scanner

3.____

4. In a system, the appearance of an additional pattern or sequence of states is referred to as

    A. autonomy   B. differentiation
    C. bifurcation   D. variation

4.____

5. Which of the following is NOT considered to be an information output?

    A. Storage   B. Expert–system advice
    C. Query response   D. Report

5.____

6. Which of the following is a direct access storage device (DASD)?

    A. Punch card   B. Sequential tape
    C. Printed page   D. Magnetic disk

6.____

7. Which of the following is most likely to be an output from a knowledge work system (KWS)?

    A. Special report   B. Model
    C. Summary report   D. Query response

7.____

8. A system resting on accepted and fixed definitions of data and procedures, operating with predefined rules, is described in systems terminology as

    A. formal   B. computer–based
    C. fixed   D. expert

8.____

9. Which of the following is a characteristic of operational data? They

    A. are stored on a single platform
    B. contain recent as well as historical data
    C. are organized around major business informational subjects
    D. are generally used by isolated legacy systems

9.____

10. Which of the following signifies a telecommunications network that requires its own dedi-   10.____
cated channels and encompasses a limited physical distance?

   A. WAN   B. KWS   C. LAN   D. ISDN

11. Which of the following terms is used for the capture or collection of raw data from within   11.____
the organization, or from its external environment, for processing in an information system?

   A. Feedback   B. Tracking   C. Entry   D. Input

12. What is the term for the high–speed storage of frequently used instructions and data?   12.____

   A. Cache   B. Index   C. Reserve   D. Packet

13. Which of the following represents the largest unit of data?   13.____

   A. Byte   B. Record   C. Field   D. File

14. In most organizations, the entire system–building effort is driven by   14.____

   A. user information requirements
   B. existing hardware
   C. user training requirements
   D. availability of packaged applications

15. Which of the following terms is used to describe a process of change governed by prob-   15.____
abilities at each step?

   A. Adiabatic   B. Stochastic
   C. Multifinal   D. Probabilistic

16. In object–oriented programming, a specific class of objects often receives the features of   16.____
a more general class. This process is referred to as

   A. aliasing   B. inheritance
   C. summation   D. incrementation

17. In a typical organization, the strategic planning of an MIS would be the responsibility of   17.____
the

   A. steering committee
   B. project teams
   C. operations personnel and end users
   D. chief information officer

18. Which of the following is a specialized computer that supervises communications traffic   18.____
between the CPU and the peripheral devices in a telecommunications system?

   A. Controller   B. Concentrator
   C. Connector   D. Compiler

19. Of the following steps in the machine cycle of a computer, which occurs FIRST?   19.____

   A. Transmission of data from main memory to storage register
   B. Placement of instruction in instruction register
   C. ALU performance
   D. Placement of instruction in address register

20. Which of the following is a process of recoding information which reduces the number of   20.____
different characters in a message while increasing the different number of characters to
be recognized?

   A. The black box method   B. Daisy chaining
   C. Aliasing   D. Chunking

21. Of the following methodologies for establishing organizational MIS requirements, which   21.____
is most explicitly oriented toward deploying information systems as a competitive
weapon?

   A. Critical success factors (CSF)
   B. Strategic cube and value chain
   C. Business sytems planning (BSP)
   D. Strategy set transformation

22. Which of the following is a type of MIS application used for tracking and monitoring?   22.____

   A. Database
   B. Decision Support System (DSS)
   C. Spreadsheet
   D. Desktop publishing

23. An organization's information requirements are often analyzed by looking at the entire   23.____
organization in terms of units, functions, processes, and data elements. What is the term
most frequently used for such an examination?

   A. Semantic networking   B. Decision support
   C. Enterprise analysis   D. Run control

24. Which of the following would most likely be classifed as an *information worker*?   24.____

   A. Engineer   B. Scientist
   C. Data processor   D. Architect

25. In an organization that uses a decision support system to make stock investment deci-   25.____
sions, which of the following would be classified as memory aids to the system?

   A. Graphs   B. Databases
   C. Menus   D. Training documents

KEY (CORRECT ANSWERS)

1.	A		11.	D
2.	D		12.	A
3.	D		13.	D
4.	C		14.	A
5.	A		15.	B
6.	D		16.	B
7.	B		17.	D
8.	A		18.	A
9.	D		19.	B
10.	C		20.	D

21.	B
22.	A
23.	C
24.	C
25.	B

———

TEST 3

DIRECTIONS: Each question or incomplete statement is followed by several suggested answers or completions. Select the one that BEST answers the question or completes the statement. *PRINT THE LETTER OF THE CORRECT ANSWER IN THE SPACE AT THE RIGHT.*

1. In the _____ process, the components of a system and their relationship to each other are laid out as they would appear to users.   1.____

    A. external integration   B. logical design
    C. file serving   D. hierarchical

2. Over the past two decades, technological trends have raised ethical issues in society, especially in the area of privacy. Which of the following trends has LEAST directly impacted the issue of privacy?   2.____

    A. Advances in data storage techniques and declining storage costs
    B. Advances in telecommunications infrastructure
    C. The doubling of computer power every 18 months
    D. Advances in data mining techniques for large databases

3. Which of the following systems exists at the strategic level of an organization?   3.____

    A. Expert system
    B. Decision support system (DSS)
    C. Value chain
    D. Executive support system (ESS)

4. Which of the following is equal to one–billionth of a second?   4.____

    A. Millisecond   B. Picosecond
    C. Nanosecond   D. Microsecond

5. A small section of a program that can be easily stored in primary storage and quickly accessed from secondary storage is a(n)   5.____

    A. sector   B. module   C. page   D. applet

6. Which of the following statements about hierarchical and network database systems is TRUE?   6.____
They

    A. do support English–language inquiries for information
    B. involve easily changeable access pathways
    C. are difficult to install
    D. are relatively inefficient processors

7. Which of the following is a programming language that is portable across different brands of soft hardware, and is used for both military and nonmilitary applications?   7.____

    A. FORTRAN   B. Pascal   C. Ada   D. C

8. Which of the following would be LEAST likely to be an output of an office automation system (OAS)?   8.____

    A. Memo   B. Schedule   C. List   D. Mail

9. At a minimum, an information system must consist of all of the following EXCEPT   9._____

    A. computers   B. data   C. people   D. procedures

10. What is the term for the strategy used to search through the rule base in an expert system?   10._____

    A. Index server   B. Key field
    C. Register   D. Inference engine

11. Which of the following communications media has the greatest frequency range?   11._____

    A. Wireless (electromagnetic)
    B. Fiber optics
    C. Wireless (PCS)
    D. Microwave

12. Models of decision–making in which decisions are shaped by the organization's standard operation procedures are described as   12._____

    A. systems–oriented   B. indexed
    C. bureaucratic   D. sequential

13. The first element involved in a standard dataflow diagram is a(n)   13._____

    A. dataflow   B. external entity
    C. data store   D. process

14. A system that seeks a set of related goals is described as   14._____

    A. purposive   B. closed   C. fixed   D. driven

15. Weaknesses in a system's _____ controls may affect the entire system of general controls, which may not be properly executed or enforced.   15._____

    A. administrative   B. software
    C. implementation   D. computer operations

16. Current and historical data from operational systems is often consolidated for management reporting and analysis into a database with reporting and query tools. This type of database is usually referred to as a(n)   16._____

    A. warehouse   B. redundancy
    C. controller   D. library

17. A project manager at an organization plans to compose letters outlining details of an upcoming trade show to be addressed individually to several dozen employees. The most appropriate type of application for this purpose is   17._____

    A. simple word processing   B. desktop publishing
    C. a mail merge   D. an automated document

18. In the process of systems analysis, which of the following procedures is typically per-   18.____
formed FIRST?

   A. Defining a problem that can be solved by a newly designed system
   B. Examining existing documents
   C. Identifying the primary owners and users of data in the organization
   D. Identifying the information requirements that must be met by a system solution

19. Each of the following is a method for performing a data quality audit EXCEPT surveying   19.____

   A. data dictionaries
   B. entire data files
   C. end users for perceptions of data quality
   D. samples from data files

20. Which of the following signifies semiconductor memory chips that contain program   20.____
instructions?

   A. RAM   B. ROM   C. CPU   D. ALU

21. The Fair Information Practices Principles set forth in 1973 include: 21.____
   I. Individuals have rights of access, inspection, review, and amendment to sys-
      tems that contain information about them
   II. Managers of systems are responsible and can be held liable for the damages
       done by systems, for the reliability, and for their security
   III. Managers do not have the right of access to any form of interorganizational
        correspondence if individuals do not wish to grant such access
   IV. Governments have the right to intervene in the information relationships
       among private parties
   The CORRECT answer is:

   A. I, II   B. II, III
   C. I, II, IV   D. II, III, IV

22. In information systems terminology, a group of records of the same type is known as a   22.____

   A. class   B. field   C. batch   D. file

23. In systems theory, communication which travels through informal rather than formal   23.____
channels is known as

   A. noise
   B. back channel communication
   C. cross–talk
   D. the grapevine

24. In order to be useful as a resource, information must satisfy each of the following condi-   24.____
tions EXCEPT it must

   A. be accurate
   B. be available when needed
   C. reinforce beliefs
   D. relate to the business or matters at hand

25. In most contemporary organizations, the role of an MIS department can be described as   25.____

    A. performing key design and analysis functions, before and after a systems design has been implemented

    B. designing, installing, testing, and maintaining all organizational computer–based information and communications systems

    C. providing and perfecting all information and communications needs at the organization's management level

    D. coordinating corporate MIS efforts and providing an overall computational infrastructure

———

KEY (CORRECT ANSWERS)

1.	B	11.	C
2.	C	12.	C
3.	D	13.	B
4.	C	14.	A
5.	C	15.	A
6.	C	16.	A
7.	C	17.	C
8.	C	18.	C
9.	A	19.	A
10.	D	20.	B

21.	C
22.	D
23.	B
24.	C
25.	D

———

EXAMINATION SECTION
TEST 1

DIRECTIONS: Each question or incomplete statement is followed by several suggested answers or completions. Select the one that BEST answers the question or completes the statement. *PRINT THE LETTER OF THE CORRECT ANSWER IN THE SPACE AT THE RIGHT.*

1. A microprocessor includes media for each of the following EXCEPT   1.____

    A. secondary storage   B. control
    C. logic   D. memory

2. Which of the following protocols is LEAST likely to be used in a wide–area network   2.____
(WAN)?

    A. SNA   B. Token passing
    C. TCP/IP   D. DEC DNA

3. In an expert system, the rule base is sometimes searched using a strategy that begins   3.____
with a hypothesis and seeks out more information until the hypothesis is either proved or
disproved. This strategy is known as

    A. backward chaining
    B. key fielding
    C. indexed sequential access
    D. process specification

4. The meaning of signs, symbols, messages or systems are involved in a body of inquiry   4.____
known as

    A. linguistics   B. semantics
    C. communications   D. syntactics

5. Which of the following is a query language?   5.____

    A. Nomad   B. Ideal   C. Systat   D. RPG–III

6. Which of the following is the typical unit of measurement used by systems designers to   6.____
estimate the length of time needed to complete a project?

    A. Data–week   B. Man–hour
    C. File–hour   D. Man–month

7. Which of the following is the oldest professional computer society in the United States?   7.____

    A. Data Processing Management Association (DPMA)
    B. Institute for Certification of Computer Professionals (ICP)
    C. Association of Computing Machinery (ACM)
    D. Information Technology Association of America (ITAA)

8. Which of the following terms is commonly used to describe the interaction of people and   8.____
machines in the work environment, especially in terms of job design and health issues?

    A. Connectivity   B. Ergonomics
    C. Feasibility   D. Interface

9. Which of the following is a likely application of the sensitivity analysis models of a decision–support system?   9.____

    A. Forecasting sales
    B. Determining the proper product mix within a given market
    C. Predicting the actions of competitors
    D. Goal seeking

10. What is the term for the temporary storage location in a control unit where small amounts of data or instructions reside for thousandths of a second just before use?   10.____

    A. Cache   B. Register   C. Sector   D. Buffer

11. Systems whose behavior includes options without specification of probabilities within the system are described as   11.____

    A. runaway   B. possibilistic
    C. stochastic   D. probabilistic

12. The physical devices and software that link various hardware components and transfer data from one physical location to another are known collectively as   12.____

    A. cyberspace
    B. wide–area networks
    C. telecommunications technology
    D. semantic networks

13. Which of the following is a tangible benefit associated with organizational information systems?   13.____

    A. Streamlined operations   B. Higher asset utilization
    C. Inventory reduction   D. Improved planning

14. Which of the following is NOT generally considered to be a physical component of an MIS?   14.____

    A. Personnel   B. Information
    C. Procedures   D. Software

15. Any undesired information in a communication channel which is not part of the intended message is typically referred to as   15.____

    A. resistance   B. noise
    C. data error   D. cross–talk

16. Which of the following is the ASCII 8–bit binary code for the number 1?   16.____

    A. 0001 0001   B. 0101 0001
    C. 0000 1000   D. 1001 0001

17. Which of the following is a method of organizing expert system knowledge into chunks in which relationships are based on shared characteristics determined by the user?   17.____

    A. Indexing   B. GUI
    C. Batch processing   D. Frames

18. Which of the following is a telecommunications requirement that is particular to the task of on–line data entry?

    A. High–capacity video and data capabilities
    B. Infrequent, high–volume bursts of information
    C. Instant response
    D. Direct response

18._____

19. What is the term for the technology which breaks blocks of text into small fixed bundles of data and routes them in an economical way through an available communications channel?

    A. Optical character recognition
    B. Frame relay
    C. Packet switching
    D. Branch exchange

19._____

20. A transaction processing system rejects a transaction on the basis that it includes a Social Security number which contains an alphabetic character. This is an example of a(n) _____ check.

    A. reasonableness   B. format
    C. dependency   D. existence

20._____

21. The smallest unit of data for defining an image in a computer is the

    A. byte   B. pixel   C. quark   D. bit

21._____

22. In a microcomputer, which of the following transmits signals specifying whether to read or write data from a given primary storage address, input device, or output device?

    A. Control bus   B. Address bus
    C. Data bus   D. CPU

22._____

23. Which of the following stages occurs the LATEST in the traditional systems life cycle model?

    A. Systems study   B. Programming
    C. Design   D. Project definition

23._____

24. The fastest and most expensive memory used in a microcomputer is located in the

    A. cache   B. register   C. hard disk   D. RAM

24._____

25. Which of the following is an optical disk system that allows users to record data only once, but to read the data indefinitely?

    A. WORM   B. EPROM   C. RAM   D. TQM

25._____

KEY (CORRECT ANSWERS)

1.	A		11.	B
2.	B		12.	C
3.	A		13.	C
4.	B		14.	B
5.	D		15.	B
6.	D		16.	B
7.	C		17.	D
8.	B		18.	D
9.	D		19.	C
10.	B		20.	B

21.	B
22.	A
23.	B
24.	B
25.	A

———————

TEST 2

1. Which of the following styles of systems development is most often used for information systems at the individual level?

    A. End–user computing
    B. Commercial software packages
    C. Prototyping
    D. Traditional life cycle

    1._____

2. Which of the following is a programming language that was developed in 1956 for scientific and mathematical applications?

    A. COBOL B. BASIC C. Pascal D. FORTRAN

    2._____

3. Which of the following personnel would be considered a *technical specialist* in an MIS department?

    A. Education specialist
    C. Applications programmer
    B. Database administrator
    D. Systems analyst

    3._____

4. Which of the following is NOT a characteristic of a fault–tolerant system?

    A. The use of special software routines to detect hardware failures
    B. Extra memory chips, processors, and disk storage
    C. Continuous detection of bugs or program defects
    D. Hardware parts that can be removed without system disruption

    4._____

5. Defining a system program in such a way that it may call itself is an example of

    A. eudemony
    C. redundancy
    B. recursion
    D. artificial intelligence

    5._____

6. What is the term used to enumerate the number of bits that can be processed at one time by a computer?

    A. Data bus width
    C. RAM capacity
    B. Word length
    D. Bandwidth

    6._____

7. Which of the following is another term for a field, or a grouping of characters into a word, group of words, or complete number?

    A. Code
    C. Data element
    B. Byte
    D. File

    7._____

8. A person in a multi–user system sends a message using the OSI model to another user at a different location. At the messenger's end of the system, after passing through the *session* layer of the model, the message will then enter the _____ layer.

    A. transport
    C. presentation
    B. network
    D. data link

    8._____

9. Which of the following is NOT a disadvantage associated with the traditional life cycle model of systems development?

    A. Time consumption   B. Oversimplification
    C. Cost   D. Inflexibility

9.____

10. Transmission speeds that would fall within the expected range of coaxial cable are _____ per second.

    A. 400 bits   B. 50 megabits
    C. 300 megabits   D. 7 gigabits

10.____

11. Which of the following is a telecommunications computer that collects and temporarily stores messages from terminals for batch transmission to the host computer?

    A. Assembler   B. Concentrator
    C. Buffer   D. Compiler

11.____

12. Which of the following is an advantage associated with the centralized or teleprocessing model of multi–user systems?

    A. Local computing   B. Scaleability
    C. Low start–up costs   D. Low technical risk

12.____

13. Software systems that can operate on different hardware platforms are referred to as _____ systems.

    A. open   B. interoperable
    C. branched   D. transmigrational

13.____

14. What is the term for the process by which the properties of a collection (i.e., of data) are described in terms of the sums of the properties of the units contained in the collection?

    A. Unity   B. Autarky
    C. Chunking   D. Aggregation

14.____

15. In systems terminology, what is the term for output that is returned to the appropriate members of an organization to help them evaluate or correct input?

    A. Exit data   B. Feedback
    C. Assessor   D. Valuation

15.____

16. The years 1957 to 1963 are generally considered to have been the _____ generation in the evolution of computer hardware technology.

    A. first   B. second   C. third   D. fourth

16.____

17. A conversion approach in which the new system completely replaces the old one on an appointed day is known as

    A. focused differentiation   B. direct cutover
    C. allied distribution   D. batch processing

17.____

18. Of the following types of business network redesign, the one that can be said to be most highly coupled is/are

    18.____

    A. interenterprise system access
    B. knowledge networks
    C. EDI
    D. interenterprise process integration

19. Which of the following terms is used to describe the shape or configuration of a telecommunications network?

    19.____

    A. Duplex
    B. Topology
    C. Protocol
    D. Transmissivity

20. Which of the following is/are recognized differences between microcomputers and workstations?

    20.____

    I. Microcomputers have more powerful mathematical processing capabilities.
    II. Microcomputers are more useful for computer–aided design (CAD).
    III. Workstations are more widely used by knowledge workers.
    IV. Workstations can more easily perform multiple tasks simultaneously.

The CORRECT answer is:

    A. I, II
    B. II, III
    C. III, IV
    D. II, IV

21. Which of the following signifies a tool for retrieving and transferring files from a remote computer?

    21.____

    A. EDI
    B. CPU
    C. TCP/IP
    D. FTP

22. Which of the following is a federal privacy law that applies to private institutions?

    22.____

    A. Freedom of Information Act of 1968 (as amended)
    B. Privacy Act of 1974 (as amended)
    C. Privacy Protection Act of 1980
    D. Computer Matching and Privacy Protection Act of 1988

23. The main contribution of end–user systems development typically occurs in the area of

    23.____

    A. productivity enhancement
    B. improved updating functions
    C. increased technical complexity
    D. improved efficiency in transaction processing

24. In cooperative processing, a mainframe and a microcomputer generally share tasks. The mainframe, however, is generally best at performing

    24.____

    A. screen presentation
    B. error processing
    C. data field editing
    D. file input and output

25. In a systems development process, users are made active members of development   25._____
project teams, and some users are placed in charge of system training and installation.
In this case, management has made use of _____ tools.

    A. external integration   B. internal integration
    C. formal planning   D. formal control

KEY (CORRECT ANSWERS)

1.	C	11.	B
2.	D	12.	D
3.	B	13.	A
4.	C	14.	D
5.	B	15.	B
6.	B	16.	B
7.	C	17.	B
8.	A	18.	B
9.	B	19.	B
10.	B	20.	C

21.	D
22.	C
23.	A
24.	D
25.	A

TEST 3

Each question or incomplete statement is followed by several suggested answers or completions. Select the one that BEST answers the question or completes the statement. *PRINT THE LETTER OF THE CORRECT ANSWER IN THE SPACE AT THE RIGHT.*

1. As a general rule, the development of a system that will be used by others can be expected to take _____ as long as the development of an individual system that will be used only by the developer.

    A. half   B. twice
    C. three times   D. five times

1.____

2. In LANs, the token ring configuration is most useful for

    A. broadcasting messages to the entire network through a single circuit
    B. multidirectional transmissions between microcomputers or between micros and a larger computer
    C. transmissions between microcomputers and a larger computer that require a degree of traffic control
    D. transmitting large volumes of data between microcomputers

2.____

3. Which of the following statements about expert systems is generally TRUE? They

    A. function best in lower–level clerical functions
    B. require minimal development resources
    C. are highly adaptable over time
    D. are capable of representing a wide range of causal models

3.____

4. A middle–range machine with a RAM capacity that measures from about 10 megabytes to over 1 gigabyte is known as a

    A. microcomputer   B. minicomputer
    C. desktop computer   D. mainframe

4.____

5. Which of the following media uses the sector method for storing data?

    A. Cache   B. Floppy disk
    C. Hard disk   D. CD–ROM

5.____

6. When mechanisms of functional subsystems are connected causally to influence each other, they are said to be

    A. aggregated   B. coupled
    C. synchronous   D. constrained

6.____

7. Which of the following storage media generally has the largest capacity?

    A. Cache   B. Magnetic disk
    C. Optical disk   D. Magnetic tape

7.____

8. In terms of information ethics, the mechanisms for assessing responsibility for decisions and actions are referred to as

    A. liability   B. capacity
    C. creditability   D. accountability

8.____

9. Which of the following signifies the central switching system that handles a firm's voice and digital communications? 9._____

    A. OSI   B. DSS   C. PBX   D. LAN

10. What is the term for the LAN channel technology that provides a single path for transmitting text, graphics, voice, or video data at one time? 10._____

    A. Bus   B. Baseband
    C. Firewall   D. Broadband

11. The stage in a system's life cycle in which testing, training, and conversion occur is termed 11._____

    A. evaluation   B. design
    C. installation   D. documentation

12. Which of the following is NOT a type of processor used in telecommunications systems? 12._____

    A. Coaxial cable   B. Controller
    C. Modem   D. Multiplexer

13. A database that is stored in more than one physical location is described as 13._____

    A. sequential   B. wide-area
    C. distributed   D. indexed

14. An organization decides to redesign its information system using only the components that are already available to it. In the language of systems theory, the resulting system would be described as a(n) 14._____

    A. ensemble   B. creod   C. kluge   D. cyborg

15. What is the term for an integrated circuit made by printing thousands or millions of transistors on a small silicon chip? 15._____

    A. Cache   B. Semiconductor
    C. Control unit   D. Microprocessor

16. Computer programming includes a logic pattern that allows for the repetition of certain actions while a specified condition occurs or until a certain conditions exists. This pattern is known as the 16._____

    A. object linkage   B. selection construct
    C. key field   D. iteration construct

17. Which of the following is the standard or reference model for allowing e-mail systems operating on different hardware to communicate? 17._____

    A. X.400   B. X.25   C. X.12   D. FDDI

18. Which of the following terms is used to denote circular tracks on the same vertical line within a disk pack? 18._____

    A. Track   B. Spindle   C. Sector   D. Cylinder

19. A system that is capable of listing the descriptions of each of a certain set of alternatives is described as

    A. generative
    C. smart
    B. contingency–based
    D. stochastic

19.____

20. Which of the following is an operating cost associated with an information system?

    A. Database establishment
    C. Personnel training
    B. Facilities
    D. Hardware acquisition

20.____

21. As a collaboration tool, the World Wide Web involves

    A. data that undergoes frequent updating
    B. documents predominantly authored by a single user
    C. applications with data at multiple sites
    D. applications with high security requirements

21.____

22. A mathematical formula used to translate a record's key field directly into its storage location is known as a(n) _____ algorithm.

    A. synchronous
    C. asynchronous
    B. genetic
    D. transform

22.____

23. Which of the following is a common DISADVANTAGE associated with outsourcing the systems development process?

    A. Loss of control over system function
    B. Increased costs
    C. Generally slow progress
    D. Increased paperwork requirements

23.____

24. Which of the following is a network topology in which all computers and other devices are connected to a central host computer?

    A. LAN
    B. Star
    C. Ring
    D. Bus

24.____

25. In terms of information systems, *processing* means the

    A. assignment of data to certain categories for later use
    B. calculation or computation of data to arrive at a solution or conclusion
    C. conversion, manipulation, and analysis of raw input into a meaningful form
    D. collection or capture of raw data for use in an information system

25.____

_____

KEY (CORRECT ANSWERS)

1.	C		11.	C
2.	D		12.	A
3.	A		13.	C
4.	B		14.	C
5.	B		15.	B
6.	B		16.	D
7.	C		17.	A
8.	D		18.	D
9.	C		19.	A
10.	B		20.	B

21.	B
22.	D
23.	A
24.	B
25.	C

EXAMINATION SECTION
TEST 1

DIRECTIONS: Each question or incomplete statement is followed by several suggested answers or completions. Select the one that BEST answers the question or completes the statement. *PRINT THE LETTER OF THE CORRECT ANSWER IN THE SPACE AT THE RIGHT.*

1. What is the term for a device that enables a single communications channel to carry data transmissions from many different sources simultaneously?   1.____

   A. Compiler
   C. Concentrator
   B. Multitasker
   D. Multiplexer

2. Which of the following represents the earliest stage in the computer language translation process?   2.____

   A. Linkage editor
   C. Compiler
   B. Load module
   D. Object code

3. Within data flow diagrams, the transformations that occur within the lowest level are described by   3.____

   A. development methodologies
   B. structure charts
   C. selection constructs
   D. process specifications

4. The time or number of operations after which a process in a system repeats itself is expressed in a measure known as   4.____

   A. periodicity
   C. loop
   B. synchronicity
   D. iteration

5. What is the term for the single steps or actions in the logic of a program that do NOT depend on the existence of any condition?   5.____

   A. Logical construct
   C. Sequence construct
   B. Run control
   D. Rule base

6. Which of the following terms is most different in meaning from the others?   6.____

   A. Data file approach
   B. Relational data model
   C. Flat file organization
   D. Traditional file environment

7. Which of the following is a tool for locating data on the Internet that performs key word searches of an actual database of documents, software, and data files available for downloading?   7.____

   A. WAIS   B. Archie   C. Acrobat   D. Gopher

8. Typical transaction processing (TPS) systems include all of the following types EXCEPT _____ systems.   8.____

   A. finance/accounting
   C. engineering/design
   B. sales/marketing
   D. human resources

9. The main weakness of the enterprise analysis approach to systems development is that it

    A. involves little input at the managerial level
    B. is relatively unstructured
    C. produces an enormous amount of data that is expensive to collect and analyze
    D. only generally identifies an organization's informational requirements

9.____

10. What is the term for special system software that translates a higher–level language into machine language for execution by the computer?

    A. Compiler   B. Translator   C. Renderer   D. Assembler

10.____

11. Compared to private branch exchanges, LANs
    I. are more expensive to install
    II. have a smaller geographical range
    III. are more inflexible
    IV. require specially trained staff
The CORRECT answer is

    A. I *only*   B. I, III
    C. I, II, IV   D. III, IV

11.____

12. Each of the following is considered to be a basic component of a database management system EXCEPT a

    A. transform algorithm
    B. data manipulation language
    C. data definition language
    D. data dictionary

12.____

13. Which of the following is a technical approach to the study of information systems?

    A. Management science   B. Sociology
    C. Political science   D. Psychology

13.____

14. In desktop publishing applications, a user may sometimes elect to alter the standard spacing between two characters. This is a technique known as

    A. weighting   B. kerning   C. pointing   D. leading

14.____

15. In systems design, the generic framework used to think '. about a problem is known as the

    A. schema   B. reference model
    C. prototype   D. operational model

15.____

16. What is the term for a small computer that manages! communications for the host com-puter in a network?

    A. Concentrator   B. Multiplexer
    C. Controller   D. Front–end processor

16.____

17. Which of the following is a competitive strategy for developing new market niches, where a business can compete in a target area better than its competitors?   17._____

   A. Vertical integration
   C. Multitasking
   B. Focused differentiation
   D. Forward engineering

18. An electronic meeting system (EMS) is considered to be a type of collaborative   18._____

   A. executive support system (ESS)
   B. management information system (MIS)
   C. office automation system (OAS)
   D. group decision support system (GDSS)

19. In systems theory, the minimum description required to distinguish a system from its environment is known as a(n)   19._____

   A. blip   B. margin   C. mediation   D. boundary

20. The principal advantage of the hierarchical and network database models is   20._____

   A. adaptability
   B. architecture simplicity
   C. minimal programming requirements
   D. processing efficiency

21. Which of the following is a character–oriented tool for locating data on the Internet which allows a user to locate textual information through a series of hierarchical menus?   21._____

   A. FTP   B. Gopher   C. Lug   D. Archie

22. The principal logical database models include each of the following types EXCEPT   22._____

   A. network
   C. relational
   B. object–oriented
   D. hierarchical

23. Computer programming includes a logic pattern where a stated condition determines which of two or more actions can be taken, depending on the condition. This pattern is known as the   23._____

   A. object linkage
   C. key field
   B. selection construct
   D. iteration construct

24. Which of the following is the tool used by database designers to document a conceptual data model?   24._____

   A. Entity–relationship diagram
   B. Partition statement
   C. Gantt chart
   D. Data–flow diagram

25. The phenomenon of _____ refers to the idea that people will avoid new uncertain alter-   25._____
natives and stick with traditional and familiar rules and procedures.

    A.   the Hawthorne effect
    B.   bounded rationality
    C.   system–oriented reasoning
    D.   case–based reasoning

KEY (CORRECT ANSWERS)

1.	D	11.	C
2.	C	12.	A
3.	D	13.	A
4.	A	14.	B
5.	C	15.	B
6.	B	16.	D
7.	B	17.	B
8.	C	18.	D
9.	C	19.	D
10.	A	20.	D

21.	B
22.	B
23.	B
24.	A
25.	B

TEST 2

DIRECTIONS: Each question or incomplete statement is followed by several suggested answers or completions. Select the one that BEST answers the question or completes the statement. *PRINT THE LETTER OF THE CORRECT ANSWER IN THE SPACE AT THE RIGHT.*

1. In systems theory, the history of a system's structural transformations is referred to as its

    A. ontology
    C. ontogeny
    B. entailment
    D. epistemology

1.____

2. Programming language that consists of the 1s and 0s of binary code is referred to as

    A. machine language
    C. object language
    B. assemblage
    D. pseudocode

2.____

3. Generally, the EBCDIC standard can be used to code up to _____ characters in one byte of information.

    A. 128   B. 256   C. 512   D. 1024

3.____

4. In MIS terminology, which of the following offers the best definition of *network?*

    A. The devices and software that link components and transfer data from one location to another
    B. The media and software governing the storage and organization of data for use
    C. Two or more computers linked to share data or resources such as a printer
    D. Formal rules for accomplishing tasks

4.____

5. Which of the following is a type of MIS application used for analysis?

    A. Database
    C. Desktop publishing
    B. Operations research
    D. Presentation

5.____

6. In computer processing, an overload sometimes results when trying to test more rules to reach a solution that the computer is capable of handling. This type of overload is referred to as

    A. combinatorial explosion
    C. transaction jam
    B. data crashing
    D. conversion error

6.____

7. In the normal processing of a workgroup information system, which of the following is an operations procedure, as opposed to a user procedure?

    A. Maintaining backup
    B. Placing constraints on processing
    C. Initiating access to network
    D. Starting hardware and programs

7.____

8. A company's European units want to share information about production schedules and inventory levels to ship excess products from one country to another. The telecommunications technology most appropriate for this is

    A. teleconferencing
    C. e–mail
    B. voice mail
    D. videoconferencing

8.____

9. As opposed to systems development, approximately how much of an organization's efforts can be expected to be spent on systems maintenance during the total system life cycle?

    A. 25   B. 45   C. 65   D. 85

9.____

10. The most critical, and often most difficult, task of the systems analyst is usually to

    A. define the specific problem that must be solved with an information system
    B. identify the causes of the problem
    C. specify the nature of the solution that will address the problem
    D. define the specific information requirements that must be met by the system solution

10.____

11. Which of the following is not a commonly recognized difference between workgroup and enterprise management information systems?

    A. An enterprise MIS is a subfunction of a company.
    B. Workgroup MIS users know and work with each other,
    C. An enterprise MIS uses several different applications.
    D. A workgroup MIS is a peripheral system.

11.____

12. The first step in testing the accuracy of a spreadsheet application is usually to

    A. verify the input
    B. stresstest the spreadsheet
    C. check the output
    D. involve others in the process

12.____

13. Programs in information systems make use of complete, unambiguous procedures for solving specified problems in a finite number of steps. These procedures are known as

    A. schema   B. protocols
    C. algorithms   D. criteria

13.____

14. Weaknesses in a system's_____ controls may permit unauthorized changes in processing.

    A. software   B. computer operations
    C. data file security   D. implementation

14.____

15. In the model of case–based reasoning, after a user describes a problem, the system

    A. modifies its solution to better fit the problem
    B. asks the user questions to narrow its search
    C. retrieves a solution
    D. searches a database for a similar problem

15.____

16. The particular form that information technology takes in a specific organization to achieve selected goals or functions is referred to as the organization's

    A. information configuration
    B. knowledge base
    C. operability
    D. information architecture

16.____

17. Which of the following applications is most likely to require real–time response from a   17._____
telecommunications network?

    A. Intercomputer data exchange
    B. Administrative message switching
    C. Process control
    D. On–line text retrieval

18. The main DISADVANTAGE associated with the use of application software packages to   18._____
solve organizational problems is that

    A. the initial costs of purchase are often prohibitive
    B. they often involve the added costs of customization and additional programming
    C. maintenance and support will usually have to come from within the purchasing organization
    D. the new program usually requires intensive training

19. Which of the following is a disadvantage associated with distributed data processing?   19._____

    A. Drains on system power
    B. Reliance on high–end telecommunications technology
    C. Increased vulnerability of storage location
    D. Reduced responsiveness to local users

20. In the current environment of systems development, end–user computing contributes   20._____
most effectively to the _____ aspects of the process.

    A. problem identification and systems study
    B. installation and maintenance
    C. systems study and installation
    D. programming and detail design

21. Which of the following steps in the machine cycle of a computer occurs during the execu-   21._____
tion cycle (e–cycle)?

    A. Instruction fetched
    B. Data sent from main memory to storage register
    C. Instruction decoded
    D. Instruction placed into instruction register

22. Of the following, which offers the least accurate definition of *information* as it applies to   22._____
the study of MIS?

    A. Data placed within a context
    B. The amount of uncertainty that is reduced when a message is received
    C. A thing or things that are known to have occurred, to exist, or to be true
    D. Knowledge derived from data

23. Programming languages in which each source code statement generates multiple state-   23._____
ments at the machine–language level are described as

    A. incremental   B. high–level
    C. first–generation   D. hierarchical

24. Which of the following types of visual representations is used as an overview, to depict an entire system as a single process with its major inputs and outputs?

    A. Context diagram   B. Decision tree
    C. Data flow diagram   D. Nomograph

24._____

25. Once an organization has developed a business telecommunications plan, it must determine the initial scope of the project, taking several factors into account. The first and most important of these factors is

    A. security   B. connectivity
    C. distance   D. multiple access

25._____

KEY (CORRECT ANSWERS)

1.	C	11.	A
2.	A	12.	C
3.	B	13.	C
4.	C	14.	A
5.	B	15.	D
6.	A	16.	D
7.	D	17.	D
8.	C	18.	B
9.	C	19.	B
10.	D	20.	D

21.	B
22.	C
23.	B
24.	A
25.	C

TEST 3

DIRECTIONS: Each question or incomplete statement is followed by several suggested answers or completions. Select the one that BEST answers the question or completes the statement. *PRINT THE LETTER OF THE CORRECT ANSWER IN THE SPACE AT THE RIGHT.*

1. Which of the following is a commonly used term for the programming environment of an expert system?

    A. Model   B. Ada   C. Schema   D. AI shell

1.____

2. In the language of dataflow diagrams, the external entity that absorbs a dataflow is known as a

    A. store   B. sink   C. cache   D. source

2.____

3. Which of the following is most clearly a fault tolerant technology?

    A. Random access memory
    B. On–line transaction processing
    C. Secondary storage
    D. Mobile data networks

3.____

4. Each of the following is a type of input control used with applications EXCEPT

    A. data conversion   B. run control totals
    C. edit checks   D. batch control totals

4.____

5. In a typical organization, approximately what percentage of total system maintenance time is spent making user enhancements, improving documentation, and recoding system components?

    A. 20   B. 40   C. 60   D. 80

5.____

6. Which of the following is NOT considered to be an operations control used with information systems?

    A. Error detection circuitry
    B. Control of equipment maintenance
    C. Regulated access to data centers
    D. Control of archival storage

6.____

7. Which of the following styles of systems development is most often used for information systems at the workgroup level?

    A. Traditional life cycle
    B. Life cycle for licensed programs
    C. Prototyping
    D. Outsourcing

7.____

8. Which of the following systems exists at the management level of an organization?

    A. Decision support system (DSS)
    B. Executive support system (ESS)
    C. Office automation system (OAS)
    D. Expert system

8.____

9. What is the term for a special language translator that translates each source code statement into machine code and executes it one at a time?

   A. Adapter   B. Assembler
   C. Compiler   D. Interpreter

   9.____

10. Which of the following is NOT perceived to be a difference between a decision support system and a management information system?

   A. In an MIS, systems analysis is aimed at identifying information requirements.
   B. The philosophy of a DSS is to provide integrated tools, data, and models to users.
   C. The design process of an MIS is never really considered to be finished.
   D. The design of a DSS is an interative process.

   10.____

11. Which of the following is a programming language that resembles machine language but substitutes mnemonics for numeric codes?

   A. Pseudocode   B. BASIC
   C. C   D. Assembly language

   11.____

12. Each of the following is a rule of thumb for handling type in desktop publishing applications EXCEPT

   A. use small capitals for acronyms
   B. use sans serif typefaces when presenting a lot of text
   C. generally limit the different number of typefaces in a document to two
   D. use distinctly different typefaces together in the same document

   12.____

13. Typically, a microcomputer is classified as a desktop or portable machine that has up to

   A. 1 gigabyte of secondary storage space
   B. 5 gigabytes of secondary storage space
   C. 64 megabytes of RAM
   D. 1 gigabyte of RAM

   13.____

14. Which of the following is NOT considered to be a basic component of a decision support system?

   A. Electronic meeting system
   B. Database
   C. DSS software system
   D. Model base

   14.____

15. Information systems that monitor the elementary activities and transactions of the organization are said to be functioning at the_____ level.

   A. tactical   B. operational
   C. strategic   D. managerial

   15.____

16. Which of the following applications would be most likely to use the sequential method of file organization in a database?

    A. Personnel evaluations
    B. Inventory
    C. Asset turnover calculations
    D. Payroll

16.____

17. Each of the following is a reason for the increased vulnerability of computerized systems to external threats EXCEPT

    A. invisible appearance of procedures
    B. inability to replicate manually
    C. wider overall impact than manual systems
    D. multiple points of access

17.____

18. Membership functions are nonspecific terms that are used to solve problems in applications of

    A. decision support
    C. neural networks
    B. expert systems
    D. fuzzy logic

18.____

19. Rules or standards used to rank alternatives in order of desirability are known as

    A. norms
    C. parameters
    B. algorithms
    D. criteria

19.____

20. In most organizations, the database administration group performs each of the following functions EXCEPT

    A. developing security procedures
    B. performing data quality audits
    C. maintaining database management software
    D. defining and organizing database structure and content

20.____

21. What is the term for on–line data that appears in the form of fixed–format reports for management executives?

    A. Browsers
    C. Modules
    B. Briefing books
    D. Web pages

21.____

22. Which of the following is a likely application of the optimization models of a decision–support system?

    A. Forecasting sales
    B. Determining the proper product mix within a given market
    C. Predicting the actions of competitors
    D. Goal seeking

22.____

23. In database management, a group of related fields is known as a(n)

    A. domain   B. register   C. record   D. file

23.____

24. Storage of _____ is NOT a function of a computer's primary. storage.

    A. operating system programs
    B. data being used by the program
    C. all or part of the program being executed
    D. long–term data in a nonvolatile space

24.____

25. Which of the following is equal to 1 billion bytes of information?

    A. Nanobyte   B. Gigabyte   C. Terabyte   D. Megabyte

25.____

KEY (CORRECT ANSWERS)

1.	D	11.	D
2.	B	12.	B
3.	B	13.	C
4.	B	14.	A
5.	C	15.	B
6.	A	16.	D
7.	B	17.	C
8.	A	18.	D
9.	D	19.	D
10.	C	20.	B

21.	B
22.	B
23.	C
24.	D
25.	B

EXAMINATION SECTION
TEST 1

DIRECTIONS: Each question or incomplete statement is followed by several suggested answers or completions. Select the one that BEST answers the question or completes the statement. *PRINT THE LETTER OF THE CORRECT ANSWER IN THE SPACE AT THE RIGHT.*

1. What is the term for the methodical simplification of a logical data model?

    A. Elucidation   B. Normalization
    C. Partitioning   D. Bit streaming

1.____

2. Systems development projects _____ are most likely to benefit from the use of internal integration tools.

    A. with high levels of technical complexity
    B. in which end-user participation is voluntary
    C. which experience counterimplementation
    D. that are small in scale and involve only specific departments

2.____

3. In a typical telecommunications system, a message that has just passed through the front-end multiplexer will then pass through

    A. a front-end processor   B. a modem or modems
    C. a controller   D. the host computer

3.____

4. Which of the following is a characteristic of data warehouse data? They

    A. are organized from a functional view
    B. are volatile to support operations within a company
    C. include enterprise-wide data, collected from legacy systems
    D. involve individual fields that may be inconsistent across the enterprise

4.____

5. Which of the following terms is used to enumerate the bits that can be moved at one time between a CPU, primary storage, and other devices of a computer?

    A. Bandwidth   B. RAM cache
    C. Data bus width   D. Register

5.____

6. In enterprise analysis, data elements are organized into groups that support related sets of organizational processes. These groups are known as

    A. data sub-units   B. critical success factors
    C. end-user interfaces   D. logical application groups

6.____

7. Which of the following terms is used to describe a system's order of complexity?

    A. Resilience   B. Eudemony
    C. Ordinality   D. Dialectics

7.____

8. Of the following file organization methods, the only one that can be used on magnetic tape is

    A. random   B. indexed sequential
    C. alphabetic   D. sequential

8.____

9. What is the term for a set of rules and procedures that govern transmissions between the components of a telecommunications network?

    A. Criteria   B. Norms
    C. Algorithms   D. Protocols

9.____

10. In what type of processing can more than one instruction be processed at once, by breaking down a problem into smaller parts and processing them simultaneously?

    A. Parallel   B. Indexed
    C. Sequential   D. Batch

10.____

11. Which of the following terms is used to describe a system in which the internal parameters can be changed when necessary through feedback?

    A. Homeostatic   B. Elastic
    C. Capacitive   D. Heuristic

11.____

12. Each of the following is a rule of thumb for handling graphics in desktop publishing applications EXCEPT

    A. using pie charts for showing parts of a whole
    B. showing data relationships with line plots
    C. using serif typefaces in graph labels
    D. using bar charts to shown quantities of a single item

12.____

13. The central liability-related ethical issue raised by new information technologies is generally considered to be

    A. whether software or other intellectual property may be copied for personal use
    B. the point at which it is justifiable to release software or services for consumption by others
    C. the conditions under which it is justifiable to invade the privacy of others
    D. whether individuals and organizations that create, produce, and sell systems are morally responsible for the consequences of their use

13.____

14. Which of the following personnel would be considered part of the development team in an MIS department?

    A. Control clerk   B. Maintenance programmer
    C. Education specialist   D. Data administrator

14.____

15. Which of the following is an object-oriented programming language that can deliver only the software functionality needed for a particular task, and which can run on any computer or operating system?

    A. Perl   B. C   C. Linux   D. Java

15.____

16. Which of the following is NOT typically an example of the inquiry/response type of telecommunications application?

    A. Point-of-sale system
    B. Airline reservation system
    C. Hospital information system
    D. Credit checking

16.____

17. Which of the following is an example of work-flow management?   17.____

    A. Financial officers at a firm use a computer program to calculate the rate of return for specific investments.

    B. A manager views a company's quarterly revenues from her own workstation without the need for printed matter.

    C. Loan officers at a bank enter application information into a central system so that the application can be evaluated by many people at once.

    D. Cashiers at a retail outlet scan the bar codes on items of merchandise to more quickly move customers through the checkout.

18. According to Simon's description, there are four stages in any decision-making process. Decision support systems are designed primarily to help monitor the _____ stage.   18.____

    A. implementation   B. design
    C. choice   D. intelligence

19. A form of organization resembling a fishnet or network, in which authority is determined by knowledge and function, is a   19.____

    A. hierarchy   B. matrix
    C. heterarchy   D. homeostat

20. What is the term used to describe the approach to software development that combines data and procedures into a single item?   20.____

    A. Operational   B. Object-oriented
    C. Output controlled   D. Transactional

21. Which of the following is a computer language that is an application generator?   21.____

    A. SQL   B. Nomad   C. AMAPS   D. FOCUS

22. Approximately what percentage of an organization's software development budget will be expended on testing?   22.____

    A. 10-20   B. 15-35   C. 30-50   D. 55-75

23. The process embodied in an input-output device, which enables it to convert or code without memory a type of signal, motion, or sequence of characters into another, is known as   23.____

    A. telematics   B. polarity
    C. reification   D. transduction

24. Which of the following steps in the business systems planning (BSP) process is typically performed FIRST?   24.____

    A. Defining business processes
    B. Analyzing current systems support
    C. Defining information architecture
    D. Developing recommendations

25. What is the term for a networking technology that parcels information into 8-byte cells, allowing data to be transmitted between computers of different vendors at any speed?   25.____

    A. Indexed sequential access method (ISAM)
    B. Asynchronous transfer mode (ATM)
    C. Private branch exchange (PBX)
    D. Domestic export

─────────

KEY (CORRECT ANSWERS)

1.	B	11.	D
2.	A	12.	C
3.	B	13.	D
4.	C	14.	B
5.	C	15.	D
6.	D	16.	C
7.	C	17.	C
8.	D	18.	A
9.	D	19.	C
10.	A	20.	B

21.	D
22.	C
23.	D
24.	A
25.	B

─────────

TEST 2

DIRECTIONS: Each question or incomplete statement is followed by several suggested answers or completions. Select the one that BEST answers the question or completes the statement. *PRINT THE LETTER OF THE CORRECT ANSWER IN THE SPACE AT THE RIGHT.*

1. *Intelligent agent* software is an appropriate tool for each of the following applications EXCEPT

    A. finding cheap airfares
    B. conducting data conferences
    C. scheduling appointments
    D. deleting junk e-mail

1.____

2. Which of the following is the general term for high-speed digital communications networks that are national or worldwide in scope and accessible by the general public?

    A. Wide-area networks (WANs)
    B. Internet
    C. World Wide Web
    D. Information superhighway

2.____

3. Which of the following types of organizations is LEAST likely to make use of a hierarchical database?

    A. Insurance companies
    B. Consultancies/service organizations
    C. Banks
    D. National retailers

3.____

4. A transmission rate of _____ per second falls within the normal range for a local-area network.

    A. 70 bits   B. 100 kilobits
    C. 100 megabits   D. 3 gigabits

4.____

5. In the history of artificial intelligence, the effort to build a physical analog to the human brain has been referred to as the _____ approach.

    A. schematic   B. sequential
    C. neuronet   D. bottom-up

5.____

6. In an individual MIS, the most commonly-used technique for conducting operations research is _____ programming.

    A. productivity   B. statistical
    C. management   D. linear

6.____

7. Of the types of organizational change that are enabled by information technology, which tends to be the most common?

    A. Paradigm shift
    B. Automation
    C. Business reengineering
    D. Rationalization of procedures

7.____

8. Which of the following is offered the clearest protection under the Electronic Communications Privacy Act of 1986? 8.____

    A. Personal e-mail received from outside by the organization's system
    B. Interoffice fax transmissions
    C. Business-related phone calls received from outside by the organization's system
    D. Interoffice e-mail

9. Which of the following systems exists at the operational level of an organization? 9.____

    A. Transaction processing system (TPS)
    B. Executive support system (ESS)
    C. Office automation system (OAS)
    D. Management information system (MIS)

10. The representation of data as they appear to an application programmer or end user is described as a(n) _____ view. 10.____

    A. schematic   B. analogous
    C. logical   D. physical

11. Which of the computer hardware *generations* involved vacuum tube technology? 11.____

    A. First   B. Second   C. Third   D. Fourth

12. Which of the following is an example of the administrative message switching application of telecommunications technology? 12.____

    A. Inventory control
    B. Electronic mail
    C. Library systems
    D. International transfer of bank funds

13. Which of the following styles of systems development is most often used for information systems at the enterprise level? 13.____

    A. Prototyping   B. Outsourcing
    C. End-user development   D. Traditional life cycle

14. Which of the following is an element of the physical design of an information system? 14.____

    A. Manual procedures   B. Input descriptions
    C. Processing functions   D. Controls

15. Which of the following functions to connect dissimilar networks by providing the translation from one protocol to another? 15.____

    A. Gateway   B. Assembler   C. Gopher   D. Buffer

16. The primary memory of most microcomputers is measured in 16.____

    A. megabytes   B. gigabytes   C. kilobytes   D. bytes

17. _____ tools is a project management technique that structures and sequences tasks, and budgets the time, money, and technical resources required to complete these tasks. 17.____

    A. Internal integration   B. Formal control
    C. External integration   D. Formal planning

18. What is the term for the capacity of a communications channel as measured by the difference between the highest and lowest frequencies that can be transmitted by that channel?

    A. Transmissivity
    C. Baud rate
    B. Broadband
    D. Bandwidth

18.____

19. Which of the following are LEAST likely to be an input into a management information system (MIS)?

    A. Design specifications
    C. Summary transaction data
    B. Simple models
    D. High-volume data

19.____

20. Which of the following is a shared network service technology that packages data into bundles for transmission but does not use error correction routines?

    A. Private branch exchange
    C. Internal integration
    B. Packet switching
    D. Frame relay

20.____

21. A purpose of a file server in a network is to

    A. collect messages for batch transmission
    B. route communications
    C. store programs
    D. connect dissimilar networks

21.____

22. _____ testing provides the final certification that a new system is ready to be used in a production setting.

    A. Parallel
    C. Acceptance
    B. Unit
    D. System

22.____

23. The number of _____ is NOT an example of software metrics.

    A. payroll checks printed per hour
    B. known users who are dissatisfied with an application's performance
    C. transactions that can be processed in one business day
    D. known bugs per hundred lines of code

23.____

24. What is the term for a set or rules that govern the manipulation of characters in a system?

    A. Synergy
    C. Aggregation
    B. Entropy
    D. Calculus

24.____

25. During the process of enterprise analysis, the results of a large managerial survey are broken down into each of the following EXCEPT

    A. processes
    C. data matrices
    B. goals
    D. functions

25.____

KEY (CORRECT ANSWERS)

1.	B		11.	A
2.	D		12.	B
3.	B		13.	D
4.	C		14.	A
5.	D		15.	A
6.	D		16.	C
7.	B		17.	D
8.	A		18.	D
9.	A		19.	A
10.	C		20.	D

21.	C
22.	C
23.	B
24.	D
25.	B

EXAMINATION SECTION
TEST 1

DIRECTIONS: Each question or incomplete statement is followed by several suggested answers or completions. Select the one that BEST answers the question or completes the statement. *PRINT THE LETTER OF THE CORRECT ANSWER IN THE SPACE AT THE RIGHT.*

1. Each of the following is a problem in long-distance data transmissions that can be overcome by converting the digital signals to analog signals EXCEPT   1.____

     A.   higher power requirements
     B.   attenuation
     C.   repeater loss
     D.   introduction of spurious signals

2. The two primary determinants of data transmission speed are   2.____

     A.   bandwidth and media   B.   baud and bandwidth
     C.   baud and distance   D.   distance and media

3. The last record on a sequential file is known as a(n)   3.____

     A.   trailer label   B.   link
     C.   end message   D.   stop bit

4. Which of the following transmission media does NOT offer analog transmission?   4.____

     A.   Twisted-pair wire   B.   Coaxial cable
     C.   Microwave   D.   Optical fiber

5. Parallel bit transmission requires AT LEAST _____ wires.   5.____

     A.   2   B.   5   C.   8   D.   16

6. Which of the following *AT* modem commands is used to reset the modem's registers?   6.____

     A.   +++   B.   R   C.   Z   D.   Reg

7. Data transmissions can be classified as each of the following EXCEPT   7.____

     A.   baseband   B.   ultraspectrum
     C.   broadband   D.   voiceband

8. A communications device which sends a message and then requires switching in order to receive a message is described as   8.____

     A.   simplex   B.   duplex
     C.   half-duplex   D.   multiplex

9. What is the common range (miles) of a typical microwave signal?   9.____

     A.   10   B.   25   C.   40   D.   80

10. Each location on a computer network is called a   10.____

     A.   node   B.   station   C.   sector   D.   terminal

11. Each of the following is an advantage associated with using synchronous data transmission EXCEPT   11._____

    A. ability to compress data
    B. fast throughput due to bit flow
    C. rapid demodulation of signals
    D. ability to address terminals directly using address codes in the frames

12. According to the X.25 standard, a PDN packet must ALWAYS contain _____ bits.   12._____

    A. 16   B. 84   C. 128   D. 248

13. The back-end processor in a hierarchical network handles   13._____

    A. input/output   B. data processing
    C. security tasks   D. data communication

14. The purpose of a CRC is to   14._____

    A. check the accuracy of a transferred file
    B. extract stop bits during data compression
    C. provide an interface during computer-to-computer communications
    D. convert a simplex device into duplex

15. The measure of signal changes in a communications channel per second is known as   15._____

    A. skip   B. baud
    C. noise   D. bandwidth

16. Each of the following is a disadvantage associated with parallel bit transmission EXCEPT   16._____

    A. cable costs
    B. relatively low transmission speed
    C. incompatibility with some public carriers
    D. differing arrival times for transmitted bits

17. What is the term for the amount of data processing work a computer can perform in a given amount of time?   17._____

    A. Capacity   B. Threshold
    C. Thrashing   D. Throughput

18. Which of the following *AT* modem commands is used to repeat a previously given command?   18._____

    A. A/   B. &   C. X   D. RR

19. If a PC has both a COMM1 port and an internal modem, which of the following steps must be taken FIRST during IRQ conflict resolution?   19._____

    A. Set the internal modem to COMM1
    B. Disabling the modem
    C. Set the COMM1 port to COMM2
    D. Disabling the COMM1 port

20. When the computers in a ring network are interconnected, a _____ network is created. 20._____

    A. mesh   B. star
    C. bus   D. token ring

21. Which of the following file transfer protocols uses small packets of 128 bits? 21._____

    A. XMODEM   B. YMODEM   C. ZMODEM   D. Kermit

22. Which of the following is NOT a use associated with wide area networks? 22._____

    A. Centralizing file information
    B. Remote data entry
    C. Interoffice voice communications
    D. Time sharing

23. A network in which each piece of computer equipment can only communicate with its adjacent neighbors is termed a 23._____

    A. mesh   B. star
    C. private branch exchange   D. ring

24. Which of the following transmission media typically offers the GREATEST maximum data rate? 24._____

    A. Twisted-pair wire   B. Coaxial cable
    C. Optical fiber   D. Microwave

25. Each of the following is a purpose of a terminal program EXCEPT 25._____

    A. automating connection process
    B. processing error bits in a transmission
    C. transferring files between two computers
    D. controlling modem setup

KEY (CORRECT ANSWERS)

1.	B		11.	C
2.	B		12.	C
3.	A		13.	B
4.	D		14.	A
5.	C		15.	B
6.	C		16.	B
7.	B		17.	D
8.	C		18.	A
9.	C		19.	D
10.	A		20.	A

21.	A
22.	C
23.	D
24.	D
25.	B

TEST 2

DIRECTIONS: Each question or incomplete statement is followed by several suggested answers or completions. Select the one that BEST answers the question or completes the statement. *PRINT THE LETTER OF THE CORRECT ANSWER IN THE SPACE AT THE RIGHT.*

1. Which of the following *AT* modem commands is used to turn the speaker off?

   A. M   B. &W   C. -   D. #

   1.____

2. What is the term for a data communications device that allows several users to share communication channels?

   A. Star   B. Multiplexer
   C. Distributor   D. Token ring

   2.____

3. Which of the following is NOT typically a component of a synchronous message frame?

   A. An 8-bit error code
   B. A 16-bit device address
   C. Two repetitive start characters, each 8 bits long
   D. A message number

   3.____

4. Which of the following steps in the file transfer process would be performed LAST?

   A. Select protocol for distant end
   B. Notify distant end of file to be transferred
   C. Select protocol for user end
   D. Notify term program of file to be transferred

   4.____

5. Which of the following is a *line of sight* transmission medium?

   A. Microwave   B. Optical fiber
   C. Radio wave   D. Coaxial cable

   5.____

6. Most of a network's operations are backed up and stored on

   A. floppy disks   B. the server's hard disk
   C. external hard disks   D. magnetic tape

   6.____

7. Each of the following is an advantage commonly associated with asynchronous data transmission EXCEPT

   A. relatively inexpensive equipment requirements
   B. no need for synchronized clocks
   C. transmission of each character can occur independently over a wire
   D. easy adaptation to bus networks

   7.____

8. The MOST common setting between PCs connected by modem is

   A. Parity, 6 data bits, 2 stop bits
   B. No parity, 7 data bits, 1 stop bit
   C. No parity, 8 data bits, 1 stop bit
   D. Parity, 8 data bits, 2 stop bits

   8.____

9. Which of the following *AT* modem commands is used to pause an operation?   9.____

   A. +++   B. *   C. ,   D. P

10. Which of the following file transfer protocols is slow, tout good for transferring files over   10.____
    noisy telephone lines?

    A. XMODEM   B. YMODEM   C. ZMODEM   D. Kermit

11. When empty and filled message frames are relayed from one device in a network to   11.____
    another, _____ occurs.

    A. capturing   B. branch exchange
    C. token passing   D. looping

12. The purpose of IRQ is to   12.____

    A. control input and output
    B. provide security to the server
    C. interpret parallel transmissions
    D. convert analog signals

13. The MAIN disadvantage associated with synchronous data transmission is   13.____

    A. dependence on accuracy of timing clocks to interpret signals
    B. frequent interference by spurious signals
    C. difficulty in processing error codes
    D. rapid signal degradation

14. Which of the following file transfer protocols is considered the BEST and MOST sophisti-   14.____
    cated?

    A. XMODEM   B. YMODEM   C. ZMODEM   D. Kermit

15. The *distant end* in a network is the   15.____

    A. server
    B. back-end processor
    C. node farthest from the server
    D. answering modem

16. What is the term for the process of temporarily storing input or output data on an inter-   16.____
    mediary storage medium?

    A. Capturing   B. Spooling
    C. Holding   D. Buffing

17. What type of computer network allows for simultaneous voice and data communications?   17.____

    A. Bus network   B. Computer branch exchange
    C. Star network   D. Private branch exchange

18. The simultaneous transmission of bits along several wires is known as _____ transmis-   18.____
    sion.

    A. wide-area   B. serial   C. analog   D. parallel

19. What is the term for the practice of computers on a bus network to check whether a channel is free before transmitting data?   19.____

    A. Contention protocol   B. Multiplexing
    C. Token passing   D. Branch exchange

20. What type of data transmission specifically uses one or more *start bits* for each eight-bit string of data?   20.____

    A. Analog   B. Asynchronous
    C. Synchronous   D. Digital

21. Which of the following *AT* modem commands is used to dial the phone number that follows a command?   21.____

    A. P   B. D   C. @   D. AT

22. Typically, which of the following steps in the file transfer process would be performed FIRST?   22.____

    A. Select protocol for distant end
    B. Notify distant end of file to be transferred
    C. Select protocol for user end
    D. Notify term program of file to be transferred

23. Which of the following file transfer protocols is equipped with the BEST error checking and correction capability?   23.____

    A. XMODEM   B. YMODEM
    C. YMODEM BATCH   D. Kermit

24. Without the use of devices such as repeaters, which of the following transmission media typically has the SHORTEST range?   24.____

    A. Analog twisted-pair wire
    B. Microwave
    C. Analog coaxial cable
    D. Digital coaxial cable

25. The MAIN disadvantage associated with asynchronous data transmission is that it   25.____

    A. permits only point-to-point transmissions
    B. requires several timed clock pulses
    C. is sometimes too slow to be useful
    D. needs a separate modulator and demodulator

KEY (CORRECT ANSWERS)

1.	A		11.	C
2.	B		12.	A
3.	A		13.	A
4.	C		14.	C
5.	A		15.	D
6.	D		16.	B
7.	D		17.	B
8.	C		18.	D
9.	C		19.	A
10.	D		20.	B

21.	B
22.	B
23.	D
24.	C
25.	A

EXAMINATION SECTION

TEST 1

DIRECTIONS: Each question or incomplete statement is followed by several suggested answers or completions. Select the one that BEST answers the question or completes the statement. *PRINT THE LETTER OF THE CORRECT ANSWER IN THE SPACE AT THE RIGHT.*

1. What is VGA?
   A. Video Graphics Array
   B. Video Graphics Adapter
   C. Visual Graphics Array
   D. None of the above

   1.____

2. IBM 1401 was a
   A. fourth generation computer
   B. second generation computer
   C. third generation computer
   D. none of the above

   2.____

3. A micro program is a collection of
   A. large scale operations
   B. DMA
   C. registers
   D. microinstructions

   3.____

4. The time a CPU takes to recognize an interrupt request is called
   A. interrupt latency
   B. timer delay
   B. response deadline
   D. throughput

   4.____

5. A _____ regulates the arrangement of the flow of microinstructions.
   A. multiplexer
   B. micro program controller
   C. DMA controller
   D. virtual memory

   5.____

6. Which of the following techniques will not be used when CPU exchanges data with a peripheral device?
   A. Interrupt driven I/O
   B. Direct Memory Access (DMA)
   C. Programmed I/O
   D. Virtual memory

   6.____

7. If a prior received character is not read by CPU and overwritten by new character received, the error will be called a _____ error.
   A. framing   B. parity   C. overrun   D. under-run

   7.____

8. Which of the following networks needs manual routing?
   A. Fiber optic   B. Bus   C. T-switched   D. Ring

   8.____

9. Which layer of TCP/IP responds to the OSI models to three layers?
   A. Application   B. Presentation   C. Session   D. Transport

   9.____

10. _____ transport layer protocols is connectionless.
    A. UDP   B. TCP   C. FTP   D. NVT

    10.____

11. _____ applications permit a user to approach and modify/change remote files without physical transfer.

    A. DNS   B. FTP   C. NFS   D. Telnet

11.____

12. Which of the following is a non-impact and quiet printer?

    A. Inkjet   B. Laser   C. Thermal   D. Dot matrix

12.____

13. Which of the following are high-end printers?

    A. Inkjet   B. Laser   C. Thermal   D. Dot matrix

13.____

14. For the purpose of plotting designs and graphs on papers, _____ is/are used.

    A. trackball   B. joystick   C. light pen   D. plotters

14.____

15. What is a Snowbol?

    A. Operating system   B. HLL

    C. Software   D. Search engine

15.____

16. Which of the following connects to a modem?

    A. Telephone line   B. Keyboard   C. Printer   D. Monitor

16.____

17. In automated organizations, _____ processing is used by large transaction processing systems.

    A. online   B. batch   C. once-a-day   D. end-of-day

17.____

18. What should a technician do after addition of a new cable segment to the network?

    A. Revise the disaster recovery plan

    B. Update the changes in document

    C. Update the wiring schematics

    D. None of the above

18.____

19. For the purpose of breaking up a broadcast domain, a _____ can be used.

    A. bridge   B. router

    C. DHCP server   D. printer

19.____

20. The secure way of transferring files between two devices is

    A. SFTP   B. SNMPv3   C. TFTP   D. FTP

20.____

21. An administrator networking closet (with all the networking and communication equipment) is on the second floor of a building and the communications lines are installed on the first floor. A _____ will be extended to connect communication lines to the networking closet.

    A. smart jack   B. demarcation point

    C. patch panel   D. router

21.____

22. To provide access to a VPN, _____ is used.

    A. IGP   B. PPTP   C. PPP   D. RAS

22.____

23. Two users are directly linked via RJ-45 and CAT5e cables and are communicating through IP. If the first user transmits data out of the RJ-45 on pins 1 and 2, the client should expect to receive a response on pins

23.____

    A. 1 and 2   B. 2 and 4   C. 3 and 6   D. 4 and 6

24. Examination of physical hardware addresses is done in _____ network access security method.

24.____

    A. IP filtering   B. L2TP   C. MAC filtering D. RAS

25. Wireless standards give the direct advantage of

25.____

    A. increased use of wireless spectrum
    B. greater device security
    C. interoperability between devices
    D. increased number of protocols can be used

KEY (CORRECT ANSWERS)

1.	A		11.	C
2.	B		12.	A
3.	D		13.	B
4.	A		14.	D
5.	B		15.	D
6.	D		16.	A
7.	C		17.	B
8.	C		18.	C
9.	A		19.	B
10.	A		20.	A

21.	C
22.	B
23.	C
24.	C
25.	C

TEST 2

DIRECTIONS: Each question or incomplete statement is followed by several suggested answers or completions. Select the one that BEST answers the question or completes the statement. *PRINT THE LETTER OF THE CORRECT ANSWER IN THE SPACE AT THE RIGHT.*

1. What is an ALU? 1._____
   A. Arithmetic Logic Unit
   B. Array Logic Unit
   C. Application Logic Unit
   D. None of the above

2. In a client-server system, which type of computers are usually client computers? 2._____
   A. Mainframe
   B. Mini computer
   C. Micro computer
   D. PDA

3. A(n) _____ is necessary for a computer to *boot*. 3._____
   A. compiler
   B. loader
   C. operating system
   D. assembler

4. In the present technology age, computers are typically 4._____
   A. digital   B. analog   C. hybrid   D. complex

5. What is the physical structure of a computer called? 5._____
   A. CPU   B. Hardware   C. Software   D. All of the above

6. Data is represented in the form of discrete signals in a(n) _____ computer. 6._____
   A. analog   B. digital   C. both A and B   D. hybrid

7. _____ is now available in the form of PC. 7._____
   A. Mainframe
   B. Micro computer
   C. Mini computer
   D. Both B and C

8. Which of the following is larger than a portable computer but is a small general function micro computer? 8._____
   A. Hybrid
   B. Digital
   C. Desktop
   D. None of the above

9. Most of the processing in a computer takes place in 9._____
   A. memory   B. RAM   C. both A and B   D. CPU

10. What does LAN stand for? 10._____
    A. Limited Area Network
    B. Logical Area Network
    C. Local Area Network
    D. Large Area Network

11. Which of the following defines the rules and procedures for regulating data transmission over the internet? 11._____
    A. IP address   B. Domains   C. Protocol   D. Gateway

12. Which of the following protocol is used by the intranets, extranets and internet?
    A. TCP/IP
    B. Protocol
    C. Open system
    D. Internet work processor

12.____

13. On which ring does the data travel in FDDI?
    A. The primary
    B. The secondary
    C. Both rings
    D. None of the above

13.____

14. _____ is the logical topology.
    A. Bus
    B. Tree
    C. Star
    D. Both A and C

14.____

15. The main drawback of ring topology is that
    A. if one computer fails, it affects the whole network
    B. adding/removing computers affects the network activity
    C. failure of the central hub makes the whole network unable to work
    D. both A and B

15.____

16. _____ is NOT anti-virus software.
    A. NAV
    B. F-Prot
    C. Oracle
    D. McAfee

16.____

17. DMA stands for
    A. Direct Memory Allocation
    B. Direct Memory Access
    C. Direct Module Access
    D. none of the above

17.____

18. Which of the following is a storage device?
    A. Tape
    B. Hard disk
    C. Floppy disk
    D. All of the above

18.____

19. Which of the following are determined by user needs?
    A. System software
    B. Application software
    C. Assemblers
    D. Compilers

19.____

20. Which tools are available with system analysis?
    A. Review of procedure and conducting interviews
    B. Review of documentation and observation of the situation
    C. Conducting interviews and questionnaire administration
    D. Both B and C

20.____

21. Programs used to catch errors and their causes are called
    A. operating system extensions
    B. cookies
    C. diagnostic software
    D. boot diskettes

21.____

22. A virus which reproduces itself by using the computer host is called
    A. time bomb
    B. worm
    C. Melissa virus
    D. macro virus

22.____

23. The best practice for implementing a basic wireless network is   23._____
    A. disabling ESSID broadcast
    B. adding two access points per area of service
    C. not configuring the ESSID point
    D. none of the above

24. For connecting a single network node to a switch, _____ wiring standards   24._____
    will usually be used.
    A. loopback   B. straight   C. rollover   D. crossover

25. Before having a db loss, a CAT5 cable can run a maximum distance of   25._____
    A. 106 feet (31 meters)   B. 203 feet (60 meters)
    C. 328 feet (100 meters)   D. none of the above

_____

KEY (CORRECT ANSWERS)

1.	A		11.	C
2.	C		12.	A
3.	C		13.	A
4.	A		14.	C
5.	B		15.	D
6.	B		16.	C
7.	B		17.	B
8.	C		18.	D
9.	D		19.	A
10.	C		20.	D

21.	C
22.	B
23.	A
24.	B
25.	C

_____

TEST 3

DIRECTIONS: Each question or incomplete statement is followed by several suggested answers or completions. Select the one that BEST answers the question or completes the statement. *PRINT THE LETTER OF THE CORRECT ANSWER IN THE SPACE AT THE RIGHT.*

1. I/O port is an interface that is used to connect microcomputer bus to
    A. flip flops   B. memory
    C. peripheral devices   D. multiplexers

    1._____

2. In _____, a CPU poll after detecting an interrupt, determines the interrupting module and branches in an interrupt service routine.
    A. daisy chain   B. software poll
    C. multiple interrupts lines   D. all of the above

    2._____

3. Where is a separate address space for an I/O operation reserved for a CPU?
    A. Isolated I/O   B. Memory mapped I/O
    C. Memory   D. None of the above

    3._____

4. In _____ for resolving the priority, the highest priority device is placed at the first position followed by less priority devices.
    A. asynchronous methods   B. daisy-chaining priority methods
    C. parallel method   D. semi-synchronous method

    4._____

5. In _____, a part of the CPU's address lines constructing an input to the address decoder is neglected.
    A. microprogramming   B. instruction pre-fetching
    C. pipelining   D. partial decoding

    5._____

6. What is the data unit in TCP/IP called?
    A. Message   B. Segment   C. Datagram   D. Frame

    6._____

7. If a host domain name is known, what can DNS obtain?
    A. Station address   B. IP address
    C. Port address   D. Checksum

    7._____

8. _____ OSI layers correspond to TCP/IP's application layer.
    A. Application   B. Presentation
    C. Session   D. All of the above

    8._____

9. Devices on different networks can communicate with each other via a
    A. file server   B. gateway
    C. printer server   D. none of the above

    9._____

10. Which of the following can combine transmissions from different input/output devices into one line?   10.____
    A. Concentrator communication device
    B. Modifier
    C. Multiplexer
    D. Full duplex line

11. For the analysis of retinal scans, fingerprints, etc. in security access systems, which of the following techniques is used?   11.____
    A. Biometrics   B. Bio measurement
    C. Computer security   D. Smart weapon machinery

12. _____ guards a computer against unauthorized access to a network.   12.____
    A. Hacker-proof antivirus   B. Firewall
    C. Encryption safe wall   D. All of the above

13. What is scrambling of code called?   13.____
    A. Encryption   B. Firewall
    C. Scrambling   D. Password proofing

14. What should be used to prevent data loss due to power failure?   14.____
    A. Encryption program   B. Surge protector
    C. Firewall   D. UPS

15. If an administrator wants to install a device which can detect and control peer-to-peer traffic, a _____ device type will be installed.   15.____
    A. bandwidth shaper   B. intrusion detection
    C. proxy server   D. load balancer

16. If a technician needs to troubleshoot an unfamiliar network, the first step taken to diagnose the problem would be to   16.____
    A. report the problem to administrative technician
    B. make use of a port analyzer to analyze the network topology
    C. analyze symptoms and draw a network diagram
    D. all of the above

17. To discover MAC address of a connecting router, _____ commands can be used.   17.____
    A. ARP   B. trace route   C. ping   D. ping sweep

18. E-mails sent to users with malicious website links are an example of   18.____
    A. viruses   B. phishing
    C. rogue access points   D. man-in-the-middle

19. To analyze that a RJ-45 jack in a cubicle responds to a specific RJ-45 jack in a patch panel, an administrator will use a   19.____
    A. punch-down tool   B. spectrum analyzer
    C. toner probe   D. multi-meter

20. _____ network types are suitable for a 10 gigabyte core network using 33 feet (10 meter) fiber runs.

    A. 10Base-FX   B. 10GBase-SR

    C. 10GBase-SW   D. None of the above

20._____

21. When an administrator troubleshoots network connectivity and wants to view which packets are going through from workstation X to server 1, he will use _____ command line tools.

    A. view route   B. route

    C. trace route   D. ping

21._____

22. For the purpose of updating physical network diagrams, revising _____ is the most appropriate policy.

    A. whenever a connection is changed

    B. before regularly scheduled network audits

    C. after new personnel are hired

    D. after weekly network support team review

22._____

23. When a firewall accepts a request packet on port 80, it allows the reply packet to pass through automatically. This behavior of firewall is best described as

    A. stateful inspection   B. intrusion detection

    C. content filtering   D. passive fingerprinting

23._____

24. A network technician can face _____ connectivity issues as a result of bundling network cables tightly together.

    A. collision   B. attenuation   C. crosstalk   D. open circuit

24._____

25. On a wireless network, a _____ mechanism uses a separate network authentication server.

    A. Kerberos   B. TKIP   C. RADIUS   D. WEP

25._____

KEY (CORRECT ANSWERS)

1.	C		11.	A
2.	B		12.	B
3.	A		13.	A
4.	C		14.	D
5.	D		15.	A
6.	D		16.	C
7.	B		17.	A
8.	D		18.	B
9.	B		19.	D
10.	C		20.	B

21.	C
22.	A
23.	A
24.	C
25.	C

———

TEST 4

DIRECTIONS: Each question or incomplete statement is followed by several suggested answers or completions. Select the one that BEST answers the question or completes the statement. *PRINT THE LETTER OF THE CORRECT ANSWER IN THE SPACE AT THE RIGHT.*

1. The electrical pathway through which the processor communicates with peripheral devices is called the
   A. computer bus B. hazard C. memory D. disk

   1.____

2. If a 0 is transmitted instead of a stop bit, a(n) _____ error will be the serial communication error condition.
   A. framing B. parity C. overrun D. under-run

   2.____

3. An interrupt can be defined as a process where
   A. an external device can speed up the working of the microprocessor
   B. input devices can take over the working of the microprocessor
   C. an external device gets the attention of the microprocessor
   D. none of the above

   3.____

4. What controls the sequence of the flow of microinstructions?
   A. Multiplexer B. Micro program controller
   C. DMA controller D. Virtual memory

   4.____

5. What is MSI?
   A. Medium Scale Integrated Circuits
   B. Medium System Intelligence
   C. Medium Scale Intelligent Circuit
   D. None of the above

   5.____

6. If a network has N number of devices and every device has N-1 ports for cables, this topology is known as
   A. mesh B. star C. bus D. ring

   6.____

7. Usenet is also known as
   A. Gopher B. Newsgroups C. Browser D. CERN

   7.____

8. Junk e-mail is also known as
   A. spam B. spoof C. sniffer script D. spool

   8.____

9. Geographical scattered office LANS can be connected by
   A. VAN B. LAN C. DAN D. WAN

   9.____

10. _____ gathers information of the user and sends it to someone over the internet.
    A. A virus B. Spybot
    C. Logic bomb D. Security patch

    10.____

11. A worm virus is terminated eventually due to the lack of   11._____
    A. memory or disk space   B. time
    C. CD drive space   D. CD-RW

12. Instructions of a computer are executed by direct involvement of the   12._____
    A. scanner   B. main storage
    C. secondary storage   D. processor

13. Most processing of a computer takes place in   13._____
    A. memory   B. RAM   C. motherboard D. CPU

14. Which of the following is NOT a storage medium?   14._____
    A. Hard disk   B. Flash drive   C. DVD   D. Scanner

15. Suppose a user calls you for network support and says that his e-mail is not   15._____
working. What will you do first?
    A. Inquire about the operation performed by the user and what was the
       expected and actual result
    B. Restart the hub the user was connected to
    C. Send a test e-mail message to see if it's sent
    D. None of the above

16. Suppose two networks in different departments are using DHCP set up for   16._____
192.168.0.0/24 and after consolidation of the officer's network we have run out
of IP addresses. The BEST cost-effective solution for this will be
    A. adding a router to connect both networks
    B. switching to static IP addressing
    C. changing the subnet mask to 255.255.254.0
    D. none of the above

17. Suppose that packets to an IP address are getting lost over the internet.   17._____
Which tools will an administrator use to find out the responsible hop?
    A. Ping   B. nslookup   C. Trace route   D. netstat

18. What should a technician check if a workstation on the network is able to   18._____
ping hosts on the network but it is not able to ping any addresses on the
internet?
    A. The DNS server entries   B. The network card
    C. The default gateway   D. The host's file

19. To find out the status of all established TCP connections by port 80, the   19._____
administrator will use the _____ command.
    A. netstat –at   B. netstat –r   C. netstat –v   D. netstat -p tcp

20. To evaluate the network traffic, which of the following tools will be used?   20._____
    A. OTDR   B. Protocol analyzer
    C. Certifier   D. Toner probe

21. Which port is usually used for FTP traffic?
    A. 20   B. 22   C. 23   D. 25

21.____

22. _____ can function as a router, support VLANs and connect multiple workstations.
    A. Repeater   B. Switch
    C. Hub   D. Multilayer switch

22.____

23. 208.177.23.1 belongs to class
    A. A   B. B   C. C   D. D

23.____

24. If 25 clients on the same network want to see a video, _____ should be configured on the user's computer to reduce network traffic.
    A. class C addresses   B. class A addresses
    C. broadcast   D. multicast

24.____

25. Suppose we have installed a new LAN switch on fiber ports. In order to allow compatibility to the existing fiber network, what will a technician need on the new switch?
    A. Router   B. Repeater
    C. Media converter   D. Hub

25.____

KEY (CORRECT ANSWERS)

1.	A		11.	A
2.	A		12.	D
3.	C		13.	D
4.	B		14.	D
5.	A		15.	A
6.	A		16.	C
7.	B		17.	C
8.	A		18.	C
9.	D		19.	D
10.	B		20.	B

21.	A
22.	D
23.	C
24.	D
25.	C

EXAMINATION SECTION
TEST 1

DIRECTIONS: Each question or incomplete statement is followed by several suggested answers or completions. Select the one that BEST answers the question or completes the statement. *PRINT THE LETTER OF THE CORRECT ANSWER IN THE SPACE AT THE RIGHT.*

1. _____ computer(s) can transmit data at a time in a network.
   A. Sender and the receiver   B. Only one
   C. All   D. Selected

   1.____

2. Switching networks are also called _____ networks.
   A. streaming   B. transmission   C. packet   D. routing

   2.____

3. Data may be lost in transmission. _____ will help the transmitter and receiver to determine correctly received data.
   A. Fair use   B. Coordination
   C. Packet layers   D. Correction bit

   3.____

4. A network has a capacity of 3 minutes to transfer a file of 3 MB. Therefore,
   A. a 3 MB file is always transferred in 3 minutes
   B. priority transfer time is 3 minutes for a 3 MB file
   C. network congestion is no more than 3 minutes
   D. wait time for each new transfer is 3 minutes

   4.____

5. While a 3 MB file is being transmitted, a 3 KB file is added for transmission.
   A. 3 MB file will be sent in the same time as previous
   B. 3 MB file is delayed
   C. 3 KB file is delayed
   D. There is no effect on transmission time

   5.____

6. All packets enter the transmission medium at
   A. demultiplexor   B. multiplexor   C. hub   D. switch

   6.____

7. Packet size
   A. must be standard for all hardware technologies
   B. targets the format of the frame used
   C. varies with the hardware used
   D. depends on the type of transmission medium

   7.____

8. Frame has a
   A. begin bit and end bit   B. start and stop bit
   C. header and trailer   D. predetermined size

   8.____

9. Sending computer will transmit frame in this sequence:
   A. End (EOT), Header (SOH), Data
   B. Data and End (EOT)
   C. End (EOT), Data and Header (SOH)
   D. Header (SOH), Data and End (EOT)

9.____

10. EOT is missing. This indicates
   A. the sender crashed
   C. the packet was discarded
   B. the receiver malfunctioned
   D. transmission medium is faulty

10.____

11. A bad frame is detected. It will be
   A. resent
   C. discarded
   B. corrected with a parity bit
   D. transmitted with error bit

11.____

12. _____ is a technique to encode reserved bytes.
   A. Bit stuffing
   C. Modulation
   B. Encryption
   D. Encapsulation

12.____

13. _____ makes a pair of bytes from Reserved Byte.
   A. Receiver
   C. Buffering algorithm
   B. Sender
   D. Packet

13.____

14. Unwanted data is generated due to
   A. transmission errors
   C. parity bit
   B. incorrect frame format
   D. byte stuffing

14.____

15. Incorrect data is rejected during
   A. error correction
   C. multiplexing
   B. demultiplexing
   D. error detection

15.____

16. In 11100011, parity is
   A. even   B. odd   C. biased   D. checksum

16.____

17. One of the bits is changed from 0 to 1. The parity of resulting bits
   A. becomes undefined
   C. always changes to 0
   B. is wrong
   D. always changes to 1

17.____

18. _____ detects erroneous data.
   A. Sender after receiving error bit
   C. Packet
   B. Error correction algorithm
   D. Receiver based on parity

18.____

19. _____ is an error detection technique.
   A. CRC   B. CSMA   C. Byte stuffing   D. CMC

19.____

20. Checksum uses
   A. parity   B. redundancy   C. collision   D. sum of data

20.____

21. Unrolling loop is an _____ technique.
    A. optimization
    B. error detection
    C. error correction
    D. error

21.____

22. CRC stands for
    A. Core Recall Cycle
    B. Critical Recycle Code
    C. Coded Redundancy Check
    D. Cyclic Redundancy Check

22.____

23. CRC will follow
    A. SOH   B. EOT   C. parity bit   D. error frame

23.____

24. In shared networks, data reaches _____ destination(s).
    A. selected
    B. all
    C. nearest node
    D. none of the above

24.____

25. Each station has a unique _____ address.
    A. frame   B. hardware   C. generic   D. operational

25.____

KEY (CORRECT ANSWERS)

1.	B	11.	C
2.	C	12.	A
3.	B	13.	B
4.	D	14.	A
5.	A	15.	D
6.	B	16.	B
7.	C	17.	B
8.	C	18.	D
9.	D	19.	A
10.	A	20.	D

21.	A
22.	D
23.	B
24.	B
25.	B

TEST 2

DIRECTIONS: Each question or incomplete statement is followed by several suggested answers or completions. Select the one that BEST answers the question or completes the statement. *PRINT THE LETTER OF THE CORRECT ANSWER IN THE SPACE AT THE RIGHT.*

1. _____ adds hardware address to outgoing frames.
   A. Byte stuffing   B. CSMA   C. DMA   D. LAN interface

   1.____

2. _____ defines access rules.
   A. DMA   B. CD/CSMA   C. Parity bit   D. Bit stuffing

   2.____

3. Each time a packet passes through the router, the number of _____ increases by 1.
   A. address bytes   B. hops
   C. subnet masks   D. processing cycles

   3.____

4. The hardware address is typically one to _____ bytes.
   A. four   B. eight   C. sixteen   D. six

   4.____

5. _____ address is used to send messages to all stations.
   A. Broadcast   B. Abstract   C. Podcast   D. Unique

   5.____

6. The data area following the header is called
   A. payload   B. frame   C. loader info   D. packet

   6.____

7. An interface which receives all frames for analysis is
   A. DMA   B. promiscuous mode
   C. NIC   D. CSMA

   7.____

8. Analyzer can display real time info by
   A. capturing specific frames   B. computing totals
   C. counting frames   D. analyzing parity bits

   8.____

9. _____ can be used over a long distance.
   A. RS-232   B. Oscillating signal carriers
   C. Encoded signaling   D. Beacon

   9.____

10. Carrier modulation can be used with _____ medium.
    A. fiber   B. copper   C. radio   D. all types of

    10.____

11. _____ modulation involves timing shifts.
    A. Amplitude   B. Frequency   C. Phase shift   D. TDM

    11.____

12. _____ is the responsibility of the modulator.
    A. Encoding of the data bits   B. Decoding of data bits
    C. Transmission of the data   D. Error detection in carrier

    12.____

13. Simultaneous _____ communication requires a modulator as well as a demodulator.
    A. half duplex
    B. full duplex
    C. asynchronous
    D. modulated

13._____

14. Transducers using modulation through sound use
    A. glass
    B. dial-up
    C. radio
    D. copper

14._____

15. Air carries multiple signals called _____ for each TV station.
    A. frequency
    B. amplitude
    C. channels
    D. modulations

15._____

16. Switching data streams sequentially is
    A. TDM
    B. FDM
    C. DTM
    D. DMA

16._____

17. Network resources are managed using _____ service in Windows server-based networks.
    A. Windows active directory
    B. Windows NT directory servicer
    C. NDM
    D. DMS

17._____

18. IP subnets connected using fast links are called
    A. domain
    B. controller
    C. site
    D. BDC

18._____

19. Object attributes in active directory are contained in
    A. configuration NC
    B. CMD log
    C. MMC
    D. Schema NC

19._____

20. For group policy objects, a folder exists on all domain controllers as
    A. SYSVOL
    B. C$
    C. $SYS
    D. \\shared

20._____

21. A minimum required services and roles will run in
    A. minimal installation option
    B. VMS
    C. server core
    D. named piping

21._____

22. Minimum storage required for active directory is
    A. 100 MB
    B. 200 MB
    C. 250 MB
    D. 512 MB

22._____

23. Administrators for duration of the schema update have the role of _____ Admins.
    A. Global
    B. Schema
    C. Security
    D. Data

23._____

24. A site created when installed in a forest root domain controller will derive its name from
    A. default first site name
    B. default site built in
    C. $wins
    D. NC

24._____

25. A server that manages site-to-site replication is
    A. Bridgehead
    B. Masthead
    C. PDC
    D. member

25._____

KEY (CORRECT ANSWERS)

1.	D		11.	D
2.	B		12.	A
3.	B		13.	B
4.	D		14.	B
5.	A		15.	C
6.	A		16.	A
7.	B		17.	A
8.	B		18.	C
9.	B		19.	D
10.	D		20.	A

21.	C
22.	B
23.	B
24.	A
25.	A

TEST 3

DIRECTIONS: Each question or incomplete statement is followed by several suggested answers or completions. Select the one that BEST answers the question or completes the statement. *PRINT THE LETTER OF THE CORRECT ANSWER IN THE SPACE AT THE RIGHT.*

1. In Unix variants, _____ command is used to generate statistics on socket connections.
   A. SS   B. NETSTAT   C. IPNET   D. ST

   1._____

2. The _____ command is used to send mail via SMTP server.
   A. MAILX   B. SMAIL   C. NETSND   D. CONM

   2._____

3. Fdisk command on Linus is used to
   A. format hard disk   B. check partition
   C. copy contents   D. remove bad sectors

   3._____

4. The _____ command is used to open the command prompt in Windows.
   A. LST   B. PRM   C. TASKMGR   D. CMD

   4._____

5. IOS stands for
   A. Internet Operating System   B. Internetwork Operating System
   C. Internal Operating System   D. Input Output System

   5._____

6. Which is TRUE of a switch connected in a star topology?
   A. Packets are sent to all recipients in the network
   B. Packets are sent to intended recipients
   C. Packets are filtered by the recipient
   D. Packets are filtered by the sender

   6._____

7. Which is NOT an Ethernet cable standard?
   A. CAT-5   B. CAT-6   C. CAT-6e   D. CAT-5e

   7._____

8. Ethernet cables physically differ by
   A. quality of material used   B. number of twists per cm
   C. color coding scheme   D. number of wire pairs

   8._____

9. The term NEXT is used for
   A. lost packets   B. cable faults   C. parity   D. cross talk

   9._____

10. A stranded cable is
    A. an unused cable
    B. loosely connected
    C. made up of multiple cables
    D. the main cause of communication error

    10._____

11. Trusted Platform Module (TPM) is a(n)
    A. application software   B. hardware chip
    C. Ethernet cabling standard   D. encryption standard

11.____

12. Which statement is TRUE for BitLocker?
    A. It secures files one by one
    B. It secures the entire operating system
    C. It locks the entire drive
    D. It removes viruses

12.____

13. Web servers use _____ virtualization.
    A. server   B. desktop   C. application   D. data

13.____

14. _____ is a Linux OS.
    A. CMOS   B. VMS   C. Novell   D. Ubuntu

14.____

15. Wi-Fi means
    A. IEEE 802   B. wireless fidelity
    C. wireless first   D. SMPTE

15.____

16. _____ computing uses unused processing cycles from different computers.
    A. Cloud   B. Network   C. Packet   D. Grid

16.____

17. The _____ command will be used to change file permissions.
    A. CHKDSK   B. CHFLS   C. CHMOD   D. CHALP

17.____

18. CDFS is used for
    A. Window Active directory permissions
    B. making file system changes permanent
    C. checking for errors
    D. while reading CD-ROM

18.____

19. _____ is a technology provided for e-mail clients.
    A. Clutter   B. NOVA   C. ARPANET   D. Outlook

19.____

20. Unix users are protected by a firewall service named
    A. TCP wrapper   B. Fast TCP
    C. Modbus TCP/IP   D. TOE

20.____

21. _____ mode allows troubleshooting of Windows critical errors.
    A. Safe   B. Command line
    C. Line operation   D. CHKLST

21.____

22. Protocol _____ allows multiple protocols to work together.
    A. stack   B. pool   C. block   D. cloud

22.____

23. BCD is a data standard representing integers in _____ bits.
    A. 4   B. 8   C. 16   D. 32

23.____

3 (#3)

24. Copying digital content from a device of one type to another is
    A. space shifting   B. CODEC
    C. openshift   D. proportional spacing

24.____

25. A zero that exists on the leftmost digit of a number is
    A. significant   B. absolute   C. rounding   D. leading

25.____

KEY (CORRECT ANSWERS)

1.	A		11.	B
2.	A		12.	C
3.	B		13.	A
4.	D		14.	D
5.	B		15.	A
6.	B		16.	D
7.	B		17.	C
8.	B		18.	D
9.	D		19.	A
10.	C		20.	A

21. A
22. A
23. A
24. A
25. D

145

TEST 4

DIRECTIONS: Each question or incomplete statement is followed by several suggested answers or completions. Select the one that BEST answers the question or completes the statement. *PRINT THE LETTER OF THE CORRECT ANSWER IN THE SPACE AT THE RIGHT.*

1. _____ interface allows a working based on body movements.
   A. Cyber   B. Nova   C. Rota   D. Haptic

   1.____

2. Computers within the same domain acting as servers can have exactly _____ role(s).
   A. one   B. three   C. two   D. four

   2.____

3. _____ is a part of an operating system.
   A. Kernel   B. Core   C. Grid   D. Cloud

   3.____

4. File servers and application servers will typically be _____ servers in a Windows environment.
   A. data server   B. active directory
   C. cluster   D. member

   4.____

5. Any of the network computers can be the server in _____ network.
   A. client server   B. VLAN   C. peer-to-peer   D. terrestrial

   5.____

6. Ad-hoc mode does NOT use any
   A. shared services   B. access point
   C. protocol   D. data standards

   6.____

7. Manchester encoding is a data _____ method.
   A. encryption   B. correction   C. compression   D. transmission

   7.____

8. _____ server stores databases.
   A. File   B. Database   C. Data   D. Information

   8.____

9. In a(n) _____ network, data may be coming from many sources but managed centrally.
   A. centralized   B. remote   C. distributed   D. isolated

   9.____

10. Users outside of network are also allowed. They are part of the
    A. intranet   B. internet   C. subnet   D. extranet

    10.____

11. Internet service providers are connected to each other using
    A. network access points (NAP)   B. access point (AP)
    C. APLink   D. virtual access points

    11.____

12. An organization's network accessible to its staff only is a
    A. LAN   B. internet   C. intranet   D. WAN

    12.____

13. _____ is memory area an application is legally allowed to access.
    A. Viber space
    C. Application memory
    B. Address space
    D. Physical memory

13.____

14. MAC OS always uses _____ addressing.
    A. segmented
    B. thunking
    C. flat
    D. virtual

14.____

15. Multicast address is assigned to _____ device(s).
    A. one
    C. NIC only
    B. any two specific
    D. multiple

15.____

16. With _____, a packet can have multiple destinations.
    A. Mbone
    B. MIDL
    C. SDS
    D. DDL

16.____

17. Rules and regulations governing the management of data are called
    A. computer law
    C. code law
    B. compliance
    D. GRC

17.____

18. An application in Windows that allows creating routing applications is
    A. RDMA
    C. social routing
    B. BRAS
    D. RRAS

18.____

19. A fiber-based distributed data interface will typically use _____ topology.
    A. star
    B. mesh
    C. bus
    D. ring

19.____

20. The number of bits transferred from one device to another in 1 second is _____ rate.
    A. adaptive
    B. bit
    C. baud
    D. passive

20.____

21. _____ is a scripting language used in Windows server OS, used for automating Windows management.
    A. Powershell
    B. Vbscript
    C. JDBC
    D. JSON

21.____

22. What tool would you use for writing snap-ins in Windows?
    A. Powershell
    C. APM
    B. WHS console
    D. MMC

22.____

23. _____ monitors the packet collision rate.
    A. NIC
    B. Switch
    C. Router
    D. API

23.____

24. Dynamic packet filtering is a feature of _____ architecture.
    A. firewall
    B. DNA
    C. FDDI
    D. service

24.____

25. WHS denotes Windows
    A. hash system
    C. hypertext service
    B. home server
    D. help service

25.____

KEY (CORRECT ANSWERS)

1.	D		11.	B
2.	C		12.	C
3.	A		13.	B
4.	D		14.	C
5.	C		15.	D
6.	B		16.	A
7.	D		17.	B
8.	B		18.	D
9.	C		19.	D
10.	D		20.	B

21.	A
22.	D
23.	C
24.	A
25.	B

EXAMINATION SECTION

TEST 1

DIRECTIONS: Each question or incomplete statement is followed by several suggested answers or completions. Select the one that BEST answers the question or completes the statement. *PRINT THE LETTER OF THE CORRECT ANSWER IN THE SPACE AT THE RIGHT.*

1. Modern day telephony uses _____ for sending voice signals.
   A. VoIP   B. modems   C. routers   D. switches

   1._____

2. A user is downloading a file using a computer on the network. The computer is a(n)
   A. node   B. entry point   C. client   D. access point

   2._____

3. A network operating system offers its services to
   A. groups of computers using desktop operating system
   B. groups of servers connected to LAN
   C. users in another network segment
   D. all of the above

   3._____

4. The program to interpret HTML files sent from a web server is called
   A. browser   B. SMTP server
   C. RAS   D. HTML engine

   4._____

5. FrameRelay is used in
   A. LAN   B. MAN   C. WAN   D. PAN

   5._____

6. The most secure network is
   A. LAN   B. MAN   C. WAN   D. PAN

   6._____

7. In a _____ network, any computer could be a client or server.
   A. peer-to-peer   B. client server
   B. VLAN   D. terrestrial

   7._____

8. User documents have been stored on a central server for printing. This is an example of a(n) _____ server.
   A. application   B. file   C. print   D. mail

   8._____

9. Small computer programs are being run from a central computer. This is a(n) _____ kind of server.
   A. application   B. file   c. print   D. mail

   9._____

10. Databases are stored in a(n) _____ server.
    A. database   B. file   C. data   D. information

    10._____

11. Data resources are placed at different geographical locations, however, they are managed from one unique location. What kind of network model is this?
    A. Centralized   B. Remote   C. Distributed   D. Isolated

    11._____

12. A company has a private network used within its premises. It has given   12._____
access to a few outside suppliers through its
    A. intranet   B. extranet   C. internet   D. subnet

13. You are using your browser to browse a web page using HTTP protocol.   13._____
_____ protocol will be used to respond to your request.
    A. HTTP   B. TCP   C. HTTPS   D. IP

14. _____ protocols are not specific to one supplier of LAN equipment.   14._____
    A. Proprietary   B. Functional   C. Universal   D. Standard

15. RFCs are used to upgrade the bandwidth requirements of a protocol. RFC   15._____
stands for
    A. Requirement for Formal Consent   B. Regional Formats Committee
    C. Request For Comments   D. Released Future Concerns

16. LAN standards for networking are developed by _____ organization.   16._____
    A. IERT   B. IEEE   C. FERS   D. OOEE

17. Standard allocation of Internet protocol addresses are insured by an   17._____
organization called
    A. ICANN   B. Internet Architecture Board (IAB)
    C. IEEE   D. Internet Society

18. A network switch is connected to 15 employees. _____ topology is in use.   18._____
    A. Star   B. Bus   C. Ring   D. Hybrid

19. _____ optic fiber cable will be used for smaller distances.   19._____
    A. Single Mode Fiber (SMF)   B. Multi-Mode Fiber (MMF)
    C. Both A and B   D. None of the above

20. The entire bandwidth of a digital signal is being used by the only channel.   20._____
It is called a(n) _____ communication.
    A. broadband   B. digital   C. analog   D. baseband

21. Frequency Division Multiplexing (FDM) is possible in   21._____
    A. baseband   B. broadband
    C. both A and B   D. none of the above

22. Gigabit Ethernet is capable of transmissions of 1000   22._____
    A. BPS   B. GBPS   C. MBPS   D. KBPS

23. Fiber distributed data interface uses _____ topology.   23._____
    A. ring   B. star   C. mesh   D. bus

24. IEEE networking standards apply to the _____ layer specifications technology.   24._____
    A. network   B. data   C. application   D. physical

25. Mutual authentication between the client and the server is called 25.____
    A. encrypted B. decrypted
    C. challenge handshake D. kerberos

_____

KEY (CORRECT ANSWERS)

1.	A		11.	C
2.	C		12.	B
3.	D		13.	A
4.	A		14.	D
5.	C		15.	C
6.	A		16.	B
7.	A		17.	A
8.	B		18.	A
9.	A		19.	A
10.	A		20.	D

21.	B
22.	C
23.	A
24.	A
25.	A

_____

TEST 2

DIRECTIONS: Each question or incomplete statement is followed by several suggested answers or completions. Select the one that BEST answers the question or completes the statement. *PRINT THE LETTER OF THE CORRECT ANSWER IN THE SPACE AT THE RIGHT.*

1. Fast Ethernet can run on   1.____
   - A. UTP
   - B. optical fiber
   - C. wireless
   - D. all of the above

2. Fiber fast Ethernet can provide speeds of up to   2.____
   - A. 1 GBPS
   - B. 512 MBPS
   - C. 100 MBPS
   - D. 256 KBPS

3. Giga-Ethernet provides speed up to _____ MBPS over fiber.   3.____
   - A. 1000
   - B. 512
   - C. 256
   - D. 1.5

4. _____ LAN is a solution to divide a single broadcast domain into multiple broadcast domains.   4.____
   - A. Virtual
   - B. Localized
   - C. Bridged
   - D. Broadcast

5. Internet uses _____ topology.   5.____
   - A. hybrid
   - B. daisy chain
   - C. dual ring
   - D. mesh

6. Unlike OSI, the Internet model uses _____ layers.   6.____
   - A. 3
   - B. 4
   - C. 7
   - D. 5

7. Infrared frequency ranges from 300 GHz to 43 THz and is used for   7.____
   - A. TV remotes
   - B. penetrating obstacles
   - C. communications of up to 1000 meters
   - D. line of sight communication

8. Frequency Division Multiplexing (FDM) uses _____ to distribute bandwidth.   8.____
   - A. frequency
   - B. channels
   - C. time slots
   - D. path

9. _____ is used to provide abstraction of services.   9.____
   - A. Abstraction layer
   - B. Network layer
   - C. Encapsulation
   - D. Collision detection

10. _____ are addressed via ports.   10.____
   - A. Processes
   - B. Memory address
   - C. NIC
   - D. Protocols

11. SMTP is _____-level protocol.
    A. higher   B. lower   C. user   D. network

    11.____

12. _____ layer provides host-to-host communications.
    A. Network   B. Data   C. Transport   D. Physical

    12.____

13. _____ is basic transport layer protocol.
    A. UDP   B. HTTP   C. HTTPS   D. FTP

    13.____

14. Adding a packet header is a function of
    A. transport   B. physical   C. data link   D. application

    14.____

15. _____ requires sending from one network to another.
    A. Internetworking   B. Transmission control
    C. TCP   D. IP

    15.____

16. A host is identified using
    A. IP addressing system   B. website address
    C. MAC address   D. Checksum

    16.____

17. 128-bit addressing is made possible by
    A. IPV4   B. IPV6   C. TCP/IP   D. UDP

    17.____

18. HDLC stands for
    A. High Level Link Control   B. High Level Data Level Checking
    C. High Definition Latency Check   D. High Definition Least Control

    18.____

19. IP (Internet Protocol) does NOT guarantee _____ delivery.
    A. reliable   B. efficient   C. error-free   D. complete

    19.____

20. Routers and _____ do not examine traffic.
    A. graphic cards   B. bridges
    C. network hubs   d switches

    20.____

21. A PAN may use _____ protocol.
    A. Bluetooth   B. IP   C. TCP   D. UDP

    21.____

22. A wireless router typically allows devices to connect to
    A. a wired network
    B. a wireless network
    C. both wired and wireless networks
    D. predefined devices on other networks

    22.____

23. _____ may refer to a Wi-Fi use without permission.
    A. Piggybacking   B. Address breach
    C. Access point hack   D. IP address violation

    23.____

24. FTTN in fiber networks denotes Fiber
    A. Technology Tracking Network
    C. Transmission Twisted Network
    B. to the Neighborhood
    D. Traceability Track Nationwide

24.____

25. PON stands for _____ Network.
    A. Passive Optic
    C. Privately Owned
    B. Private Optic
    D. Primary Operational

25.____

KEY (CORRECT ANSWERS)

1. D	11. A
2. C	12. C
3. A	13. A
4. A	14. C
5. A	15. A
6. B	16. A
7. A	17. B
8. B	18. A
9. C	19. A
10. A	20. D

21. A
22. C
23. A
24. B
25. A

TEST 3

DIRECTIONS: Each question or incomplete statement is followed by several suggested answers or completions. Select the one that BEST answers the question or completes the statement. *PRINT THE LETTER OF THE CORRECT ANSWER IN THE SPACE AT THE RIGHT.*

1. MIMO stands for
   A. Multiple Input Multiple Output
   B. Multiple Inter Modular Operations
   C. Metropolitan Inter Module Onset
   D. Metropolitan Intra Modular Offnet

   1.____

2. Beamforming characterizes
   A. merging of optic fiber streams
   B. merging of signals
   C. line of sight light beams
   D. unidirectional radio streams

   2.____

3. Speed of transmission will be SLOWEST in
   A. LAN   B. WAN   C. MAN   D. PAN

   3.____

4. Network Interface Cards (NIC) use a(n) _____ to distinguish one computer from another.
   A. network address
   B. IP address
   C. MAC address
   D. Checksum

   4.____

5. Which of the following amplify communication signals and filter noise?
   A. Hubs   B. Switches   C. Routers   D. Repeaters

   5.____

6. _____ send information/data to be copied unmodified to all computers.
   A. Hubs   B. Bridges   C. Firewalls   D. Switches

   6.____

7. Which of the following reject network access requests from unsafe sources?
   A. Filter services
   B. Hubs
   C. Security protocols
   D. Firewalls

   7.____

8. A _____ normally represents the smallest amount of data that can traverse over a network at a single time.
   A. byte   B. bit   C. word   D. packet

   8.____

9. OSPF is a
   A. routing protocol
   B. unique addressing scheme
   C. end user identification technique
   D. open source software

   9.____

10. _____ route is used when failure occurs with a routing device.
    A. Adaptive   B. Alternate   C. Access   D. Appropriate

    10.____

11. _____ is a parameter used for calculating a routing metric.
    A. Path speed   B. Load   C. Hop count   D. All of the above

    11.____

12. Algorithm in computer operations is a

    A. software   B. hardware   C. method   D. pseudo code

    12.____

13. _____ is the total time a packet takes to transmit from one place to another.

    A. Response time   B. Latency

    C. Delay   D. Bandwidth

    13.____

14. Media portion in an OSI model includes

    A. presentation and data layer

    B. application and network layer

    C. transport and data layer

    D. all of the network data link and physical layers

    14.____

15. OSI stands for Open

    A. Systems Interconnection   B. Standards International

    C. Systems Integration   D. Standards for Internet

    15.____

16. Collision occurs when

    A. packets collide due to throttling

    B. more than one computer sends data at the same time

    C. data is sent out of sequence

    D. network traffic exceeds its limit

    16.____

17. CSMA is a method used by

    A. Ethernet   B. Internet

    C. operating system   D. error detection services

    17.____

18. The term broadband is used when a media type

    A. can carry multiple data signals

    B. can carry one signal at one time

    C. has separate lines for sending and receiving

    D. has error detection and correction mechanism

    18.____

19. Fast Ethernet is also known as

    A. 10 Base-T   B. 100 Base-T

    C. Gigabit Ethernet   D. 1000 Base-X

    19.____

20. _____ is called beacon frame.

    A. Periodically broadcasted frame   B. Identification frame

    C. Header frame   D. Frame beginning the broadcast

    20.____

21. Channel bonding allows multiple _____ at the same time.

    A. packets   B. channels   C. media   D. data streams

    21.____

22. Gigabit Ethernet works on _____ media.

    A. fiber optic   B. copper

    C. both fiber and copper   D. wireless

    22.____

23. FDDI uses _____ rings.
    A. four   B. two   C. one   D. three

      23.____

24. IPV6 addresses are _____ bits.
    A. 32   B. 65   C. 128   D. 256

      24.____

25. IPV6 addresses are binary numbers represented in
    A. decimal   B. binary   C. octal   D. hexadecimal

      25.____

KEY (CORRECT ANSWERS)

1.	A		11.	D
2.	D		12.	C
3.	C		13.	B
4.	C		14.	D
5.	D		15.	A
6.	A		16.	B
7.	D		17.	A
8.	D		18.	A
9.	A		19.	B
10.	A		20.	A

21.	B
22.	C
23.	B
24.	C
25.	D

TEST 4

DIRECTIONS: Each question or incomplete statement is followed by several suggested answers or completions. Select the one that BEST answers the question or completes the statement. *PRINT THE LETTER OF THE CORRECT ANSWER IN THE SPACE AT THE RIGHT.*

1. VoIP allows sending voice data using
   A. fiber optics
   C. standard IP
   B. PSTN
   D. copper wires

   1.____

2. Bootstrapping refers to the _____ process.
   A. self-starting
   C. infinite
   B. batch processing
   D. automatically ending

   2.____

3. NOS stands for Network
   A. Operation Starter
   C. Optic Stream
   B. On Standby
   D. Operating System

   3.____

4. Compared to LANs, WANS are more
   A. reliable   B. congested   C. error-free   D. cheaper

   4.____

5. The initial setup costs for LAN are _____ compared to WAN.
   A. the same   B. low   C. high   D. very high

   5.____

6. WANs are often built using
   A. more than one adjacent LAN
   C. fiber optic cables
   B. leased lines
   D. extranet

   6.____

7. The operating and maintenance costs of WAN are _____ compared to LAN.
   A. very low   B. low   C. high   D. very high

   7.____

8. Nowadays, most LAN(s) use _____ as standard.
   A. Ethernet
   C. frame relay
   B. VPN over Internet
   D. leased lines

   8.____

9. WANs may use _____ as standard.
   A. Ethernet
   C. VPN
   B. Subnet
   D. Fast Ethernet

   9.____

10. A computer network spanning three university campuses within remote geographical locations is a typical example of a _____ area network.
    A. campus   B. wide   C. metropolitan   D. local

    10.____

11. Client server networks require a _____ server.
    A. dedicated   B. parallel   C. data   D. file

    11.____

12. A file server will typically run _____ protocol.
    A. HTTP   B. IP   C. HTTPs   D. FTP

    12.____

13. _____ servers allow central administration of user and network resources.

    A. Print   B. Directory   C. File   D. Application

13.____

14. Network resources will be optimally used from a central resource in a _____ computer network model.

    A. central   B. distributed   C. remote   D. wireless

14.____

15. An internetwork will connect at least two

    A. internets   B. extranets   C. intranets   D. networks

15.____

16. Internet Protocol Security (IPSec) is a(n) _____ part of the IPV4.

    A. optional   B. integral/mandatory

    C. built-in   D. missing

16.____

17. Features of _____ can be extended by adding headers.

    A. IPV4   B. IPV6   C. IP   D. TCP

17.____

18. The available types of communication in IPV4 are unicast, multicast and

    A. podcast   B. broadcast   C. lancast   D. delicast

18.____

19. In backup terminology, a cold site means

    A. needs time to switch to normal operations

    B. readily available backup

    C. a backup on Cloud

    D. a separate backup

19.____

20. An overlapping frame is called a(n)

    A. header   B. packet

    C. collision   D. extended frame

20.____

21. _____ is a set of checks/rules for communication.

    A. Protocol   B. Syntax

    C. Lexical grammar   D. Encryption

21.____

22. Multiplexing collects data from different

    A. networks   B. applications   C. addresses   D. routers

22.____

23. When a block of data is transmitted, supplement data is attached to the _____ for use from one layer to another.

    A. datagram   B. packet   C. FIN bit   D. header

23.____

24. De-multiplexing is done in a(n) _____ layer.

    A. transport   B. network   C. data   D. application

24.____

25. In large networks, a _____ will divide the network into logical parts called segments to handle data traffic.

    A. switch   B. hub   C. router   D. bridge

25.____

KEY (CORRECT ANSWERS)

1.	C		11.	A
2.	A		12.	D
3.	D		13.	C
4.	B		14.	A
5.	B		15.	D
6.	B		16.	B
7.	C		17.	B
8.	A		18.	B
9.	C		19.	A
10.	C		20.	C

21.	A
22.	B
23.	D
24.	A
25.	C

EXAMINATION SECTION
TEST 1

DIRECTIONS: Each question or incomplete statement is followed by several suggested answers or completions. Select the one that BEST answers the question or completes the statement. *PRINT THE LETTER OF THE CORRECT ANSWER IN THE SPACE AT THE RIGHT.*

1. _____ is commonly used to report on project performance.
   A. Earned Value Management
   B. WBS
   C. Quality Management Plan
   D. RBS

1._____

2. Which of the following is NOT a process associated with communications management?
   A. Distribute information
   B. Manage stakeholder expectations
   C. Plan communication
   D. Survey questionnaire

2._____

3. As a project manager, you are expected to make relevant information available to project stakeholders as planned. Which process does this relate to?
   A. Distribute information
   B. Manage stakeholder expectations
   C. Plan communication
   D. Report performance

3._____

4. Report performance involves all of the following EXCEPT
   A. collecting and distributing performance data
   B. collecting and distributing progress measurements
   C. collecting stakeholder information needs
   D. collecting and distributing forecasts

4._____

5. Of the following examples listed, which is a sign of feedback from the receiver?
   A. No written response from the receiver
   B. An acknowledgement or additional questions from the receiver
   C. Encoding the message by the receiver
   D. Decoding the message by the receiver

5._____

6. As a project manager you are expected to create a scope statement. Once you have the statement, you find it to be useful in all the following ways EXCEPT
   A. describing the purpose of the project
   B. describing the objectives of the project
   C. distributing information
   D. explaining the business problems the project is expected to solve

6._____

7. What are project deliverables?   7._____
    A. Tangible products that the project is expected to deliver
    B. Prioritized list of deliverables
    C. Project scope statement
    D. Project documents

8. As a project manager, you are arranging criteria for project completion criteria.   8._____
   You could organize it using all of the following EXCEPT
    A. functional department
    B. milestones
    C. tasks of projects
    D. project phase

9. Which of the following is not a task under "Developing human resource plan"?   9._____
    A. Documenting organizational relationships
    B. Looking for the availability of required human resources
    C. Identification and documentation of project roles and responsibilities
    D. Creating a staffing plan

10. If you are a project manager who is keen in managing a project team, you would   10._____
    undertake any of the following EXCEPT
    A. creating a staffing plan
    B. evaluating individual team member performance
    C. providing feedback
    D. resolving conflicts

11. Nurturing the team is a vital role of a project manager. If you have to do so, what   11._____
    would you avoid?
    A. Guide the team members as required
    B. Provide mentoring throughout the project
    C. Remove the team member who is found to be less skilled
    D. On-the-job training

12. War room creation is an example of   12._____
    A. co-location
    B. management skills
    C. rewards and recognitions
    D. establishing ground rules

13. The team member roles and responsibilities could be documented using all of the   13._____
    following EXCEPT
    A. functional chart
    B. text-oriented format
    C. hierarchical type organizational chart
    D. matrix-based responsibility chart

14. _____ is NOT an example of constraints placed upon the project by current organizational policies.
    A. Hiring freeze
    B. Reduced training funds
    C. Organizational chart templates
    D. Rewards and Increments Freeze

14._____

15. As a project manager, you have decided to have a virtual team. What kind of limitation would this create with regards to team development?
    A. Rewards and recognition
    B. Establishing ground rules
    C. Team building
    D. Co-location

15._____

16. Unplanned training means
    A. team building using virtual team arrangement
    B. competencies developed as a result of project performance appraisals
    C. on-the-job training
    D. training that is done without any planning in advance

16._____

17. Resource break down structure is an example of
    A. functional chart
    B. text-oriented format
    C. hierarchical type organizational chart
    D. matrix-based responsibility chart

17._____

18. A project manager would consider the following as inputs to define scope EXCEPT
    A. requirements document
    B. project Charter
    C. product management plan
    D. organizational process charts

18._____

19. Aldo is a project manager and has to terminate a project earlier than planned. The level and extent of completion should be documented. Under which is this done?
    A. Verify scope
    B. Create scope
    C. Control scope
    D. Define scope

19._____

20. Sam, an IT project manager, is having difficulty in getting resources for his project, and hence has to depend highly on department heads. Which type of organization is Sam most likely working with?
    A. Functional
    B. Tight matrix
    C. Weak matrix
    D. Projectized

20._____

Questions 21-25.

Len is a project manager of an infrastructure project manager of a well-known company. He is involved in various processes of scope management. Look at the following chart and align the different processes to various tasks listed. Choose the appropriate answer for each process and list them under corresponding tasks.

	Processes	Corresponding tasks	List of tasks
21.	Define scope	21._____	A. Monitoring project scope and project status
22.	Control scope	22._____	B. Defining and documenting stakeholder needs
23.	Collect requirements	23._____	C. Formalizing acceptance of the complete project deliverables
24.	Verify scope	24._____	D. Breaking down the project into smaller, more manageable tasks
25.	Create WBS	25._____	E. Developing a detailed description of the project and its ultimate product

_____

KEY (CORRECT ANSWERS)

1. A	11. C	21. E
2. D	12. A	22. A
3. A	13. A	23. B
4. C	14. C	24. C
5. B	15. D	25. D
6. C	16. B	
7. A	17. C	
8. C	18. C	
9. B	19. A	
10. A	20. A	

_____

TEST 2

DIRECTIONS: Each question or incomplete statement is followed by several suggested answers or completions. Select the one that BEST answers the question or completes the statement. *PRINT THE LETTER OF THE CORRECT ANSWER IN THE SPACE AT THE RIGHT.*

1. In which of the following processes would risk be identified?
   A. Risk identification
   B. Risk monitoring and control
   C. Qualitative risk analysis
   D. Risk identification, monitoring and control

1._____

2. Jack has prepared a risk management plan for his project and also identified risks in his project. Which of the following processes should Jack do next?
   A. Plan risk responses
   B. Perform qualitative analysis
   C. Perform quantitative analysis
   D. Monitor and control risk

2._____

3. Which of the following is NOT a step in risk management?
   A. Perform qualitative analysis
   B. Monitor and control risk
   C. Risk identification
   D. Risk breakdown structure

3._____

4. Sue is a project manager for an IT project at a corporate office. She is engaged in the process of identifying risks. To do so, she collects inputs from experts from the field through a questionnaire. What is this technique called?
   A. Interview
   B. Documentation review
   C. Delphi technique
   D. Register risk

4._____

5. Positive risks may be responded by which of the following:
   I. Exploit   II. Accept   III. Mitigate   IV. Share

   A. I and III
   B. All of the above
   C. I, II and IV
   D. I, II and III

5._____

6. Risk _____ is a response to negative risks.
   A. identification
   B. mitigation
   C. response plan
   D. management plan

6._____

7. Which of the following statements is NOT true about risk management? 7._____
   A. Risk register documents all the risks in detail
   B. Risks always have negative impacts and not positive
   C. Risk mitigation is a response to negative risks
   D. Risk register documents the risks in detail

8. _____ is the document that lists all the risks in a hierarchical fashion. 8._____
   A. Risk breakdown structure
   B. Lists of risks
   C. Risk management plan
   D. Monte Carlo diagram

9. Nicole is a project manager of a reforestation project. In one of the project 9._____
   reviews, she realizes that a risk has occurred. Which document should Nicole
   refer to take an appropriate action?
   A. Risk response plan
   B. Risk register
   C. Risk management plan
   D. Risk breakdown structure

10. As a project manager, you have invited experts for an effective brainstorming 10._____
   session to identify risks involved in the project. What is the ideal group size?
   A. 3   B. 6   C. 4   D. 5

11. Of the following personnel, who is NOT involved in project risk identification 11._____
   activities?
   A. Clerical staff
   B. Subject matter experts
   C. Other project managers
   D. Risk management experts

12. _____ is one of the tools/techniques used in risk identification. 12._____
   A. Risk tracker
   B. Checklist analysis
   C. Risk register
   D. Project scope

13. Jim is a project manager in a bank. He is collecting input for the risk 13._____
   identification process. What input would he be collecting to identify risks?
   I.   Project scope statement
   II. Enterprise environmental factors
   III. Project management plan
   IV. Diagramming techniques

   A. I and IV only
   B. III and IV only
   C. All of the above
   D. I, II and III only

14. Which of the following could a project manager collect from a risk tracker?   14._____
   I.   Root causes of risk and updated risk categories
   II. List of identified risks
   III. Risk register
   IV. List of potential responses

   A. I and IV only
   B. III and IV only
   C. I, II and IV
   D. II only

15. The risk management plan should describe the entire risk management   15._____
   process, including auditing of the process, and should also define _____.
   A. reporting
   B. environmental factors
   C. organizational process assets
   D. project management plan

16. What do risk categories define?   16._____
   A. How to communicate risk activities and their results
   B. Types and sources of risks
   C. How risk management will be done on the process
   D. When and how the risk management activities appear in the project
      schedule

17. Which of the following is not a method of risk identification?   17._____
   A. Diagramming
   B. Interviewing
   C. SWOT
   D. RBS

18. Shauna is conducting a qualitative risk analysis for her project. What is she   18._____
   required to do?
   A. Apply a numerical rating to each risk
   B. Assess the probability and impact of each identified risk
   C. Assign each major risk to a risk owner
   D. Outline a course of action for each major risk identified

19. Which of the following is not a criterion to close a risk?   19._____
   A. Risk is no longer valid
   B. Risk event has occurred
   C. Risk activities are recorded regularly
   D. Risk closure at the direction of a project manager

20. As a project manager, you establish a risk contingency budget. Which of the following is not a purpose of establishing a risk contingency budget?
    A. To be reviewed as a standing agenda item for project team meetings
    B. To prepare in advance to manage the risks successfully
    C. To have some reserve funds
    D. To avoid going over the budget allotted

20._____

21. Which of the following statements is NOT correct in terms of designing a risk management?
    A. Risk is inherent to project work
    B. In any organization, projects will have common risks
    C. Some risks may occur more than once in the life a project
    D. Risks identified will definitely occur

21._____

22. All identified potential risk events that are viewed to be relevant to the project are to be recorded using the
    A. risk register
    B. risk management matrix
    C. risk report
    D. SOW

22._____

23. _____ is/are an example of a business risk.
    A. Poorly understood requirements
    B. A merger
    C. Introduction of new technology to the organization
    D. Work outside the project scope

23._____

24. Personnel turnover in a project is a
    A. Business risk
    B. Not a risk at all
    C. Technology risk
    D. Project risk

24._____

25. Which of the following is not an example of mitigation?
    A. Set expectations
    B. Involve customer in early planning process
    C. Provide training for personnel
    D. Hiring a backup person for a key team member

25._____

KEY (CORRECT ANSWERS)

1.	D	11.	A
2.	B	12.	B
3.	D	13.	D
4.	C	14.	C
5.	C	15.	A
6.	B	16.	B
7.	B	17.	D
8.	A	18.	B
9.	A	19.	C
10.	A	20.	A

21.	D
22.	B
23.	B
24.	D
25.	D

TEST 3

DIRECTIONS: Each question or incomplete statement is followed by several suggested answers of completions. Select the one that best answers the question or complete the statement. *PRINT THE LETTER OF THE CORRECT ANSWER IN THE SPACE AT THE RIGHT.*

1. Project cost management deals with all the following EXCEPT:
   A. Estimating costs
   B. Budgeting
   C. Controlling costs
   D. Communicating costs

   1.____

2. Which of the following is not a process associated with project cost management?
   A. Control costs
   B. Maintain reserves
   C. Estimate costs
   D. Determine budget

   2.____

3. _____ is not a key deliverable of project cost processes.
   A. Cost performance baseline
   B. Activity cost estimates
   C. Results of estimates
   D. Work performance measurements

   3.____

4. As a project manager, you are calculating depreciation for an object. You are doing this by depreciating the same amount from the cost each year.
   What kind of depreciation technique are you applying?
   A. Sum of year depreciation
   B. Double-declining balance
   C. Multiple depreciation
   D. Straight line depreciation

   4.____

5. Which of the following is not a characteristic of analogous estimating?
   A. It is a top-down approach
   B. It is a form of an expert judgment
   C. It makes less time when compared to bottom-up estimation
   D. It is more accurate when compared to bottom-up estimation

   5.____

6. CPI = EV/AC. If CPI is less than 1, the project
   A. is over the budget
   B. is within the budget
   C. would be left over with unused budget
   D. efficiency is less

   6.____

7. Which of the following is not a tool used for estimating cost?
   A. Cost of quality
   B. Expert judgment
   C. Two point estimates
   D. Three point estimates

   7.____

8. What are the traditional project management triple constraints?
   A. Time, cost, resources
   B. Scope, cost, resources
   C. Scope, time, cost
   D. Resources, scope, budget

   8.____

9. Sam, an IT project manager, is having difficulty getting resources for his project, and hence has to depend highly on department heads.
   Which type of organization is Sam most likely working with?
   A. Functional
   B. Tight Matrix
   C. Weak Matrix
   D. Projectized

9._____

10. After-project costs are called _____.
    A. cost of quality
    B. extra costs
    C. life cycle costs
    D. over budget costs

10._____

11. Critical chain is a tool and technique for _____.
    A. developing schedule process
    B. defining critical path
    C. sequencing activities process
    D. estimating activity duration

11._____

12. The following are outputs for sequencing activities:
    A. Project schedule network diagram, Milestone list
    B. Project document updates, Project schedule network diagram
    C. Project schedule, Project document updates
    D. Schedule data, Schedule baseline

12._____

13. The schedule performance index is a measure of:
    A. Difference between earned value and planned value
    B. Ratio between earned value and planned value
    C. Difference between earned value and estimate at completion
    D. Ratio between estimate at completion and earned value

13._____

14. Which of the following is not an input, output or tools and technique for control schedule process?
    A. Project schedule, work performance measurements and variance analysis
    B. Project management plan, project document updates and schedule compression
    C. Work performance information, schedule baseline and schedule data
    D. Project schedule, change requests and resource leveling

14._____

15. Contracts, resource calendar, risk register and forecasts are all termed as
    A. inputs to administer procurements process
    B. outputs from close procurements process
    C. project documents
    D. tools and techniques of conduct procurement process

15._____

16. Fast tracking can be best described as
    A. one of the schedule compression techniques
    B. adding resources to activities on critical path
    C. shared or critical resources available only at specific times
    D. performing activities in parallel to shorten project duration

16._____

17. Which of the following contract types places the highest risk on the seller?   17.____
    A. Cost plus fixed fee
    B. Firm fixed price
    C. Cost plus incentive fee
    D. Time and material

18. Using the Power/Interest grid, a stakeholder with low power and having high interest on   18.____
    the project should be
    A. monitored
    B. managed closely
    C. kept satisfied
    D. kept informed

19. Stakeholder classification information is found in which of the following documents?   19.____
    A. Communications management plan
    B. Stakeholder register
    C. Stakeholder management strategy document
    D. Human resource plan

20. Thomas is a project manager of a well-reputed organization. One of your senior   20.____
    managers approaches you to explain constraints on labor utilization followed by a
    request to delay a couple of your projects. What is the best way to approach this
    situation?
    A. Agree with the senior manager and delay a couple of your projects
    B. Perform an impact analysis of the requested change
    C. Report the situation to the senior management and make a complaint against the
       senior manager
    D. Disagree with the senior manager and continue with the progress of the projects
       managed by you

21. Project management is defined as   21.____
    A. completion of a project
    B. gaining trust of the people involved in the project
    C. completing a WBS
    D. the application of specific knowledge, skills and tools

22. The most common form of dependency is   22.____
    A. Start to Start
    B. Finish to Start
    C. Finish to Finish
    D. Start to Finish

23. Kelly is a project manager who is in phase of project evaluation. Which of the   23.____
    following has to be considered during project evaluation phase?
    I. Give feedback to team members
    II. Learn from experiences
    III. Monitor
    IV. Celebrate

The correct answer(s) is/are:
- A. I only
- B. I, IV and III
- C. III only
- D. I, II and IV

24. Which of the following are very vital for the implementation of the project, and also must be repeated over and over during project's life.
- I. Correct
- II. Monitor
- III. Estimate time and cost
- IV. Analyze

The correct answer(s) is/are:
- A. I, II and III
- B. III only
- C. I, III and IV
- D. I, II and IV

24._____

25. What is the average amount of time is to be allocated to project planning?
- A. 10%
- B. 25%
- C. 22%
- D. 2%

25._____

KEY (CORRECT ANSWERS)

1. D		11. A	
2. B		12. B	
3. C		13. B	
4. C		14. C	
5. D		15. C	
6. A		16. D	
7. C		17. B	
8. C		18. D	
9. A		19. B	
10. C		20. B	

21. D
22. B
23. D
24. D
25. A

TEST 4

DIRECTIONS: Each question or incomplete statement is followed by several suggested answers of completions. Select the one that best answers the question or complete the statement. *PRINT THE LETTER OF THE CORRECT ANSWER IN THE SPACE AT THE RIGHT.*

1. Imagine you are assigned a project for which you do not have the required competency and experience to manage. What is the best plan of action?
    - A. Make sure that you disclose any areas of improvement that need to be immediately addressed with the project sponsor before accepting the assignment
    - B. Do not inform anyone about the gaps and learn as much as you can before any critical activity is due for delivery
    - C. Consider the opportunity as a stepping stone for your career development and accept it
    - D. Tell your boss that you cannot manage as you do not have the relevant experience and decline it

1._____

2. You are the project manager of a new project and are involved in selecting a vendor for acquiring products required for the project. Your close friend is running a company that is also very competitive and a reputed one along with other vendors who are competing for the bid. How can you handle this situation?
    - A. Do not participate in the vendor selection process as this may be considered a conflict of interest
    - B. Provide information to help your friend get the contract as you are the project manager of the project
    - C. Do not inform anyone about your personal contact and be involved in the vendor selection process as normal
    - D. Discuss with your project sponsor the possibility of a conflict of interest and leave the decision to him on the next steps

2._____

3. You have provided good guidance to your team members and this has resulted in successful execution of all of the phases involved. There was a particular phase that has been identified as very critical and the presence of a technical expert helped achieve this success. In the senior management review meeting you were credited with the success of the project, with specific mention of that particular phase. What do you do in this situation?
    - A. Accept the appreciation and feel proud about the success of the project
    - B. Do not mention anything about the technical expert role as you were the project manager for this project
    - C. Give credit to the technical expert and let the senior management know how the presence of the technical expert helped the team to be successful
    - D. Accept the appreciation from the senior management and thank the technical expert in private for achieving this success

3._____

4. As a project manager you are preparing status reports for a meeting with the stakeholders. One of your team members has come out with an issue that will cause some delay in the project timeline. You have a plan that can be implemented to make sure that this issue can be managed without causing any delay in the timeline, but you currently do not have the time to update the project plan. How will you handle this situation?

    A. Present the status of the project as *on-track* without discussing anything about this issue as you will have time to prepare before the next meeting

    B. Cancel the meeting as you do not have the time to update the details to be provided to the stakeholders

    C. Present the status of the project *as-is* without minimizing the effect of the delay and discuss details of the planned approach to solve this issue

    D. Fire your team that is responsible for causing this delay as it has created a bad impression of you amongst the stakeholders

4._____

5. John is an Associate Director in a pharmaceutical company managing its internal projects. He has presented whitepapers on project execution methodologies and is highly respected within the organization. He also regularly conducts workshops & lectures in coordination with PMO. What kind of power does John possess?

    A. Referent power   C. Reward power

    B. Coercive power   D. Expert power

5._____

6. You are a project manager working for a non-profit organization. You had been assigned a project that is in the initial stage and involves development of an eco-system in a large community. You are reviewing the deliverables and templates from similar projects that are available in the company lessons learnt knowledge base. Which item will be of much importance to you?

    A. Project Information Management System

    B. Enterprise Environmental Factors

    C. Organization Process Assets

    D. Standard Templates

6._____

7. A project that you were managing is nearing completion. As part of the deliverables you are required to complete lessons-learned documentation of the project. What is the primary purpose of creating lessons-learned documentation?

    A. Provide information of project success

    B. Help identify all the failures

    C. Provide information on minimizing negative impacts and maximizing positive events for future projects of similar nature

    D. Comply with the organization's objectives

7._____

8. You are managing project teams that work from different locations and there has been issues with the teams' ability to effectively perform. This has resulted in delay in timeline. Which kind of team development technique would be most effective in this situation?

    A. Mediation   C. Co-location

    B. Training   D. Rewards

8._____

9. The project sponsor has requested that you create a project charter for a new project that you will manage next month. Which document will you utilize to create the project charter that will justify the need for the project?

    A. Project SOW   C. Business Case

    B. Business Need   D. Cost-benefit Analysis

9._____

10. An audit is being performed by a team for the project you are managing. The team reports that the standards utilized need to be analyzed as several processes that are not relevant to the current project. What is the process that the team is currently involved?
    A. Quality planning   C. Quality assurance
    B. Quality control   D. Benchmark creation

       10.____

11. The change control board of your organization has approved changes that were submitted and the project team is executing them. What would this process be considered?
    A. Executing the change request
    B. Implementing a corrective action
    C. Gold-plating
    D. Approving the change request

       11.____

12. Which is the primary technique that is carried out to ensure that a contract award is executed correctly or not?
    A. Litigation   C. Inspections
    B. Contract negotiation   D. Procurement audit

       12.____

13. In the final stages of completing a project, you and your team are involved in creating the project report that will be presented to the stakeholders. Which of the following information is not appropriate to be included in the final report?
    A. Recommendations from your team
    B. Project success factors
    C. WBS dictionary
    D. Details of the process improvements

       13.____

14. At the completion of a project, your team has completed the lessons-learned documentation and archived in the database. Who should have access to these documents?
    A. Project team members
    B. Operations department
    C. All of the company's members
    D. Functional managers

       14.____

15. You are project manager for a large project that is in the final stages of completion and you need to formally provide information on the major milestone achieved. You are also in need of immediate feedback from the stakeholders. Which is the best communication method to meet this requirement?
    A. E-mail   C. Meeting
    B. Web publishing   D. Videoconferencing

       15.____

16. Which document will formally authorize a project manager to start the project?
    A. Project SOW   C. Business Case
    B. Project Charter   D. Stakeholder Register

       16.____

17. Which of the following documents would be utilized to ascertain the project's investment worthiness?
    A. Project Charter   C. Business Need
    B. Business Case   D. Procurement documents

       17.____

18. Which of the following conflict resolution is considered as Lose-lose solution?
    A. Problem-solving
    B. Forcing
    C. Compromising
    D. Withdrawing

18._____

19. McGregor's Theory states that all workers fit into one of the two groups. Which of the following theories believes that people are willing to work on their own and need less supervision?
    A. Theory X
    B. Theory Y
    C. Maslow's Hierarchy
    D. Expectancy

19._____

20. The major cause for conflicts on a project are schedule, project priorities and _____.

    A. cost
    B. resources
    C. personality
    D. management

20._____

21. The project manager is responsible for
    A. the success of the project
    B. achieving the project objectives
    C. authorizing the project
    D. performing the project work

21._____

22. Which of the following actions correspond to reducing the consequences of future problems?
    A. Corrective action
    B. Preventive action
    C. Defect repair
    D. Change request

22._____

23. As a project manager for a large-scale project, you are in the process of procuring materials required for the project. Which of the following documents will you not be responsible for?
    A. Procurement documents
    B. Procurement statements of work
    C. Source selection criteria
    D. Proposals

23._____

24. During which process group will the detailed requirements be gathered?
    A. Initiating
    B. Planning
    C. Executing
    D. Closing

24._____

25. The values that illustrate PMIs code of ethics and professional conduct are
    A. respect, honesty, responsibility and honorability
    B. honesty, cultural diversity, integrity and responsibility
    C. fairness, responsibility, honesty and respect
    D. honorability, fairness, respect and responsibility

25._____

KEY (CORRECT ANSWERS)

1. A	11. A
2. D	12. D
3. C	13. C
4. C	14. C
5. D	15. D
6. C	16. B
7. C	17. B
8. C	18. C
9. C	19. B
10. C	20. B

21. B
22. B
23. D
24. B
25. C

___

EXAMINATION SECTION
TEST 1

DIRECTIONS: Each question or incomplete statement is followed by several suggested answers of completions. Select the one that best answers the question or Complete the statement. *PRINT THE LETTER OF THE CORRECT ANSWER IN THE SPACE AT THE RIGHT.*

1. In the OSI model, a hub is defined in which of the following layers?

    A. Session
    B. Application
    C. Data link
    D. Physical

1._____

2. A simple definition of bandwidth is the

    A. number of computers in a network
    B. transmission capacity
    C. classification of network IPs
    D. none of the above

2._____

3. _____ topology makes use of terminators.

    A. Star
    B. Ring
    C. Bus
    D. Token ring

3._____

4. Which of the following is an advantage of the use of multimedia in the learning process?

    A. Students can express their abilities in many different ways
    B. It is useful for the students to develop their career in media sciences
    C. It enhances students' motivation for learning
    D. None of the above

4._____

5. For the purpose of transfer of technology, companies/organizations must

    A. allocate much better budget for research and development
    B. have a good networking structure
    C. have willingness to spend on technology to gain long-term benefits
    D. all of the above

5._____

6. The focus of teacher education must be on the development of

    A. professional identity
    B. personal identity
    C. academic identity
    D. none of the above

6._____

7. System Study is a study that

    A. studies an existing system
    B. performs the documentation of the existing system
    C. highlights existing deficiencies and establishes new goals
    D. all of the above

7._____

8. Which of these is the starting point for the establishment of an MIS?   8._____

    A. Development of physical hardware and networking structure
    B. Development of a DBMS
    C. Understanding and identification of business processes
    D. None of the above

9. A new system is designed by the system analyst by   9._____

    A. identifying the subsystems and then creating links among these subsystems
    B. customizing an existing system to the new system
    C. creating a one unit larger system
    D. proposing new system alternatives

10. Process mapping may be defined by which of the following?   10._____

    A. Activities are related to the different functional units of the organization
    B. It is developed by the placement of different activities with the help of symbols in a logical order
    A. It is used to present different activities of a process in a hierarchical form
    B. Process efficiency is measured with the help of process mapping

11. Which of the following is an example of a payment system?   11._____

    A. E-commerce shopping
    B. Travel reimbursement
    C. Accounts payable
    D. All of the above

12. _____ phase performs problem analysis.   12._____

    A. Systems Analysis
    B. System Design
    C. System Implementation
    D. None of the above

13. Top management is most concerned with   13._____

    A. daily transactions
    B. strategic decisions
    C. tactical decisions
    D. both (B) and (C)

14. Most companies and organizations have their _____ MIS plans.   14._____

    A. master
    B. broad
    C. prototype
    D. control

15. Data integrity refers to

    A. simplicity
    B. security
    C. validity
    D. none of the above

15._____

16. The desired outcome for project integration is

    A. better focus on the organization
    B. ideal usage of resources of the organization
    C. better communication among projects and their teams
    D. all of the above

16._____

17. If you are working on more than one project and you frequently need to put work on one project on hold and move to another project, then return later to the original project, this is known as

    A. excessive burden
    B. flexible Processing
    C. multitasking
    D. burnout

17._____

18. Which of the following may be defined as a project aim?

    A. Meeting the specific quality requirements
    B. On-time delivery
    C. Working within budget constraints
    D. All of the above

18._____

19. The progressive phases of management over large projects are best described as

    A. planning, evaluating and scheduling
    B. planning, scheduling and operating
    C. scheduling, planning and operating
    D. planning, scheduling and controlling

19._____

20. Variance of the total project completion time is computed in the PERT analysis as

    A. project final activity variance
    B. the aggregation of variances of the project activities
    C. the aggregation of all the activities variance on the critical path
    D. the aggregation of all the activities variance not on the critical path

20._____

21. What will be critical path standard deviation if there are three activities -- X, Y and Z -- in the path? X has a deviation of 2, Y has a deviation of 1 and there is a deviation of 2 for Z. In this case, what is the standard deviation of critical path?

    A. 20
    B. 3
    C. 12
    D. 5

21._____

22. Linear regression is much similar to

22._____

    A. simple moving average forecasting approach
    B. trend project forecasting approach
    C. weighted moving average forecasting approach
    D. naïve forecasting approach

23. The purpose of risk tolerance is to

23._____

    A. observe that how much risk can be tolerated by the project
    B. rank project risks
    C. help the project manager in project estimation
    D. help in project scheduling

24. The process group for project management is ordered

24._____

    A. initiating, planning, executing, controlling, and closeout
    B. starting, planning, accelerating, and control
    C. planning, establishing, developing, and control
    D. none of the above

25. Which risk management process identifies the workaround?

25._____

    A. Risk identification
    B. Risk monitoring
    C. Risk measurement
    D. Risk monitoring and control

_____

KEY (CORRECT ANSWERS)

1. D		11. D	
2. B		12. A	
3. C		13. B	
4. C		14. A	
5. D		15. C	
6. A		16. C	
7. D		17. C	
8. C		18. D	
9. A		19. D	
10. A		20. C	

21. B
22. B
23. B
24. A
25. D

_____

TEST 2

DIRECTIONS: Each question or incomplete statement is followed by several suggested answers of completions. Select the one that best answers the question or Complete the statement. *PRINT THE LETTER OF THE CORRECT ANSWER IN THE SPACE AT THE RIGHT.*

1. What is a computer network?   1._____

    A. Information and resource sharing
    B. A combination of computer systems and other hardware elements
    C. A network of communication channels
    D. All of above

2. A network bridge _____.   2._____

    A. monitors network traffic
    B. distinguishes LANs
    C. is a source of connection among LANs
    D. none of the above

3. Which topology is best for the larger networks?   3._____

    A. Ring token
    B. Star
    C. Ring
    D. Bus

4. Interactive books are used in the form of   4._____

    A. educational games
    B. interactive storybooks
    C. interactive texts
    D. both B and C

5. Which of the following are used for GSM technology?   5._____

    A. OFDMA
    B. FDMA/TDMA
    C. CDMA
    D. None of the above

6. What is the main objective of a MIS department?   6._____

    A. To aid the other business areas in performing their tasks
    B. Information processing for the better utilization of data
    C. To be useful for chief executives
    D. To generate useful information

7. Documentation is prepared at   7._____

    A. every phase
    B. the system analysis phase
    C. the system design phase
    D. the system implementation phase

8. System prototyping is useful for the 8._____

    A. programmer in regards to understanding the whole system
    B. purpose of communication with the users, telling them how the system will look after development
    A. purpose of system demo to the higher project management
    B. Both A and B

9. Mistakes made during the requirements analysis phase normally show up in 9._____

    A. system design
    B. system testing
    C. system implementation
    D. none of the above

10. Use case analysis is best described by which of the following statements? 10._____

    A. It is used for interface design by highlighting the stages of user interaction with the system
    A. It minimizes the number of steps in order to access the content
    B. A consistent site design with the products and services
    C. It is used for the purpose of information categorization

11. Who is responsible for the analysis and design of the systems? 11._____

    A. Developer
    B. System analyst
    C. System operator
    D. Project manager

12. _____ is an outline for the development of bugs-free information systems. 12._____

    A. System development life cycle
    B. System conversion
    C. Case tools
    D. System analysis

13. Top-down analysis and design is performed by 13._____

    A. the creation of system flow chart after design process
    B. identifying the top-level functions and development of subsequent lower-level components
    C. identifying the root elements and then moving gradually up to the top level
    D. none of the above

14. Which of the following is not the part of marketing mix? 14._____

    A. Place
    B. Product
    C. Part
    D. Promotion

15. A distributed MIS mainly deals with the

    A. local data processing
    B. multiprocessing
    C. sharing of workload
    D. all of the above

15._____

16. Project managers unaware of the importance of a project for the organization might tend to

    A. focus on less important things
    B. emphasize too much on the use of technology
    C. concentrate more on the customer in hand
    D. all of the above

16._____

17. Why is it necessary for the project managers to understand the organization's mission?

    A. To make better decisions and required adjustments
    B. To advocate for projects in a better way
    C. In order to perform their jobs more effectively
    D. Both (A) and (B) are correct

17._____

18. Common multi-criteria selection models include

    A. checklist
    B. NPV
    C. weighted criteria model
    D. both A and C

18._____

19. The project management process does not involve

    A. project scheduling
    B. project planning
    C. system analysis
    D. project estimation

19._____

20. Which of the following is the best tool for monitoring projects against the original plan?

    A. Network diagrams
    B. Gantt Charts
    C. Data Flow diagrams
    D. All of the above

20._____

21. A project can be treated as a failed project if

    A. project requirements are met on schedule
    B. the project is completed on time but with flaws that require additional work
    C. costs are in line with original projections
    D. all of the above

21._____

22. Which of the following is a basic assumption of PERT?

    A. There is no repetition of any activity within the network
    B. There is known time for the completion of each activity
    C. Only the activities in the critical path must be performed
    D. Project start to project end contains only one route

22._____

23. Sharing of confidential information with some bidders with the purpose of providing them some undue favor is considered as

    A. bribery
    B. bid rigging
    C. bid fixing
    D. favoritism

23._____

24. The advantages of centralized contracting include

    A. provision of easier access to contracting expertise
    B. enhanced organizational contracting expertise
    C. higher level of loyalty
    D. none of the above

24._____

25. All of the following are features and characteristics of a project EXCEPT

    A. a defined start and end
    B. a network of related activities
    C. repeated at a regular interval
    D. temporary in nature

25._____

KEY (CORRECT ANSWERS)

1. D		11. B
2. C		12. A
3. B		13. B
4. D		14. C
5. B		15. C
6. A		16. D
7. A		17. D
8. B		18. D
9. C		19. C
10. A		20. B

21. B
22. A
23. B
24. B
25. C

TEST 3

DIRECTIONS: Each question or incomplete statement is followed by several suggested answers of completions. Select the one that best answers the question or Complete the statement. *PRINT THE LETTER OF THE CORRECT ANSWER IN THE SPACE AT THE RIGHT.*

1. The number of layers in the OSI Reference Model are   1._____

    A. 5
    B. 6
    C. 7
    D. 8

2. Which of these is a source of connection oriented message communication?   2._____

    A. TCP
    B. UDP
    C. IP
    D. None of the above

3. Which buffer is used by the print server for the holding of data before printing?   3._____

    A. Node
    B. Spool
    C. Queue
    D. None of above

4. Criteria for evaluating commercial hypermedia products include   4._____

    A. instructional design
    B. low cost
    C. portability
    D. use of all media channels

5. The domain of .net is used by   5._____

    A. universities
    B. internet service providers
    C. government organizations
    D. none of the above

6. Which of the following is a technology used for the routing of phone calls over a network?   6._____

    A. Video-conferencing
    B. VOIP
    C. Teleconferencing
    D. None of the above

7. The maintenance phase   7._____

    A. defines system requirements
    B. develops system design
    C. performs system testing
    D. none of the above

8. Reconstruction of a system requires the consideration of   8._____

    A. system inputs and outputs
    B. control and processors
    C. comprehensive user feedback
    D. all of the above

9. Cost-Benefit analysis   9._____

    A. performs an estimation of the cost of hardware and software
    B. performs a comparison of costs with the benefits of development of new system
    C. considers both the tangible and non-tangible elements
    D. all of the above

10. Who is responsible for the sponsoring and funding of the project development and its   10._____
     maintenance?

    A. System manager
    B. Project manager
    C. Systems owner
    D. External system user

11. The system implementation approach used in the event you want to run both the old   11._____
     and new systems is called

    A. parallel
    B. pilot
    C. synchronized
    D. phased

12. DBMS advantages include   12._____

    A. data integrity
    B. minimization of storage space
    C. centralized access to the data
    D. all of the above

13. Which of the following is a well-known and popular forecasting approach?   13._____

    A. Chi Square
    B. Correlation
    C. Regression Analysis
    D. None of the above

14. Who is responsible for the tactical decisions of allocation of resources and establishment   14._____
     of control over project activities?

    A. Middle-level management
    B. Higher-level management
    C. Lower-level management
    D. All of the above

15. The mission statement of an organization answers which of the following questions?   15._____

    A. How do we utilize resources?
    B. What are our goals and intentions as an organization?
    C. What are our plans in the long run?
    D. What is the mode of operations in the current environment?

16. What is the benefit of network approach?   16._____

    A. Forecasts may be carried on
    B. Structured approach is avoided
    C. Project progress against the original plan can be monitored
    D. Requirement of management judgment is eliminated

17. A Gantt chart is composed of   17._____

    A. activities in a sequence
    B. mention of different project activities with the elapsed time
    C. overall project elapsed time
    D. all of the above

18. What does *slack* mean with reference to PERT and CPM?   18._____

    A. It is the latest time on which a project may be started without causing any delay for the project
    B. It is a task which must be completed
    C. This reflects the amount of time a specific task may be delayed without having a need to change the overall time of completion of the project
    D. It reflects the start and end time of a task

19. The direct responsibilities of the project manager include   19._____

    A. calculation of probability of the task's completion
    B. design of the network diagrams
    C. acting on all aspects of the project
    D. ensuring that all people assigned to a project carry out their required duties and utilize appropriate resources and information in order to perform their tasks

20. What is standard error in a regression forecast?   20._____

    A. The highest error level for the forecast
    B. The regression line variability
    C. Time to be consumed for the computation of regression forecast
    D. Forecast validity time

21. Which management process helps in risk identification?   21._____

    A. Risk identification, monitoring and control
    B. Qualitative risk analysis
    C. Quantitative risk analysis
    D. Risk detection

22. The cost reimbursable contracts are termed as _____ contracts.   22._____

    A. gradual payment
    B. cost plus
    C. back charge
    D. secure cost

23. The style of conflict resolution that typically has the best impact is   23._____

    A. empathy
    B. problem solving
    C. willingness
    D. mapping

24. Decomposition of deliverables into more manageable components is termed as   24._____

    A. scope segmentation
    B. scope certification
    C. scoping
    D. scope definition

25. What is quality?   25._____

    A. The level at which project requirements are met
    B. Providing output beyond customer demand
    C. Meeting the objectives of management
    D. Meeting customer demands

_____

KEY (CORRECT ANSWERS)

1. C		11. A	
2. A		12. D	
3. B		13. C	
4. A		14. A	
5. B		15. B	
6. B		16. C	
7. D		17. D	
8. D		18. C	
9. D		19. D	
10. C		20. B	

21. A
22. B
23. B
24. D
25. A

_____

TEST 4

DIRECTIONS: Each question or incomplete statement is followed by several suggested answers of completions. Select the one that best answers the question or Complete the statement. *PRINT THE LETTER OF THE CORRECT ANSWER IN THE SPACE AT THE RIGHT.*

1. A firewall is a

    A. tool for web browsing
    B. network boundary established physically
    C. system that blocks unauthorized access
    D. computer's network

1._____

2. For data transfer in both directions, which communication approach is utilized?

    A. Simplex
    B. Half duplex
    C. Full duplex
    D. None of the above

2._____

3. Which of the following is utilized for the purpose of modulation and demodulation?

    A. Satellite
    B. Fiber optics
    C. Modem
    D. Coaxial Cable

3._____

4. After looking at the header of the data packet, a _____ decides the destination of the packet.

    A. hub
    B. switch
    C. router
    D. firewall

4._____

5. Which of the following is software for video editing?

    A. iMovie
    B. ScanImage
    C. PhotoShop
    D. HyperStudio

5._____

6. The use of educational technology must be considered as a(n)

    A. alternative to less technological strategies
    B. necessity for learning
    C. supplement to other teaching tools
    D. none the above

6._____

7. Parallel Run refers to

    A. job processing of two different tasks at two different terminals to compare the outputs
    B. concurrent running of old and new systems in order to identify the likely mistakes of the new system and to perform the daily routine tasks
    C. a job run at two different systems for the purpose of speed comparison
    D. all of the above

7._____

8. The purpose of a context diagram is to 8._____

    A. establish system context
    B. present the flow of data of the system in order to provide a broader system overview
    C. provide a detailed system description
    D. none of the above

9. The number of steps in the systems development life cycle (SDLC) is 9._____

    A. 4
    B. 5
    C. 6
    D. 10

10. Who is the person responsible for ensuring that the project is completed on time with the defined quality and specified budget constraints? 10._____

    A. Systems designer
    B. Project manager
    C. Systems owner
    D. Systems manager

11. Which of the following is the deliverable at the system implementation phase? 11._____

    A. A solution meeting the specific business needs
    B. Defined business problem
    C. Clear identification of business requirements
    D. A blueprint and sketch of the desired system

12. What type of mail requires proof of delivery? 12._____

    A. Express post
    B. External post
    C. Licensed post
    D. Registered post

13. Which of these is a good quality measure? 13._____

    A. Authority
    B. Correctness
    C. Precision
    D. All of the above

14. A group of related projects combine to form a _____. 14._____

    A. projects classification
    B. product
    C. department
    D. program

15. _____ analysis performs an assessment of internal and external environment.

    A. SWOT
    B. Comprehensive
    C. Organizational
    D. Strategic

15._____

16. A dummy activity is required when there is/are

    A. different ending events for more than one activity
    B. one ending event for more than one activity
    C. one starting event for two or more activities
    D. one starting and ending event for more than one activity in the network

16._____

17. Limitations of PERT and CPM include

    A. only a limited type of projects can be applied to these
    B. too much consideration is given to the critical path
    C. these are only to monitor the schedules
    D. it is difficult to interpret because of the graphical nature of the network

17._____

18. If there is a negative tracking signal against a forecasting, it means

    A. this forecast approach regularly underpredicts
    B. MAPE, too, will be negative
    C. this forecast approach regularly overpredicts
    D. MSE, too, will be negative

18._____

19. Quality management is the responsibility of

    A. team Leader
    B. team member
    C. quality assurance coordinator
    D. project manager

19._____

20. Purchasing insurance is considered what type of risk?

    A. Recognition
    B. Prevention
    C. Mitigation
    D. Transfer

20._____

21. Project costs may be monitored with respect to different categories with the help of

    A. standard accounting practices
    B. chart of accounts
    C. WBS
    D. UAS

21._____

22. What is the output of an administrative closure?

    A. Project documentation
    B. Project archives
    C. Risk analysis
    D. None of the above

22._____

23. A detailed project budget is created in the _____ process.   23._____

    A. establishment
    B. execution
    C. planning
    D. control

24. The person who can gain or lose something from the result of a project activity is the   24._____

    A. team member
    B. team leader
    C. supporter
    D. project manager

25. When a project manager apologizes for failing to deal with some issue, this is considered which of the following conflict resolutions?   25._____

    A. Forcing
    B. Withdrawal
    C. Compromising
    D. Collaborating

KEY (CORRECT ANSWERS)

1. C		11. A	
2. C		12. D	
3. C		13. D	
4. C		14. D	
5. A		15. A	
6. C		16. D	
7. B		17. B	
8. B		18. C	
9. C		19. D	
10. B		20. D	

21. B
22. B
23. C
24. C
25. B

EXAMINATION SECTION
TEST 1

DIRECTIONS: Each question or incomplete statement is followed by several suggested answers or completions. Select the one that BEST answers the question or completes the statement. *PRINT THE LETTER OF THE CORRECT ANSWER IN THE SPACE AT THE RIGHT.*

1.   A systems analyst is beginning interviews in an operational area where he is expected to make a complete analysis. At first glance, the operation has poor supervision, poor working conditions, low morale, staff shortages, and general opposition to change. The first interview with the section chief is not very helpful to the analyst in understanding the operation.
Of the following, it would be BEST for the analyst to

    A.   bypass the section chief and speak directly to the workers
    B.   pressure the section chief into being more open with him
    C.   explain to the section chief how the analysis can help him with some of his problems
    D.   formulate alternate plans for general systems improvement on the basis of obvious faults in the operation

1.____

2.   The user requests changes after a system has been substantially coded.
As the systems analyst implementing the system, you should

    A.   ignore the request; at this stage there is no way of making any changes in the system
    B.   determine the importance and impact of each change; be sure that user and system management sign-offs on the proposed changes include a statement of impact
    C.   grant the changes; any change not made may have great implications on the effectiveness of the completed system
    D.   grant the change only on condition that you are relieved of any responsibility for the performance of the system or the impact of modification

2.____

3.   After having initially trained workers of a user section in their new job tasks, it is BEST for you as a trainer to

    A.   turn the group over completely to their regular supervisor for any further training
    B.   follow up very closely to see that they are doing the work properly
    C.   restrict any further contact with the group to those workers who seem to have the most difficulty
    D.   begin your training role but make yourself unavailable as a consultant

3.____

4.   Which of the following statements offers the BEST guideline in drawing up schedules for analysis and coding?

    A.   If you break down the work assignments into small enough units, you should be able to make good estimates of the time necessary to complete the project.
    B.   Put enough good analysts and coders on a project, and you can meet practically any deadline.
    C.   In order to avoid the effects of Parkinson's Law (work expands to fill the time allotted), you should usually draw up a tight schedule.
    D.   Additional time for unforeseen problems should be added to time estimates when trying to predict a relatively accurate final completion target date.

4.____

5. In replacing a manual system with an EDP system, the FIRST concern of the analyst in charge should be

    A. the overall framework of the new system
    B. the accuracy of the specific procedures
    C. correct definition and explanation of the instruments to be used
    D. cross-referencing between manual and EDP procedures

5._____

6. In the course of instructing a trainee in the operation of a machine, there comes a time when it is best to let the trainee make an initial trial under the instructor's direct supervision.
This step in the learning sequence is *usually* IMMEDIATELY _____ of the machine.

    A. *before* the instructor demonstrates the operation
    B. *before* the instructor explains the purpose
    C. *after* the instructor demonstrates the operation
    D. *after* the instructor explains the purpose

6._____

7. Assume that a new EDP system is being installed for a division. The analyst observes suspicion and indifference in the user's staff toward the new project.
Of the following, what is the BEST course of action to be taken?

    A. Arrange for transfers for the discontented workers
    B. Assign more work to the employees
    C. Develop greater competition among the workers and a stronger interest in management functions
    D. Educate the workers in the purposes and objectives of the project

7._____

8. While doing a systems study, an analyst often observes the activities in the area under study to clarify the jobs of the employees and the methods utilized in processing the work of the section.
One general rule ESSENTIAL for observing and being accepted as an observer is to

    A. discuss the work being done in the area, giving frank criticism of current methods
    B. tell the employees the details of all possible changes
    C. avoid voicing criticism to the employees being observed
    D. avoid showing interest so as to maintain a formal distance from the employees

8._____

9. Assume that, in the course of making a feasibility study for the installation of an EDP system, older workers show extreme resistance to converting the manual system. The resistance takes the form of far-fetched reasons why EDP will not work in their situation.
Of the following, the BEST course of action to take in dealing with these workers is to tell them

    A. that they are as good as the younger workers and should adapt well to EDP
    B. exactly what changes in their work will be made because of the change to EDP
    C. that their reasons for disliking EDP are ill-founded and that they have nothing to fear
    D. that the methods used in their unit will be adapted to their desires, if possible

9._____

10. As a supervisor, you have received a rather complicated set of instructions for a new project which is to begin immediately. Some of the instructions are confusing. Your FIRST step should be to

    A. attempt to clear up with your supervisor any ambiguities before beginning the project

    B. instruct your staff to get started on the project immediately while you try to clarify the instructions

    C. discuss the matter with other supervisors at your level to find out if they have received clarification

    D. figure out the instructions as best you can and provide firm guidelines for your subordinates on the basis of your own good judgment

10.____

11. During the course of your work on the development of a new system, you realize that there is a big difference between what you think is needed and what the head of your agency thinks is needed. The agency head does not have a technical background in computer work.
Your BEST course of action is to

    A. develop a system based on what the agency head thinks is needed

    B. create a system based on what you think is needed

    C. base your system on what you believe would be acceptable compromise between the two viewpoints

    D. discuss the differences between the two points of view with the agency head and abide by his decision

11.____

12. As part of the unit under your supervision, you have been assigned a recent college graduate who is learning computer systems analysis. Although he has had computer systems and programming courses in college, he appears to be slow in doing the analysis preparatory to designing a subsystem.
The BEST course of action for you to follow FIRST in dealing with this worker is to

    A. check the possibility of his reassignment to a unit that has less strenuous work demands

    B. reduce the size of the subsystem assigned to him so that he can finish his work with little assistance

    C. let him work at his own pace, but help him with any parts of the analysis that are especially troublesome

    D. remind him of the need for meeting production demands and threaten to terminate his employment if his production does not improve

12.____

13. While working on a system design, a systems analyst is told by the user that certain changes must be made that will affect the system specification.
Of the following, which method would you use to handle these changes?

    A. Establish a formal procedure, including an approval mechanism requiring sign-offs by user and systems management.

    B. Make changes as the requests are made since there is usually no need to consult management.

    C. Refuse to permit changes in specifications that will impact the project schedule.

    D. Permit changes in specifications to be handled informally if they do not substantially alter the cost of system implementation.

13.____

14. The BEST attitude for you to assume in conducting interviews with user staff during the preliminary analysis is to

    A. act superior; their increased respect will cause them to be more open with you
    B. try to gain the respect of the staff by giving them a great deal of technical information on computers
    C. be personal; exchange views on management innovations including the proposed computer installation
    D. get the staff involved in the study; let them know that the information they are supplying is important

14._____

15. Observation of work procedures is used for many purposes in the process of systems analysis.
Which of the following represents a FAULTY purpose of observation in an analytic situation?
To

    A. give the analyst an overall view of the flow of routine tasks
    B. identify workers who are performing poorly in a manual operation
    C. confirm information secured in an interview
    D. clarify information secured in written form

15._____

16. The input requirements of a new system are such that the workflow in a clerical division will have to radically change. The supervisor of the division has asked you to help him in the training and instruction of his staff.
Your PRIMARY consideration in this task is to

    A. perform it as quickly as possible so as to promote a rapid readjustment
    B. concentrate on what you know best, the input requirements of the EDP system
    C. organize a thorough training course and help the supervisor reorganize the work assignments
    D. concentrate on those staff members who are reacting to the changeover in a negative emotional manner

16._____

17. On-the-job training is one of the most common methods used to teach the employees of a user section the skills necessary for job performance in a changeover from a manual system to an EDP system.
Which of the following is *most* likely to be a DISADVANTAGE of this type of training?

    A. In most instances, on-the-job training is carried out with little or no planning, causing a lack of focus.
    B. The employee gains experience in the environment in which he will be working.
    C. Employees usually resent this type of training because they must learn from their own mistakes.
    D. After the employee has developed sufficient skills, the trainer must follow up to determine the results of the training.

17._____

18. Most of the analysts working under your supervision are consistently submitting sub-   18._____
systems as ready for coding which actually have logical inconsistencies of one sort or
another. You have called this to their attention but the problem persists.
Of the following, the BEST method of improving their performance is to

     A.   constantly make them aware of the delays caused by incomplete analysis
     B.   correct the deficiencies yourself before submitting subsystems to programmer
     C.   encourage the analysts to do more exchanging of flow charts among themselves
        so that they can find each other's mistakes
     D.   reduce your criticism since it can be harmful to team productivity

19. A research technique which would be applied to determine the optimum number of win-   19._____
dow clerks or interviewers to have in an agency serving the public would MOST likely be
the use of

     A.   line of balance   B.   queuing theory
     C.   simulation   D.   work sampling

20. The technique of work measurement in which the analyst observes the work at random   20._____
times of the day is BEST termed

     A.   indirect observation   B.   logging
     C.   ratio delay   D.   wrist watch

21. A technique by which the supervisor or an assistant distributes a predetermined batch of   21._____
work to the employees at periodic intervals of the day is generally BEST known as

     A.   backlog control scheduling
     B.   production control scheduling
     C.   short interval scheduling
     D.   workload balancing

22. If an analyst is required to recommend the selection of a machine for an office operation,   22._____
he can BEST judge the expected output of a particular machine by pursuing which of the
following courses of action?
Obtaining

     A.   an actual test run of the machine in his office
     B.   data from the manufacturer of the machine
     C.   information on the percentage of working time the machine will be used
     D.   the experience of actual users of similar machines elsewhere

23. Theoretically, an ideal organizational structure can be set up for each enterprise. In   23._____
actual practice, the ideal organizational structure is seldom, if ever, obtained.
Of the following, the one that normally is of LEAST influence in determining the organizational structure is the

     A.   existence of agreements and favors among members of the division
     B.   funds available
     C.   opinions and beliefs of top executives
     D.   tendency of management to discard established forms in favor of new forms

24. An IMPORTANT aspect to keep in mind during the decision-making process is that   24._____

    A. all possible alternatives for attaining goals should be sought out and considered
    B. considering various alternatives only leads to confusion
    C. once a decision has been made it cannot be retracted
    D. there is only one correct method to reach any goal

25. Implementation of accountability requires   25._____

    A. a leader who will not hesitate to take punitive action
    B. an established system of communication from the bottom to the top
    C. explicit directives from leaders
    D. too much expense to justify it

_____

KEY (CORRECT ANSWERS)

1.	C	11.	D
2.	B	12.	C
3.	B	13.	A
4.	D	14.	D
5.	A	15.	B
6.	C	16.	C
7.	D	17.	A
8.	C	18.	C
9.	B	19.	B
10.	A	20.	C

21.	C
22.	A
23.	D
24.	A
25.	B

_____

TEST 2

DIRECTIONS: Each question or incomplete statement is followed by several suggested answers or completions. Select the one that BEST answers the question or completes the statement. *PRINT THE LETTER OF THE CORRECT ANSWER IN THE SPACE AT THE RIGHT.*

1. Of the following, the MAJOR difference between systems and procedures analysis and work simplification is:

    A. The former complicates organization routine and the latter simplifies it
    B. The former is objective and the latter is subjective
    C. The former generally utilizes expert advice and the latter is a *do-it-yourself* improvement by supervisors and workers
    D. There is no difference other than in name

1.____

2. Systems development is concerned with providing

    A. a specific set of work procedures
    B. an overall framework to describe general relationships
    C. definitions of particular organizational functions
    D. organizational symbolism

2.____

3. Organizational systems and procedures should be

    A. developed as problems arise as no design can anticipate adequately the requirements of an organization
    B. developed jointly by experts in systems and procedures and the people who are responsible for implementing them
    C. developed solely by experts in systems and procedures
    D. eliminated whenever possible to save unnecessary expense

3.____

4. The CHIEF danger of a decentralized control system is that

    A. excessive reports and communications will be generated
    B. problem areas may not be detected readily
    C. the expense will become prohibitive
    D. this will result in too many *chiefs*

4.____

5. Of the following, management guides and controls clerical work PRINCIPALLY through

    A. close supervision and constant checking of personnel
    B. spot checking of clerical procedures
    C. strong sanctions for clerical supervisors
    D. the use of printed forms

5.____

6. Which of the following is MOST important before conducting fact-finding interviews?

    A. Becoming acquainted with all personnel to be interviewed
    B. Explaining the techniques you plan to use
    C. Explaining to the operating officials the purpose and scope of the study
    D. Orientation of the physical layout

6.____

7. Of the following, the one that is NOT essential in carrying out a comprehensive work improvement program is

    A. standards of performance
    B. supervisory training
    C. work count/task list
    D. work distribution chart

7._____

8. Which of the following control techniques is MOST useful on large, complex systems projects?
A

    A. general work plan
    C. monthly progress report
    B. Gantt chart
    D. PERT chart

8._____

9. The action which is MOST effective in gaining acceptance of a study by the agency which is being studied is

    A. a directive from the agency head to install a study based on recommendations included in a report
    B. a lecture-type presentation following approval of the procedures
    C. a written procedure in narrative form covering the proposed system with visual presentations and discussions
    D. procedural charts showing the *before* and *after* situation, forms, steps, etc. to the employees affected

9._____

10. Which organizational principle is MOST closely related to procedural analysis and improvement?

    A. Duplication, overlapping, and conflict should be eliminated.
    B. Managerial authority should be clearly defined.
    C. The objectives of the organization should be clearly defined.
    D. Top management should be freed of burdensome detail.

10._____

11. Which one of the following is the MAJOR objective of operational audits?

    A. Detecting fraud
    B. Determining organizational problems
    C. Determining the number of personnel needed
    D. Recommending opportunities for improving operating and management practices

11._____

12. Of the following, the formalization of organizational structure is BEST achieved by

    A. a narrative description of the plan of organization
    B. functional charts
    C. job descriptions together with organizational charts
    D. multi-flow charts

12._____

13. Budget planning is MOST useful when it achieves

    A. cost control   B. forecast of receipts
    C. performance review   D. personnel reduction

                                                13.____

14. The underlying principle of sound administration is to

    A. base administration on investigation of facts
    B. have plenty of resources available
    C. hire a strong administrator
    D. establish a broad policy

                                                  14.____

15. Although questionnaires are not the best survey tool the management analyst has to use, there are times when a good questionnaire can expedite the *fact-finding* phase of a management survey.
One Which of the following should be AVOIDED in the design and distribution of the questionnaire?

    A. Questions should be framed so that answers can be classified and tabulated for analysis.
    B. Those receiving the questionnaire must be knowledgeable enough to accurately provide the information desired.
    C. The questionnaire should enable the respondent to answer in a narrative manner.
    D. The questionnaire should require a minimum amount of writing.

                                                  15.____

16. The term that may be defined as a systematic analysis of all factors affecting work being done or all factors that will affect work to be done, in order to save effort, time or money is

    A. flow process charting   B. work flow analysis
    C. work measurement   D. work simplification

                                                  16.____

17. Generally, the LEAST important basic factor to be considered in developing office layout improvements is to locate

    A. office equipment, reference facilities, and files as close as practicable to those using them
    B. persons as close as practicable to the persons from whom they receive their work
    C. persons as close as practicable to windows and/or adequate ventilation
    D. persons who are friendly with each other close together to improve morale

                                                17.____

18. Of the following, the one which is LEAST effective in reducing administrative costs is

    A. applying objective measurement techniques to determine the time required to perform a given task
    B. establishing budgets on the basis of historical performance data
    C. motivating supervisors and managers in the importance of cost reduction
    D. selecting the best method—manual, mechanical, or electronic—to process the essential work

                                                18.____

19. *Fire-fighting* is a common expression in management terminology.
Of the following, which BEST describes *fire-fighting* as an analyst's approach to solving paperwork problems?

19.____

   A. A complete review of all phases of the department's processing functions
   B. A studied determination of the proper equipment to process the work
   C. An analysis of each form that is being processed and the logical reasons for its processing
   D. The solution of problems as they arise, usually at the request of operating personnel

20. Assume that an analyst with a proven record of accomplishment on many projects is having difficulties on his present assignment.
Of the following, the BEST course of action for his supervisor to take is to

20.____

   A. assume there is a personality conflict involved and transfer the analyst to another project
   B. give the analyst some time off
   C. review the nature of the project to determine whether or not the analyst is equipped to handle the assignment
   D. suggest that the analyst seek counseling

21. Downward communication from upper management to lower levels in an organization will often not be fully accepted at the lowest levels of an organization UNLESS high-level management

21.____

   A. communicates through several levels of mid-level management where the message can be properly modified and interpreted
   B. communicates directly with the level of the organization it wishes to reach, bypassing any intermediate levels
   C. first establishes an atmosphere in which upward communication is encouraged and listened to
   D. establishes penalties for non-compliance with its communications

22. A top-level manager sometimes has an inaccurate view of the actual lower-level operations of his agency, particularly of those operations which are not running well. Of the following, the MOST frequent cause of this is the

22.____

   A. general unconcern of top-level management with the way an agency actually operates
   B. tendency of the people at the lowest level in an agency to lie about their actual performance
   C. unwillingness of top level management to deal with unfavorable information when it is presented
   D. tendency of mid-level management to edit bad news and unpleasant information from reports directed to top management

23. In the conduct of productivity analyses, work measurement is a *useful* technique for

23.____

   A. substantiating executive decisions
   B. designing a research study
   C. developing performance yardsticks
   D. preparing a manual of procedure

24. What organizational concept is illustrated when a group is organized on an *ad hoc* basis to accomplish a specific goal?   24.____

   A. Functional teamwork   B. Line/staff
   C. Task force   D. Command

25. In order to give line personnel some insight into staff problems and vice versa, it has been suggested that line and staff assignments within a particular city agency be rotated. Which of the following criticisms would be MOST valid for OPPOSING such a proposal?   25.____

   A. Generally speaking, line and staff personnel have different perspectives on organizational structures which makes rotation in assignments extremely difficult.
   B. Since their educational backgrounds are often quite diverse, staff personnel are often at a disadvantage when serving in line assignments.
   C. Line personnel frequently resent having to perform the more difficult tasks that staff assignments entail.
   D. Serving in a rotating assignment may not necessarily provide the personnel with any significant degree of insight as anticipated.

KEY (CORRECT ANSWERS)

1.	C		11.	D
2.	B		12.	C
3.	B		13.	A
4.	B		14.	A
5.	D		15.	C
6.	C		16.	D
7.	B		17.	D
8.	D		18.	B
9.	C		19.	D
10.	A		20.	C

21.	C
22.	D
23.	C
24.	C
25.	D

GLOSSARY OF COMPUTER TERMS

Contents

GLOSSARY OF COMPUTER TERMS

Basic

application & app

An application (often called "app" for short) is simply a program with a GUI. Note that it is different from an applet.

boot

Starting up an OS is booting it. If the computer is already running, it is more often called rebooting.

browser

A browser is a program used to browse the web. Some common browsers include Netscape, MSIE (Microsoft Internet Explorer), Safari, Lynx, Mosaic, Amaya, Arena, Chimera, Opera, Cyberdog, HotJava, etc.

bug

A bug is a mistake in the design of something, especially software. A really severe bug can cause something to crash.

chat

Chatting is like e-mail, only it is done instantaneously and can directly involve multiple people at once. While e-mail now relies on one more or less standard protocol, chatting still has a couple competing ones. Of particular note are IRC and Instant Messenger. One step beyond chatting is called MUDding.

click

To press a mouse button. When done twice in rapid succession, it is referred to as a double-click.

cursor

A point of attention on the computer screen, often marked with a flashing line or block. Text typed into the computer will usually appear at the cursor.

database

A database is a collection of data, typically organized to make common retrievals easy and efficient. Some common database programs include Oracle, Sybase, Postgres, Informix, Filemaker, Adabas, etc.

desktop

A desktop system is a computer designed to sit in one position on a desk somewhere and not move around. Most general purpose computers are desktop systems. Calling a system a desktop implies nothing about its platform. The fastest desktop system at any given time is typically either an Alpha or PowerPC based system, but the SPARC and PA-RISC based systems are also often in the running. Industrial strength desktops are typically called workstations.

directory

Also called "folder", a directory is a collection of files typically created for organizational purposes. Note that a directory is itself a file, so a directory can generally contain other directories. It differs in this way from a partition.

disk

A disk is a physical object used for storing data. It will not forget its data when it loses power. It is always used in conjunction with a disk drive. Some disks can be removed from their drives, some cannot. Generally it is possible to write new information to a disk in addition to reading data from it, but this is not always the case.

drive

A device for storing and/or retrieving data. Some drives (such as disk drives, zip drives, and tape drives) are typically capable of having new data written to them, but some others (like CD-ROMs or DVD-ROMs) are not. Some drives have random access (like disk drives, zip drives, CD-ROMs, and DVD-ROMs), while others only have sequential access (like tape drives).

e-book

The concept behind an e-book is that it should provide all the functionality of an ordinary book but in a manner that is (overall) less expensive and more environmentally friendly. The actual term e-book is somewhat confusingly used to refer to a variety of things: custom software to play e-book titles, dedicated hardware to play e-book titles, and the e-book titles themselves. Individual e-book titles can be free or commercial (but will always be less expensive than their printed counterparts) and have to be loaded into a player to be read. Players vary wildly in capability level. Basic ones allow simple reading and bookmarking; better ones include various features like hypertext, illustrations, audio, and even limited video. Other optional features allow the user to mark-up sections of text, leave notes, circle or diagram things, highlight passages, program or customize settings, and even use interactive fiction. There are many types of e-book; a couple popular ones include the Newton book and Palm DOC.

e-mail

E-mail is short for electronic mail. It allows for the transfer of information from one computer to another, provided that they are hooked up via some sort of network (often the Internet. E-mail works similarly to FAXing, but its contents typically get printed out on the other end only on demand, not immediately and automatically as with FAX. A machine receiving e-mail will also not reject other incoming mail messages as a busy FAX machine will; rather they will instead be queued up to be received after the current batch has been completed. E-mail is only seven-bit clean, meaning that you should not expect anything other than ASCII data to go through uncorrupted without prior conversion via something like uucode or bcode. Some mailers will do some conversion automatically, but unless you know your mailer is one of them, you may want to do the encoding manually.

file

A file is a unit of (usually named) information stored on a computer.

firmware

Sort of in-between hardware and software, firmware consists of modifiable programs embedded in hardware. Firmware updates should be treated with care since they can literally destroy the underlying hardare if done improperly. There are also cases where neglecting to apply a firmware update can destroy the underlying hardware, so user beware.

floppy

An extremely common type of removable disk. Floppies do not hold too much data, but most computers are capable of reading them. Note though that there are different competing format used for floppies, so that a floppy written by one type of computer might not directly work on another. Also sometimes called "diskette".

format

The manner in which data is stored; its organization. For example, VHS, SVHS, and Beta are three different formats of video tape. They are not 100% compatible with each other, but information can be transferred from one to the other with the proper equipment (but not always without loss; SVHS contains more information than either of the other two). Computer information can be stored in literally hundreds of different formats, and can represent text, sounds, graphics, animations, etc. Computer information can be exchanged via different computer types provided both computers can interpret the format used.

function keys

On a computer keyboard, the keys that start with an "F" that are usually (but not always) found on the top row. They are meant to perform user-defined tasks.

graphics
Anything visually displayed on a computer that is not text.

hardware
The physical portion of the computer.

hypertext
A hypertext document is like a text document with the ability to contain pointers to other regions of (possibly other) hypertext documents.

Internet
The Internet is the world-wide network of computers. There is only one Internet, and thus it is typically capitalized (although it is sometimes referred to as "the 'net"). It is different from an intranet.

keyboard
A keyboard on a computer is almost identical to a keyboard on a typewriter. Computer keyboards will typically have extra keys, however. Some of these keys (common examples include Control, Alt, and Meta) are meant to be used in conjunction with other keys just like shift on a regular typewriter. Other keys (common examples include Insert, Delete, Home, End, Help, function keys,etc.) are meant to be used independently and often perform editing tasks. Keyboards on different platforms will often look slightly different and have somewhat different collections of keys. Some keyboards even have independent shift lock and caps lock keys. Smaller keyboards with only math-related keys are typically called "keypads".

language
Computer programs can be written in a variety of different languages. Different languages are optimized for different tasks. Common languages include Java, C, C++, ForTran, Pascal, Lisp, and BASIC. Some people classify languages into two categories, higher-level and lower-level. These people would consider assembly language and machine language lower-level languages and all other languages higher-level. In general, higher-level languages can be either interpreted or compiled; many languages allow both, but some are restricted to one or the other. Many people do not consider machine language and assembly language at all when talking about programming languages.

laptop
A laptop is any computer designed to do pretty much anything a desktop system can do but run for a short time (usually two to five hours) on batteries. They are designed to be carried around but are not particularly convenient to carry around. They are significantly more expensive than desktop systems and have far worse battery life than PDAs. Calling a system a laptop implies nothing about its platform. By far the fastest laptops are the PowerPC based Macintoshes.

memory
Computer memory is used to temporarily store data. In reality, computer memory is only capable of remembering sequences of zeros and ones, but by utilizing the binary number system it is possible to produce arbitrary rational numbers and through clever formatting all manner of representations of pictures, sounds, and animations. The most common types of memory are RAM, ROM, and flash.

MHz & megahertz
One megahertz is equivalent to 1000 kilohertz, or 1,000,000 hertz. The clock speed of the main processor of many computers is measured in MHz, and is sometimes (quite misleadingly) used to represent the overall speed of a computer. In fact, a computer's speed is based upon many factors, and since MHz only reveals how many clock cycles the main processor has per second (saying nothing about how much is actually accomplished per cycle), it can really only accurately be used to gauge two computers with the same generation and family of processor plus similar configurations of memory, co-processors, and other peripheral hardware.

modem
A modem allows two computers to communicate over ordinary phone lines. It derives its name

from **mod**ulate / **dem**odulate, the process by which it converts digital computer data back and forth for use with an analog phone line.

monitor
The screen for viewing computer information is called a monitor.

mouse
In computer parlance a mouse can be both the physical object moved around to control a pointer on the screen, and the pointer itself. Unlike the animal, the proper plural of computer mouse is "mouses".

multimedia
This originally indicated a capability to work with and integrate various types of things including audio, still graphics, and especially video. Now it is more of a marketing term and has little real meaning. Historically the Amiga was the first multimedia machine. Today in addition to AmigaOS, IRIX and Solaris are popular choices for high-end multimedia work.

NC
The term **n**etwork **c**omputer refers to any (usually desktop) computer system that is designed to work as part of a network rather than as a stand-alone machine. This saves money on hardware, software, and maintenance by taking advantage of facilities already available on the network. The term "Internet appliance" is often used interchangeably with NC.

network
A network (as applied to computers) typically means a group of computers working together. It can also refer to the physical wire etc. connecting the computers.

notebook
A notebook is a small laptop with similar price, performance, and battery life.

organizer
An organizer is a tiny computer used primarily to store names, addresses, phone numbers, and date book information. They usually have some ability to exchange information with desktop systems. They boast even better battery life than PDAs but are far less capable. They are extremely inexpensive but are typically incapable of running any special purpose applications and are thus of limited use.

OS
The **o**perating **s**ystem is the program that manages a computer's resources. Common OSes include Windows '95, MacOS, Linux, Solaris, AmigaOS, AIX, Windows NT, etc.

PC
The term **p**ersonal **c**omputer properly refers to any desktop, laptop, or notebook computer system. Its use is inconsistent, though, and some use it to specifically refer to x86 based systems running MS-DOS, MS-Windows, GEOS, or OS/2. This latter use is similar to what is meant by a WinTel system.

PDA
A **p**ersonal **d**igital **a**ssistant is a small battery-powered computer intended to be carried around by the user rather than left on a desk. This means that the processor used ought to be power-efficient as well as fast, and the OS ought to be optimized for hand-held use. PDAs typically have an instant-on feature (they would be useless without it) and most are grayscale rather than color because of battery life issues. Most have a pen interface and come with a detachable stylus. None use mouses. All have some ability to exchange data with desktop systems. In terms of raw capabilities, a PDA is more capable than an organizer and less capable than a laptop (although some high-end PDAs beat out some low-end laptops). By far the most popular PDA is the Pilot, but other common types include Newtons, Psions, Zauri, Zoomers, and Windows CE hand-helds. By far the fastest current PDA is the Newton (based around a StrongARM RISC processor). Other PDAs are optimized for other tasks; few computers are as personal as PDAs and care must be taken in their purchase. Feneric's PDA / Handheld Comparison Page is perhaps the most detailed comparison of PDAs and handheld computers

to be found anywhere on the web.

platform

Roughly speaking, a platform represents a computer's family. It is defined by both the processor type on the hardware side and the OS type on the software side. Computers belonging to different platforms cannot typically run each other's programs (unless the programs are written in a language like Java).

portable

If something is portable it can be easily moved from one type of computer to another. The verb "to port" indicates the moving itself.

printer

A printer is a piece of hardware that will print computer information onto paper.

processor

The processor (also called central processing unit, or CPU) is the part of the computer that actually works with the data and runs the programs. There are two main processor types in common usage today: CISC and RISC. Some computers have more than one processor and are thus called "multiprocessor". This is distinct from multitasking. Advertisers often use megahertz numbers as a means of showing a processor's speed. This is often extremely misleading; megahertz numbers are more or less meaningless when compared across different types of processors.

program

A program is a series of instructions for a computer, telling it what to do or how to behave. The terms "application" and "app" mean almost the same thing (albeit applications generally have GUIs). It is however different from an applet. Program is also the verb that means to create a program, and a programmer is one who programs.

run

Running a program is how it is made to do something. The term "execute" means the same thing.

software

The non-physical portion of the computer; the part that exists only as data; the programs. Another term meaning much the same is "code".

spreadsheet

An program used to perform various calculations. It is especially popular for financial applications. Some common spreadsheets include Lotus 123, Excel, OpenOffice Spreadsheet, Octave, Gnumeric, AppleWorks Spreadsheet, Oleo, and GeoCalc.

user

The operator of a computer.

word processor

A program designed to help with the production of textual documents, like letters and memos. Heavier duty work can be done with a desktop publisher. Some common word processors include MS-Word, OpenOffice Write, WordPerfect, AbiWord, AppleWorks Write, and GeoWrite.

www

The World-Wide-Web refers more or less to all the publically accessible documents on the Internet. It is used quite loosely, and sometimes indicates only HTML files and sometimes FTP and Gopher files, too. It is also sometimes just referred to as "the web".

65xx
The 65xx series of processors includes the 6502, 65C02, 6510, 8502, 65C816, 65C816S, etc. It is a CISC design and is not being used in too many new stand-alone computer systems, but is still being used in embedded systems, game systems (such as the Super NES), and processor enhancement add-ons for older systems. It was originally designed by MOS Technologies, but is now produced by The Western Design Center, Inc. It was the primary processor for many extremely popular systems no longer being produced, including the Commodore 64, the Commodore 128, and all the Apple][series machines.

68xx
The 68xx series of processors includes the 6800, 6805, 6809, 68000, 68020, 68030, 68040, 68060, etc. It is a CISC design and is not being used in too many new stand-alone computer systems, but is still being used heavily in embedded systems. It was originally designed by Motorola and was the primary processor for older generations of many current machines, including Macintoshes, Amigas, Sun workstations, HP workstations, etc. and the primary processor for many systems no longer being produced, such as the TRS-80. The PowerPC was designed in part to be its replacement.

a11y
Commonly used to abbreviate the word "accessibility". There are eleven letters between the "a" and the "y".

ADA
An object-oriented language at one point popular for military and some academic software. Lately C++ and Java have been getting more attention.

AI
Artificial intelligence is the concept of making computers do tasks once considered to require thinking. AI makes computers play chess, recognize handwriting and speech, helps suggest prescriptions to doctors for patients based on imput symptoms, and many other tasks, both mundane and not.

AIX
The industrial strength OS designed by IBM to run on PowerPC and x86 based machines. It is a variant of UNIX and is meant to provide more power than OS/2.

AJaX
AJaX is a little like DHTML, but it adds asynchronous communication between the browser and Web site via either XML or JSON to achieve performance that often rivals desktop applications.

Alpha
An Alpha is a RISC processor invented by Digital and currently produced by Digital/Compaq and Samsung. A few different OSes run on Alpha based machines including Digital UNIX, Windows NT, Linux, NetBSD, and AmigaOS. Historically, at any given time, the fastest processor in the world has usually been either an Alpha or a PowerPC (with sometimes SPARCs and PA-RISCs making the list), but Compaq has recently announced that there will be no further development of this superb processor instead banking on the release of the somewhat suspect Merced.

AltiVec
AltiVec (also called the "Velocity Engine") is a special extension built into some PowerPC CPUs to provide better performance for certain operations, most notably graphics and sound. It is similar to MMX on the x86 CPUs. Like MMX, it requires special software for full performance benefits to be realized.

Amiga

A platform originally created and only produced by Commodore, but now owned by Gateway 2000 and produced by it and a few smaller companies. It was historically the first multimedia machine and gave the world of computing many innovations. It is now primarily used for audio / video applications; in fact, a decent Amiga system is less expensive than a less capable video editing system. Many music videos were created on Amigas, and a few television series and movies had their special effects generated on Amigas. Also, Amigas can be readily synchronized with video cameras, so typically when a computer screen appears on television or in a movie and it is not flickering wildly, it is probably an Amiga in disguise. Furthermore, many coin-operated arcade games are really Amigas packaged in stand-up boxes. Amigas have AmigaOS for their OS. New Amigas have either a PowerPC or an Alpha for their main processor and a 68xx processor dedicated to graphics manipulation. Older (and low end) Amigas do everything with just a 68xx processor.

AmigaOS

The OS used by Amigas. AmigaOS combines the functionality of an OS and a window manager and is fully multitasking. AmigaOS boasts a pretty good selection of games (many arcade games are in fact written on Amigas) but has limited driver support. AmigaOS will run on 68xx, Alpha, and PowerPC based machines.

Apple][

The Apple][computer sold millions of units and is generally considered to have been the first home computer with a 1977 release date. It is based on the 65xx family of processors. The earlier Apple I was only available as a build-it-yourself kit.

AppleScript

A scripting language for Mac OS computers.

applet

An applet differs from an application in that is not meant to be run stand-alone but rather with the assistance of another program, usually a browser.

AppleTalk

AppleTalk is a protocol for computer networks. It is arguably inferior to TCP/IP.

Aqua

The default window manager for Mac OS X.

Archie

Archie is a system for searching through FTP archives for particular files. It tends not to be used too much anymore as more general modern search engines are significantly more capable.

ARM

An ARM is a RISC processor invented by Advanced RISC Machines, currently owned by Intel, and currently produced by both the above and Digital/Compaq. ARMs are different from most other processors in that they were not designed to maximize speed but rather to maximize speed per power consumed. Thus ARMs find most of their use on hand-held machines and PDAs. A few different OSes run on ARM based machines including Newton OS, JavaOS, and (soon) Windows CE and Linux. The StrongARM is a more recent design of the original ARM, and it is both faster and more power efficient than the original.

ASCII

The ASCII character set is the most popular one in common use. People will often refer to a bare text file without complicated embedded format instructions as an ASCII file, and such files can usually be transferred from one computer system to another with relative ease. Unfortunately there are a few minor variations of it that pop up here and there, and if you receive a text file that seems subtly messed up with punctuation marks altered or upper and lower case reversed, you are probably encountering one of the ASCII variants. It is usually fairly straightforward to translate from one ASCII variant to another, though. The ASCII character set is seven bit while pure binary is usually eight bit, so transferring a binary file through ASCII channels will result in corruption and loss of data. Note also that the ASCII character set is a subset of the Unicode character set.

ASK

A protocol for an infrared communications port on a device. It predates the IrDA compliant infrared communications protocol and is not compatible with it. Many devices with infrared communications support both, but some only support one or the other.

assembly language

Assembly language is essentially machine language that has had some of the numbers replaced by somewhat easier to remember mnemonics in an attempt to make it more human-readable. The program that converts assembly language to machine language is called an assembler. While assembly language predates FORTRAN, it is not typically what people think of when they discuss computer languages.

Atom

Atom is an intended replacement for RSS and like it is used for syndicating a web site's content. It is currently not nearly as popular or well-supported by software applications, however.

authoring system

Any GUIs method of designing new software can be called an authoring system. Any computer language name with the word "visual" in front of it is probably a version of that language built with some authoring system capabilities. It appears that the first serious effort to produce a commercial quality authoring system took place in the mid eighties for the Amiga.

AWK

AWK is an interpreted language developed in 1977 by Aho, Weinberger, & Kernighan. It gets its name from its creators' initials. It is not particularly fast, but it was designed for creating small throwaway programs rather than full-blown applications -- it is designed to make the writing of the program fast, not the program itself. It is quite portable with versions existing for numerous platforms, including a free GNU version. Plus, virtually every version of UNIX in the world comes with AWK built-in.

BASIC

The **B**eginners' **A**ll-purpose **S**ymbolic **I**nstruction **C**ode is a computer language developed by Kemeny & Kurtz in 1964. Although it is traditionally interpreted, compilers exist for many platforms. While the interpreted form is typically fairly slow, the compiled form is often quite fast, usually faster than Pascal. The biggest problem with BASIC is portability; versions for different machines are often completely unlike each other; Amiga BASIC at first glance looks more like Pascal, for example. Portability problems actually go beyond even the cross platform level; in fact, most machines have multiple versions of incompatible BASICs available for use. The most popular version of BASIC today is called Visual BASIC. Like all BASICs it has portability issues, but it has some of the advantages of an authoring system so it is relatively easy to use.

baud

A measure of communications speed, used typically for modems indicating how many bits per second can be transmitted.

BBS

A **b**ulletin **b**oard **s**ystem is a computer that can be directly connected to via modem and provides various services like e-mail, chatting, newsgroups, and file downloading. BBSs have waned in popularity as more and more people are instead connecting to the Internet, but they are still used for product support and local area access. Most current BBSs provide some sort of gateway connection to the Internet.

bcode

Identical in intent to uucode, bcode is slightly more efficient and more portable across different computer types. It is the preferred method used by MIME.

BeOS

A lightweight OS available for both PowerPC and x86 based machines. It is often referred to simply as "Be".

beta

A beta version of something is not yet ready for prime time but still possibly useful to related developers and other interested parties. Expect beta software to crash more than properly released software does. Traditionally beta versions (of commercial software) are distributed only to selected testers who are often then given a discount on the proper version after its release in exchange for their testing work. Beta versions of non-commercial software are more often freely available to anyone who has an interest.

binary

There are two meanings for binary in common computer usage. The first is the name of the number system in which there are only zeros and ones. This is important to computers because all computer data is ultimately a series of zeros and ones, and thus can be represented by binary numbers. The second is an offshoot of the first; data that is not meant to be interpreted through a common character set (like ASCII) is typically referred to as binary data. Pure binary data is typically eight bit data, and transferring a binary file through ASCII channels without prior modification will result in corruption and loss of data. Binary data can be turned into ASCII data via uucoding or bcoding.

bit

A bit can either be on or off; one or zero. All computer data can ultimately be reduced to a series of bits. The term is also used as a (very rough) measure of sound quality, color quality, and even procesor capability by considering the fact that series of bits can represent binary numbers. For example (without getting too technical), an eight bit image can contain at most 256 distinct colors while a sixteen bit image can contain at most 65,536 distinct colors.

bitmap

A bitmap is a simplistic representation of an image on a computer, simply indicating whether or not pixels are on or off, and sometimes indicating their color. Often fonts are represented as bitmaps. The term "pixmap" is sometimes used similarly; typically when a distinction is made, pixmap refers to color images and bitmap refers to monochrome images.

blog

Short for web log, a blog (or weblog, or less commonly, 'blog) is a web site containing periodic (usually frequent) posts. Blogs are usually syndicated via either some type of RSS or Atom and often supports TrackBacks. It is not uncommon for blogs to function much like newspaper columns. A blogger is someone who writes for and maintains a blog.

boolean

Boolean algebra is the mathematics of base two numbers. Since base two numbers have only two values, zero and one, there is a good analogy between base two numbers and the logical values "true" & "false". In common usage, booleans are therefore considered to be simple logical values like true & false and the operations that relate them, most typically "and", "or" and "not". Since everyone has a basic understanding of the concepts of true & false and basic conjunctions, everyone also has a basic understanding of boolean concepts -- they just may not realize it.

byte

A byte is a grouping of bits. It is typically eight bits, but there are those who use non-standard byte sizes. Bytes are usually measured in large groups, and the term "kilobyte" (often abbreviated as K) means one-thousand twenty-four (1024) bytes; the term "megabyte" (often abbreviated as M) means one-thousand twenty-four (1024) K; the term gigabyte (often abbreviated as G) means one-thousand twenty-four (1024) M; and the term "terabyte" (often abbreviated as T) means one-thousand twenty-four (1024) G. Memory is typically measured in kilobytes or megabytes, and disk space is typically measured in megabytes or gigabytes. Note that the multipliers here are 1024 instead of the more common 1000 as would be used in the metric system. This is to make it easier to work with the binary number system. Note also that some hardware manufacturers will use the smaller 1000 multiplier on M & G quantities to make their disk drives seem larger than they really are; buyer beware.

bytecode
Sometimes computer languages that are said to be either interpreted or compiled are in fact neither and are more accurately said to be somewhere in between. Such languages are compiled into bytecode which is then interpreted on the target system. Bytecode tends to be binary but will work on any machine with the appropriate runtime environment (or virtual machine) for it.

C
C is one of the most popular computer languages in the world, and quite possibly *the* most popular. It is a compiled langauge widely supported on many platforms. It tends to be more portable than FORTRAN but less portable than Java; it has been standardized by ANSI as "ANSI C" -- older versions are called either "K&R C" or "Kernighan and Ritchie C" (in honor of C's creators), or sometimes just "classic C". Fast and simple, it can be applied to all manner of general purpose tasks. C compilers are made by several companies, but the free GNU version (gcc) is still considered one of the best. Newer C-like object-oriented languages include both Java and C++.

C#
C# is a compiled object-oriented language based heavily on C++ with some Java features.

C++
C++ is a compiled object-oriented language. Based heavily on C, C++ is nearly as fast and can often be thought of as being just C with added features. It is currently probably the second most popular object-oriented language, but it has the drawback of being fairly complex -- the much simpler but somewhat slower Java is probably the most popular object-oriented language. Note that C++ was developed independently of the somewhat similar Objective-C; it is however related to Objective-C++.

C64/128
The Commodore 64 computer to this day holds the record for being the most successful model of computer ever made with even the lowest estimates being in the tens of millions. Its big brother, the Commodore 128, was not quite as popular but still sold several million units. Both units sported ROM-based BASIC and used it as a default "OS". The C128 also came with CP/M (it was a not-often-exercized option on the C64). In their later days they were also packaged with GEOS. Both are based on 65xx family processors. They are still in use today and boast a friendly and surprisingly active user community. There is even a current effort to port Linux to the C64 and C128 machines.

CDE
The **c**ommon **d**esktop **e**nvironment is a popular commercial window manager (and much more -- as its name touts, it is more of a desktop environment) that runs under X-Windows. Free work-alike versions are also available.

chain
Some computer devices support chaining, the ability to string multiple devices in a sequence plugged into just one computer port. Often, but not always, such a chain will require some sort of terminator to mark the end. For an example, a SCSI scanner may be plugged into a SCSI CD-ROM drive that is plugged into a SCSI hard drive that is in turn plugged into the main computer. For all these components to work properly, the scanner would also have to have a proper terminator in use. Device chaining has been around a long time, and it is interesting to note that C64/128 serial devices supported it from the very beginning. Today the most common low-cost chainable devices in use support USB while the fastest low-cost chainable devices in use support FireWire.

character set
Since in reality all a computer can store are series of zeros and ones, representing common things like text takes a little work. The solution is to view the series of zeros and ones instead as

a sequence of bytes, and map each one to a particular letter, number, or symbol. The full mapping is called a character set. The most popular character set is commonly referred to as ASCII. The second most popular character set these days is Unicode (and it will probably eventually surpass ASCII). Other fairly common character sets include EBCDIC and PETSCII. They are generally quite different from one another; programs exist to convert between them on most platforms, though. Usually EBCDIC is only found on really old machines.

CISC

Complex instruction set computing is one of the two main types of processor design in use today. It is slowly losing popularity to RISC designs; currently all the fastest processors in the world are RISC. The most popular current CISC processor is the x86, but there are also still some 68xx, 65xx, and Z80s in use.

CLI

A command-line interface is a text-based means of communicating with a program, especially an OS. This is the sort of interface used by MS-DOS, or a UNIX shell window.

COBOL

The **Common Business Oriented Language** is a language developed back in 1959 and still used by some businesses. While it is relatively portable, it is still disliked by many professional programmers simply because COBOL programs tend to be physically longer than equivalent programs written in almost any other language in common use.

compiled

If a program is compiled, its original human-readable source has been converted into a form more easily used by a computer prior to it being run. Such programs will generally run more quickly than interpreted programs, because time was pre-spent in the compilation phase. A program that compiles other programs is called a compiler.

compression

It is often possible to remove redundant information or capitalize on patterns in data to make a file smaller. Usually when a file has been compressed, it cannot be used until it is uncompressed. Image files are common exceptions, though, as many popular image file formats have compression built-in.

cookie

A cookie is a small file that a web page on another machine writes to your personal machine's disk to store various bits of information. Many people strongly detest cookies and the whole idea of them, and most browsers allow the reception of cookies to be disabled or at least selectively disabled, but it should be noted that both Netscape and MSIE have silent cookie reception enabled by default. Sites that maintain shopping carts or remember a reader's last position have legitimate uses for cookies. Sites without such functionality that still spew cookies with distant (or worse, non-existent) expiration dates should perhaps be treated with a little caution.

CP/M

An early DOS for desktops, CP/M runs on both Z80 and the x86 based machines. CP/M provides only a CLI and there really is not any standard way to get a window manager to run on top of it. It is fairly complex and tricky to use. In spite of all this, CP/M was once the most popular DOS and is still in use today.

crash

If a bug in a program is severe enough, it can cause that program to crash, or to become inoperable without being restarted. On machines that are not multitasking, the entire machine will crash and have to be rebooted. On machines that are only partially multitasking the entire machine will sometimes crash and have to be rebooted. On machines that are fully multitasking, the machine should never crash and require a reboot.

Cray

A Cray is a high-end computer used for research and frequently heavy-duty graphics applications. Modern Crays typically have Solaris for their OS and sport sixty-four RISC processors; older ones had various other configurations. Current top-of-the-line Crays can have over 2000 processors.

crippleware

Crippleware is a variant of shareware that will either self-destruct after its trial period or has built-in limitations to its functionality that get removed after its purchase.

CSS

Cascading style sheets are used in conjunction with HTML and XHTML to define the layout of web pages. While CSS is how current web pages declare how they should be displayed, it tends not to be supported well (if at all) by ancient browsers. XSL performs this same function more generally.

desktop publisher

A program for creating newspapers, magazines, books, etc. Some common desktop publishing programs include FrameMaker, PageMaker, InDesign, and GeoPublish.

DHTML

Dynamic HTML is simply the combined use of both CSS and JavaScript together in the same document; a more extreme form is called AJaX. Note that DHTML is quite different from the similarly named DTML.

dict

A protocol used for looking up definitions across a network (in particular the Internet).

digital camera

A digital camera looks and behaves like a regular camera, except instead of using film, it stores the image it sees in memory as a file for later transfer to a computer. Many digital cameras offer additional storage besides their own internal memory; a few sport some sort of disk but the majority utilize some sort of flash card. Digital cameras currently lack the resolution and color palette of real cameras, but are usually much more convenient for computer applications. Another related device is called a scanner.

DIMM

A physical component used to add RAM to a computer. Similar to, but incompatible with, SIMMs.

DNS

Domain name service is the means by which a name (like www.saugus.net or ftp.saugus.net) gets converted into a real Internet address that points to a particular machine.

DoS

In a denial of service attack, many individual (usually compromised) computers are used to try and simultaneously access the same public resource with the intent of overburdening it so that it will not be able to adequately serve its normal users.

DOS

A disk operating system manages disks and other system resources. Sort of a subset of OSes, sort of an archaic term for the same. MS-DOS is the most popular program currently calling itself a DOS. CP/M was the most popular prior to MS-DOS.

download

To download a file is to copy it from a remote computer to your own. The opposite is upload.

DR-DOS

The DOS currently produced by Caldera (originally produced by Design Research as a successor to CP/M) designed to work like MS-DOS. While similar to CP/M in many ways, it utilizes simpler commands. It provides only a CLI, but either Windows 3.1 or GEOS may be run on top of it to provide a GUI. It only runs on x86 based machines.

driver

A driver is a piece of software that works with the OS to control a particular piece of hardware, like a printer or a scanner or a mouse or whatever.

DRM

Depending upon whom you ask, DRM can stand for either Digital Rights Management or Digital Restrictions Management. In either case, DRM is used to place restrictions upon the usage of digital media ranging from software to music to video.

DTML

The **D**ocument **T**emplate **M**ark-up **L**anguage is a subset of SGML and a superset of HTML used for creating documents that dynamically adapt to external conditions using its own custom tags and a little bit of Python. Note that it is quite different from the similarly named DHTML.

EDBIC

The EDBIC character set is similar to (but less popular than) the ASCII character set in concept, but is significantly different in layout. It tends to be found only on old machines..

emacs

Emacs is both one of the most powerful and one of the most popular text editing programs in existence. Versions can be found for most platforms, and in fact multiple companies make versions, so for a given platform there might even be a choice. There is even a free GNU version available. The drawback with emacs is that it is not in the least bit lightweight. In fact, it goes so far in the other direction that even its advocates will occasionally joke about it. It is however extremely capable. Almost anything that one would need to relating to text can be done with emacs and is probably built-in. Even if one manages to find something that emacs was not built to do, emacs has a built-in Lisp interpreter capable of not only extending its text editing capabilities, but even of being used as a scripting language in its own right.

embedded

An embedded system is a computer that lives inside another device and acts as a component of that device. For example, current cars have an embedded computer under the hood that helps regulate much of their day to day operation.

An embedded file is a file that lives inside another and acts as a portion of that file. This is frequently seen with HTML files having embedded audio files; audio files often embedded in HTML include AU files, MIDI files, SID files, WAV files, AIFF files, and MOD files. Most browsers will ignore these files unless an appropriate plug-in is present.

emulator

An emulator is a program that allows one computer platform to mimic another for the purposes of running its software. Typically (but not always) running a program through an emulator will not be quite as pleasant an experience as running it on the real system.

endian

A processor will be either "big endian" or "little endian" based upon the manner in which it encodes multiple byte values. There is no difference in performance between the two encoding methods, but it is one of the sources of difficulty when reading binary data on different platforms.

environment

An environment (sometimes also called a runtime environment) is a collection of external variable items or parameters that a program can access when run. Information about the computer's hardware and the user can often be found in the environment.

EPOC

EPOC is a lightweight OS. It is most commonly found on the Psion PDA.

extension

Filename extensions originate back in the days of CP/M and basically allow a very rough grouping of different file types by putting a tag at the end of the name. To further complicate matters, the tag is sometimes separated by the name proper by a period "." and sometimes by a tab. While extensions are semi-enforced on CP/M, MS-DOS, and MS-Windows, they have no real meaning aside from convention on other platforms and are only optional.

FAQ

A frequently **asked questions** file attempts to provide answers for all commonly asked questions related to a given topic.

FireWire

An incredibly fast type of serial port that offers many of the best features of SCSI at a lower price. Faster than most types of parallel port, a single FireWire port is capable of chaining many devices without the need of a terminator. FireWire is similar in many respects to USB but is significantly faster and somewhat more expensive. It is heavily used for connecting audio/video devices to computers, but is also used for connecting storage devices like drives and other assorted devices like printers and scanners.

fixed width

As applied to a font, fixed width means that every character takes up the same amount of space. That is, an "i" will be just as wide as an "m" with empty space being used for padding. The opposite is variable width. The most common fixed width font is Courier.

flash

Flash memory is similar to RAM. It has one significant advantage: it does not lose its contents when power is lost; it has two main disadvantages: it is slower, and it eventually wears out. Flash memory is frequently found in PCMCIA cards.

font

In a simplistic sense, a font can be thought of as the physical description of a character set. While the character set will define what sets of bits map to what letters, numbers, and other symbols, the font will define what each letter, number, and other symbol looks like. Fonts can be either fixed width or variable width and independently, either bitmapped or vectored. The size of the large characters in a font is typically measured in points.

Forth

A language developed in 1970 by Moore. Forth is fairly portable and has versions on many different platforms. While it is no longer an very popular language, many of its ideas and concepts have been carried into other computer programs. In particular, some programs for doing heavy-duty mathematical and engineering work use Forth-like interfaces.

FORTRAN

FORTRAN stands for **formula tran**slation and is the oldest computer language in the world. It is typically compiled and is quite fast. Its primary drawbacks are portability and ease-of-use -- often different FORTRAN compilers on different platforms behave quite differently in spite of standardization efforts in 1966 (FORTRAN 66 or FORTRAN IV), 1978 (FORTRAN 77), and 1991 (FORTRAN 90). Today languages like C and Java are more popular, but FORTRAN is still heavily used in military software. It is somewhat amusing to note that when FORTRAN was first released back in 1958 its advocates thought that it would mean the end of software bugs. In truth of course by making the creation of more complex software practical, computer languages have merely created new types of software bugs.

FreeBSD

A free variant of Berkeley UNIX available for Alpha and x86 based machines. It is not as popular as Linux.

freeware

Freeware is software that is available for free with no strings attached. The quality is often superb as the authors are also generally users.

FTP

The file **transfer protocol** is one of the most commonly used methods of copying files across the Internet. It has its origins on UNIX machines, but has been adapted to almost every type of computer in existence and is built into many browsers. Most FTP programs have two modes of operation, ASCII, and binary. Transmitting an ASCII file via the ASCII mode of operation is more efficient and cleaner. Transmitting a binary file via the ASCII mode of operation will result in a broken binary file. Thus the FTP programs that do not support both modes of operation will typically only do the binary mode, as binary transfers are capable of transferring both kinds of data without corruption.

gateway

A gateway connects otherwise separate computer networks.

GEOS

The **g**raphic **e**nvironment **o**perating **s**ystem is a lightweight OS with a GUI. It runs on several different processors, including the 65xx (different versions for different machines -- there are versions for the C64, the C128, and the Apple][, each utilizing the relevant custom chip sets), the x86 (although the x86 version is made to run on top of MS-DOS (or PC-DOS or DR-DOS) and is not strictly a full OS or a window manager, rather it is somewhat in between, like Windows 3.1) and numerous different PDAs, embedded devices, and hand-held machines. It was originally designed by Berkeley Softworks (no real relation to the Berkeley of UNIX fame) but is currently in a more interesting state: the company GeoWorks develops and promotes development of GEOS for hand-held devices, PDAs, & and embedded devices and owns (but has ceased further development on) the x86 version. The other versions are owned (and possibly still being developed) by the company CMD.

GHz & gigahertz

One gigahertz is equivalent to 1000 megahertz, or 1,000,000,000 hertz.

Glulx

A virtual machine optimized for running interactive fiction, interactive tutorials, and other interactive things of a primarily textual nature. Glulx has been ported to several platforms, and in in many ways an upgrade to the Z-machine.

GNOME

The **G**NU **n**etwork **o**bject **m**odel **e**nvironment is a popular free window manager (and much more -- as its name touts, it is more of a desktop environment) that runs under X-Windows. It is a part of the GNU project.

GNU

GNU stands for **G**NU's **n**ot **U**NIX and is thus a recursive acronym (and unlike the animal name, the "G" here is pronounced). At any rate, the GNU project is an effort by the Free Software Foundation (FSF) to make all of the traditional UNIX utilities free for whoever wants them. The Free Software Foundation programmers know their stuff, and the quality of the GNU software is on par with the best produced commercially, and often better. All of the GNU software can be downloaded for free or obtained on CD-ROM for a small service fee. Documentation for all GNU software can be downloaded for free or obtained in book form for a small service fee. The Free Software Foundation pays its bills from the collection of service fees and the sale of T-shirts, and exists mostly through volunteer effort. It is based in Cambridge, MA.

gopher

Though not as popular as FTP or http, the gopher protocol is implemented by many browsers and numerous other programs and allows the transfer of files across networks. In some respects it can be thought of as a hybrid between FTP and http, although it tends not to be as good at raw file transfer as FTP and is not as flexible as http. The collection of documents available through gopher is often called "gopherspace", and it should be noted that gopherspace is older than the web. It should also be noted that gopher is not getting as much attention as it once did, and surfing through gopherspace is a little like exploring a ghost town, but there is an interesting VR interface available for it, and some things in gopherspace still have not been copied onto the web.

GUI

A **g**raphical **u**ser **i**nterface is a graphics-based means of communicating with a program, especially an OS or window manager. In fact, a window manager can be thought of as a GUI for a CLI OS.

HP-UX

HP-UX is the version of UNIX designed by Hewlett-Packard to work with their PA-RISC and

68xx based machines.

HTML

The **H**ypertext **M**ark-up **L**anguage is the language currently most frequently used to express web pages (although it is rapidly being replaced by XHTML). Every browser has the built-in ability to understand HTML. Some browsers can additionally understand Java and browse FTP areas. HTML is a proper subset of SGML.

http

The **h**ypertext **t**ransfer **p**rotocol is the native protocol of browsers and is most typically used to transfer HTML formatted files. The secure version is called "https".

Hurd

The Hurd is the official GNU OS. It is still in development and is not yet supported on too many different processors, but promises to be the most powerful OS available. It (like all the GNU software) is free.

Hz & hertz

Hertz means cycles per second, and makes no assumptions about what is cycling. So, for example, if a fluorescent light flickers once per jiffy, it has a 60 Hz flicker. More typical for computers would be a program that runs once per jiffy and thus has a 60 Hz frequency, or larger units of hertz like kHz, MHz, GHz, or THz.

i18n

Commonly used to abbreviate the word "internationalization". There are eighteen letters between the "i" and the "n". Similar to (and often used along with) i18n.

iCalendar

The iCalendar standard refers to the format used to store calendar type information (including events, to-do items, and journal entries) on the Internet. iCalendar data can be found on some World-Wide-Web pages or attached to e-mail messages.

icon

A small graphical display representing an object, action, or modifier of some sort.

IDE

Loosely speaking, a disk format sometimes used by MS-Windows, Mac OS, AmigaOS, and (rarely) UNIX. EIDE is enhanced IDE; it is much faster. Generally IDE is inferior (but less expensive) to SCSI, but it varies somewhat with system load and the individual IDE and SCSI components themselves. The quick rundown is that: SCSI-I and SCSI-II will almost always outperform IDE; EIDE will almost always outperform SCSI-I and SCSI-II; SCSI-III and UltraSCSI will almost always outperform EIDE; and heavy system loads give an advantage to SCSI. Note that although loosely speaking it is just a format difference, it is deep down a hardware difference.

Inform

A compiled, object-oriented language optimized for creating interactive fiction.

infrared communications

A device with an infrared port can communicate with other devices at a distance by beaming infrared light signals. Two incompatible protocols are used for infrared communications: IrDA and ASK. Many devices support both.

Instant Messenger

AOL's Instant Messenger is is a means of chatting over the Internet in real-time. It allows both open group discussions and private conversations. Instant Messenger uses a different, proprietary protocol from the more standard IRC, and is not supported on as many platforms.

interactive fiction

Interactive fiction (often abbreviated "IF" or "I-F") is a form of literature unique to the computer. While the reader cannot influence the direction of a typical story, the reader plays a more active role in an interactive fiction story and completely controls its direction. Interactive fiction works come in all the sizes and genres available to standard fiction, and in fact are not always even fiction per se (interactive tutorials exist and are slowly becoming more common).

interpreted

If a program is interpreted, its actual human-readable source is read as it is run by the computer. This is generally a slower process than if the program being run has already been compiled.

intranet

An intranet is a private network. There are many intranets scattered all over the world. Some are connected to the Internet via gateways.

IP

IP is the family of protocols that makes up the Internet. The two most common flavors are TCP/IP and UDP/IP.

IRC

Internet relay chat is a means of chatting over the Internet in real-time. It allows both open group discussions and private conversations. IRC programs are provided by many different companies and will work on many different platforms. AOL's Instant Messenger utilizes a separate incompatible protocol but is otherwise very similar.

IrDA

The Infrared Data Association (IrDA) is a voluntary organization of various manufacturers working together to ensure that the infrared communications between different computers, PDAs, printers, digital cameras, remote controls, etc. are all compatible with each other regardless of brand. The term is also often used to designate an IrDA compliant infrared communications port on a device. Informally, a device able to communicate via IrDA compliant infrared is sometimes simply said to "have IrDA". There is also an earlier, incompatible, and usually slower type of infrared communications still in use called ASK.

IRI

An Internationalized Resource Identifier is just a URI with i18n.

IRIX

The variant of UNIX designed by Silicon Graphics, Inc. IRIX machines are known for their graphics capabilities and were initially optimized for multimedia applications.

ISDN

An integrated service digital network line can be simply looked at as a digital phone line. ISDN connections to the Internet can be four times faster than the fastest regular phone connection, and because it is a digital connection a modem is not needed. Any computer hooked up to ISDN will typically require other special equipment in lieu of the modem, however. Also, both phone companies and ISPs charge more for ISDN connections than regular modem connections.

ISP

An Internet service provider is a company that provides Internet support for other entities. AOL (America Online) is a well-known ISP.

Java

A computer language designed to be both fairly lightweight and extremely portable. It is tightly bound to the web as it is the primary language for web applets. There has also been an OS based on Java for use on small hand-held, embedded, and network computers. It is called JavaOS. Java can be either interpreted or compiled. For web applet use it is almost always interpreted. While its interpreted form tends not to be very fast, its compiled form can often rival languages like C++ for speed. It is important to note however that speed is not Java's primary purpose -- raw speed is considered secondary to portabilty and ease of use.

JavaScript

JavaScript (in spite of its name) has nothing whatsoever to do with Java (in fact, it's arguably more like Newton Script than Java). JavaScript is an interpreted language built into a browser to provide a relatively simple means of adding interactivity to web pages. It is only supported on a few different browsers, and tends not to work exactly the same on different versions. Thus its use on the Internet is somewhat restricted to fairly simple programs. On intranets where there are usually fewer browser versions in use, JavaScript has been used to implement much more complex and impressive programs.

jiffy

A jiffy is 1/60 of a second. Jiffies are to seconds as seconds are to minutes.

joystick

A joystick is a physical device typically used to control objects on a computer screen. It is frequently used for games and sometimes used in place of a mouse.

JSON

The JSON is used for data interchange between programs, an area in which the ubiquitous XML is not too well-suited. JSON is lightweight and works extremely cleanly with languages languages including JavaScript, Python, Java, C++, and many others.

JSON-RPC

JSON-RPC is like XML-RPC but is significantly more lightweight since it uses JSON in lieu of XML.

KDE

The **K** desktop environment is a popular free window manager (and much more -- as its name touts, it is more of a desktop environment) that runs under X-Windows.

Kerberos

Kerberos is a network authentication protocol. Basically it preserves the integrity of passwords in any untrusted network (like the Internet). Kerberized applications work hand-in-hand with sites that support Kerberos to ensure that passwords cannot be stolen.

kernel

The very heart of an OS is often called its kernel. It will usually (at minimum) provide some libraries that give programmers access to its various features.

kHz & **kilohertz**

One kilohertz is equivalent to 1000 hertz. Some older computers have clock speeds measured in kHz.

l10n

Commonly used to abbreviate the word "localization". There are ten letters between the "l" and the "n". Similar to (and often used along with) i18n.

LDAP

The **L**ightweight **D**irectory **A**ccess **P**rotocol provides a means of sharing address book type of information across an intranet or even across the Internet. Note too that "address book type of information" here is pretty broad; it often includes not just human addresses, but machine addresses, printer configurations, and similar.

library

A selection of routines used by programmers to make computers do particular things.

lightweight

Something that is lightweight will not consume computer resources (such as RAM and disk space) too much and will thus run on less expensive computer systems.

Linux

Believe it or not, one of the fastest, most robust, and powerful multitasking OSes is available for free. Linux can be downloaded for free or be purchased on CD-ROM for a small service charge. A handful of companies distribute Linux including Red Hat, Debian, Caldera, and many others. Linux is also possibly available for more hardware combinations than any other OS (with the possible exception of NetBSD. Supported processors include: Alpha, PowerPC, SPARC, x86, and 68xx. Most processors currently not supported are currently works-in-progress or even available in beta. For example, work is currently underway to provide support for PA-RISC, 65xx, StrongARM, and Z80. People have even successfully gotten Linux working on PDAs. As you may have guessed, Linux can be made quite lightweight. Linux is a variant of UNIX and as such, most of the traditional UNIX software will run on Linux. This especially includes the GNU software, most of which comes with the majority of Linux distributions. Fast, reliable, stable, and inexpensive, Linux is popular with ISPs, software developers, and home hobbyists alike.

Lisp

Lisp stands for **lis**t **p**rocessing and is the second oldest computer language in the world. Being developed in 1959, it lost the title to FORTRAN by only a few months. It is typically interpreted, but compilers are available for some platforms. Attempts were made to standardize the language, and the standard version is called "Common Lisp". There have also been efforts to simplify the language, and the results of these efforts is another language called Scheme. Lisp is a fairly portable language, but is not particularly fast. Today, Lisp is most widely used with AI software.

load

There are two popular meanings for load. The first means to fetch some data or a program from a disk and store it in memory. The second indicates the amount of work a component (especially a processor) is being made to do.

Logo

Logo is an interpreted language designed by Papert in 1966 to be a tool for helping people (especially kids) learn computer programming concepts. In addition to being used for that purpose, it is often used as a language for controlling mechanical robots and other similar devices. Logo interfaces even exist for building block / toy robot sets. Logo uses a special graphics cursor called "the turtle", and Logo is itself sometimes called "Turtle Graphics". Logo is quite portable but not particularly fast. Versions can be found on almost every computer platform in the world. Additionally, some other languages (notably some Pascal versions) provide Logo-like interfaces for graphics-intensive programming.

lossy

If a process is lossy, it means that a little quality is lost when it is performed. If a format is lossy, it means that putting data into that format (or possibly even manipulating it in that format) will cause some slight loss. Lossy processes and formats are typically used for performance or resource utilization reasons. The opposite of lossy is lossless.

Lua

Lua is a simple interpreted language. It is extremely portable, and free versions exist for most platforms.

Mac OS

Mac OS is the OS used on Macintosh computers. There are two distinctively different versions of it; everything prior to version 10 (sometimes called Mac OS Classic) and everything version 10 or later (called Mac OS X).

Mac OS Classic

The OS created by Apple and originally used by Macs is frequently (albeit slightly incorrectly) referred to as Mac OS Classic (officially Mac OS Classic is this original OS running under the modern Mac OS X in emulation. Mac OS combines the functionality of both an OS and a window manager and is often considered to be the easiest OS to use. It is partially multitasking but will still sometimes crash when dealing with a buggy program. It is probably the second most popular OS, next only to Windows 'XP (although it is quickly losing ground to Mac OS X) and has excellent driver support and boasts a fair selection of games. Mac OS will run on PowerPC and 68xx based machines.

Mac OS X

Mac OS X (originally called Rhapsody) is the industrial strength OS produced by Apple to run on both PowerPC and x86 systems (replacing what is often referred to as Mac OS Classic. Mac OS X is at its heart a variant of UNIX and possesses its underlying power (and the ability to run many of the traditional UNIX tools, including the GNU tools). It also was designed to mimic other OSes on demand via what it originally refered to as "boxes" (actually high-performance emulators); it has the built-in capability to run programs written for older Mac OS (via its "BlueBox", officially called Mac OS Classic) and work was started on making it also run Windows '95 / '98 / ME software (via what was called its "YellowBox"). There are also a few rumors going around that future versions may even be able to run Newton software (via the "GreenBox"). It provides a selection of two window managers built-in: Aqua and X-Windows (with Aqua being the default).

machine language

Machine language consists of the raw numbers that can be directly understood by a particular processor. Each processor's machine language will be different from other processors' machine language. Although called "machine language", it is not usually what people think of when talking about computer languages. Machine language dressed up with mnemonics to make it a bit more human-readable is called assembly language.

Macintosh

A Macintosh (or a Mac for short) is a computer system that has Mac OS for its OS. There are a few different companies that have produced Macs, but by far the largest is Apple. The oldest Macs are based on the 68xx processor; somewhat more recent Macs on the PowerPC processor, and current Macs on the x86 processor. The Macintosh was really the first general purpose computer to employ a GUI.

MacTel

An x86 based system running some flavor of Mac OS.

mainframe

A mainframe is any computer larger than a small piece of furniture. A modern mainframe is more powerful than a modern workstation, but more expensive and more difficult to maintain.

MathML

The **Math M**ark-up **L**anguage is a subset of XML used to represent mathematical formulae and equations. Typically it is found embedded within XHTML documents, although as of this writing not all popular browsers support it.

megahertz

A million cycles per second, abbreviated MHz. This is often used misleadingly to indicate processor speed, because while one might expect that a higher number would indicate a faster processor, that logic only holds true within a given type of processors as different types of processors are capable of doing different amounts of work within a cycle. For a current example, either a 200 MHz PowerPC or a 270 MHz SPARC will outperform a 300 MHz Pentium.

Merced

The Merced is a RISC processor developed by Intel with help from Hewlett-Packard and possibly Sun. It is just starting to be released, but is intended to eventually replace both the x86 and PA-RISC processors. Curiously, HP is recommending that everyone hold off using the first release and instead wait for the second one. It is expected some day to be roughly as fast as an Alpha or PowerPC. It is expected to be supported by future versions of Solaris, Windows-NT, HP-UX, Mac OS X, and Linux. The current semi-available Merced processor is called the Itanium. Its overall schedule is way behind, and some analysts predict that it never will really be released in significant quanitities.

MFM

Loosely speaking, An old disk format sometimes used by CP/M, MS-DOS, and MS-Windows. No longer too common as it cannot deliver close to the performance of either SCSI or IDE.

middleware

Software designed to sit in between an OS and applications. Common examples are Java and Tcl/Tk.

MIME

The **m**ulti-purpose **I**nternet **m**ail **e**xtensions specification describes a means of sending non-

ASCII data (such as images, sounds, foreign symbols, etc.) through e-mail. It commonly utilizes bcode.

MMX

Multimedia extensions were built into some x86 CPUs to provide better performance for certain operations, most notably graphics and sound. It is similar to AltiVec on the PowerPC CPUs. Like AltiVec, it requires special software for full performance benefits to be realized.

MOB

A movable object is a graphical object that is manipulated separately from the background. These are seen all the time in computer games. When implemented in hardware, MOBs are sometimes called sprites.

Modula-2 & Modula-3

Modula-2 is a procedural language based on Pascal by its original author in around the 1977 - 1979 time period. Modula-3 is an intended successor that adds support for object-oriented constructs (among other things). Modula-2 can be either compiled or interpreted, while Modula-3 tends to be just a compiled language.

MOTD

A message of the day. Many computers (particularly more capable ones) are configured to display a MOTD when accessed remotely.

Motif

Motif is a popular commercial window manager that runs under X-Windows. Free work-alike versions are also available.

MS-DOS

The DOS produced by Microsoft. Early versions of it bear striking similarities to the earlier CP/M, but it utilizes simpler commands. It provides only a CLI, but either OS/2, Windows 3.1, Windows '95, Windows '98, Windows ME, or GEOS may be run on top of it to provide a GUI. It only runs on x86 based machines.

MS-Windows

MS-Windows is the name collectively given to several somewhat incompatible OSes all produced by Microsoft. They are: Windows CE, Windows NT, Windows 3.1, Windows '95, Windows '98, Windows ME, Windows 2000, and Windows XP.

MUD

A multi-user dimension (also sometimes called multi-user dungeon, but in either case abbreviated to "MUD") is sort of a combination between the online chatting abilities provided by something like IRC and a role-playing game. A MUD built with object oriented principles in mind is called a "Multi-user dimension object-oriented", or MOO. Yet another variant is called a "multi-user shell", or MUSH. Still other variants are called multi-user role-playing environments (MURPE) and multi-user environments (MUSE). There are probably more. In all cases the differences will be mostly academic to the regular user, as the same software is used to connect to all of them. Software to connect to MUDs can be found for most platforms, and there are even Java based ones that can run from within a browser.

multitasking

Some OSes have built into them the ability to do several things at once. This is called multitasking, and has been in use since the late sixties / early seventies. Since this ability is built into the software, the overall system will be slower running two things at once than it will be running just one thing. A system may have more than one processor built into it though, and such a system will be capable of running multiple things at once with less of a performance hit.

nagware

Nagware is a variant of shareware that will frequently remind its users to register.

NetBSD

A free variant of Berkeley UNIX available for Alpha, x86, 68xx, PA-RISC, SPARC, PowerPC, ARM, and many other types of machines. Its emphasis is on portability.

netiquette

The established conventions of online politeness are called netiquette. Some conventions vary from site to site or online medium to online medium; others are pretty standard everywhere. Newbies are often unfamiliar with the conventional rules of netiquette and sometimes embarrass themselves accordingly. Be sure not to send that incredibly important e-mail message before reading about netiquette.

newbie

A newbie is a novice to the online world or computers in general.

news

Usenet news can generally be thought of as public e-mail as that is generally the way it behaves. In reality, it is implemented by different software and is often accessed by different programs. Different newsgroups adhere to different topics, and some are "moderated", meaning that humans will try to manually remove off-topic posts, especially spam. Most established newsgroups have a FAQ, and people are strongly encouraged to read the FAQ prior to posting.

Newton

Although Newton is officially the name of the lightweight OS developed by Apple to run on its MessagePad line of PDAs, it is often used to mean the MessagePads (and compatible PDAs) themselves and thus the term "Newton OS" is often used for clarity. The Newton OS is remarkably powerful; it is fully multitasking in spite of the fact that it was designed for small machines. It is optimized for hand-held use, but will readily transfer data to all manner of desktop machines. Historically it was the first PDA. Recently Apple announced that it will discontinue further development of the Newton platform, but will instead work to base future hand-held devices on either Mac OS or Mac OS X with some effort dedicated to making the new devices capable of running current Newton programs.

Newton book

Newton books provide all the functionality of ordinary books but add searching and hypertext capabilities. The format was invented for the Newton to provide a means of making volumes of data portable, and is particularly popular in the medical community as most medical references are available as Newton books and carrying around a one pound Newton is preferable to carrying around twenty pounds of books, especially when it comes to looking up something. In addition to medical books, numerous references, most of the classics, and many contemporary works of fiction are available as Newton books. Most fiction is available for free, most references cost money. Newton books are somewhat more capable than the similar Palm DOC; both are specific types of e-books.

Newton Script

A intepreted, object-oriented language for Newton MessagePad computers.

nybble

A nybble is half a byte, or four bits. It is a case of computer whimsy; it only stands to reason that a small byte should be called a nybble. Some authors spell it with an "i" instead of the "y", but the "y" is the original form.

object-oriented

While the specifics are well beyond the scope of this document, the term "object-oriented" applies to a philosophy of software creation. Often this philosophy is referred to as object-oriented design (sometimes abbreviated as OOD), and programs written with it in mind are referred to as object-oriented programs (often abbreviated OOP). Programming languages designed to help facilitate it are called object-oriented languages (sometimes abbreviated as OOL) and databases built with it in mind are called object-oriented databases (sometimes abbreviated as OODB or less fortunately OOD). The general notion is that an object-oriented approach to creating software starts with modeling the real-world problems trying to be solved in familiar real-world ways, and carries the analogy all the way down to structure of the program. This is of course a great over-simplification. Numerous object-oriented programming languages exist including: Java, C++, Modula-2, Newton Script, and ADA.

Objective-C & ObjC

Objective-C (often called "ObjC" for short) is a compiled object-oriented language. Based heavily on C, Objective-C is nearly as fast and can often be thought of as being just C with added features. Note that it was developed independently of C++; its object-oriented extensions are more in the style of Smalltalk. It is however related to Objective-C++.

Objective-C++ & ObjC++

Objective-C++ (often called "ObjC++" for short) is a curious hybrid of Objective-C and C++, allowing the syntax of both to coexist in the same source files.

office suite

An office suite is a collection of programs including at minimum a word processor, spreadsheet, drawing program, and minimal database program. Some common office suites include MS-Office, AppleWorks, ClarisWorks, GeoWorks, Applixware, Corel Office, and StarOffice.

open source

Open source software goes one step beyond freeware. Not only does it provide the software for free, it provides the original source code used to create the software. Thus, curious users can poke around with it to see how it works, and advanced users can modify it to make it work better for them. By its nature, open souce software is pretty well immune to all types of computer virus.

OpenBSD

A free variant of Berkeley UNIX available for Alpha, x86, 68xx, PA-RISC, SPARC, and PowerPC based machines. Its emphasis is on security.

OpenDocument & ODF

OpenDocument (or ODF for short) is the suite of open, XML-based office suite application formats defined by the OASIS consortium. It defines a platform-neutral, non-proprietary way of storing documents.

OpenGL

A low-level 3D graphics library with an emphasis on speed developed by SGI.

OS/2

OS/2 is the OS designed by IBM to run on x86 based machines. It is semi-compatible with MS-Windows. IBM's more industrial strength OS is called AIX.

PA-RISC

The PA-RISC is a RISC processor developed by Hewlett-Packard. It is currently produced only by HP. At the moment only one OS runs on PA-RISC based machines: HP-UX. There is an effort underway to port Linux to them, though.

Palm DOC

Palm DOC files are quite similar to (but slightly less capable than) Newton books. They were designed for Palm Pilots but can now be read on a couple other platforms, too. They are a specific type of e-book.

Palm Pilot

The Palm Pilot (also called both just Palm and just Pilot, officially now just Palm) is the most popular PDA currently in use. It is one of the least capable PDAs, but it is also one of the smallest and least expensive. While not as full featured as many of the other PDAs (such as the Newton) it performs what features it does have quite well and still remains truly pocket-sized.

parallel

Loosely speaking, parallel implies a situation where multiple things can be done simultaneously, like having multiple check-out lines each serving people all at once. Parallel connections are by their nature more expensive than serial ones, but usually faster. Also, in a related use of the word, often multitasking computers are said to be capable of running multiple programs in parallel.

partition

Sometimes due to hardware limitations, disks have to be divided into smaller pieces. These pieces are called partitions.

Pascal

Named after the mathematician Blaise Pascal, Pascal is a language designed by Niklaus Wirth originally in 1968 (and heavily revised in 1972) mostly for purposes of education and training people how to write computer programs. It is a typically compiled language but is still usually slower than C or FORTRAN. Wirth also created a more powerful object-oriented Pascal-like language called Modula-2.

PC-DOS

The DOS produced by IBM designed to work like MS-DOS. Early versions of it bear striking similarities to the earlier CP/M, but it utilizes simpler commands. It provides only a CLI, but either Windows 3.1 or GEOS may be run on top of it to provide a GUI. It only runs on x86 based machines.

PCMCIA

The **P**ersonal **C**omputer **M**emory **C**ard **I**nternational **A**ssociation is a standards body that concern themselves with PC Card technology. Often the PC Cards themselves are referred to as "PCMCIA cards". Frequently flash memory can be found in PC card form.

Perl

Perl is an interpreted language extremely popular for web applications.

PET

The Commodore PET (**P**ersonal **E**lectronic **T**ransactor) is an early (circa 1977-1980, around the same time as the Apple][) home computer featuring a ROM-based BASIC developed by Microsoft which it uses as a default "OS". It is based on the 65xx family of processors and is the precursor to the VIC-20.

PETSCII

The PETSCII character set gets its name from "**PET** ASCII; it is a variant of the ASCII character set originally developed for the Commodore PET that swaps the upper and lower case characters and adds over a hundred graphic characters in addition to other small changes. If you encounter some text that seems to have uppercase where lowercase is expected and vice-versa, it is probably a PETSCII file.

PHP

Named with a recursive acronym (PHP: Hypertext Preprocessor), PHP provides a means of creating web pages that dynamically modify themselves on the fly.

ping

Ping is a protocol designed to check across a network to see if a particular computer is "alive" or not. Computers that recognize the ping will report back their status. Computers that are down will not report back anything at all.

pixel

The smallest distinct point on a computer display is called a pixel.

plug-in

A plug-in is a piece of software designed not to run on its own but rather work in cooperation with a separate application to increase that application's abilities.

point

There are two common meanings for this word. The first is in the geometric sense; a position in space without size. Of course as applied to computers it must take up some space in practise (even if not in theory) and it is thus sometimes synonomous with pixel. The other meaning is related most typically to fonts and regards size. The exact meaning of it in this sense will unfortunately vary somewhat from person to person, but will often mean 1/72 of an inch. Even when it does not exactly mean 1/72 of an inch, larger point sizes always indicate larger fonts.

PowerPC

The PowerPC is a RISC processor developed in a collaborative effort between IBM, Apple, and Motorola. It is currently produced by a few different companies, of course including its original developers. A few different OSes run on PowerPC based machines, including Mac OS, AIX, Solaris, Windows NT, Linux, Mac OS X, BeOS, and AmigaOS. At any given time, the fastest processor in the world is usually either a PowerPC or an Alpha, but sometimes SPARCs and PA-RISCs make the list, too.

proprietary

This simply means to be supplied by only one vendor. It is commonly misused. Currently, most processors are non-proprietary, some systems are non-proprietary, and every OS (except for arguably Linux) is proprietary.

protocol

A protocol is a means of communication used between computers. As long as both computers recognize the same protocol, they can communicate without too much difficulty over the same network or even via a simple direct modem connection regardless whether or not they are themselves of the same type. This means that WinTel boxes, Macs, Amigas, UNIX machines, etc., can all talk with one another provided they agree on a common protocol first.

Psion

The Psion is a fairly popular brand of PDA. Generally, it is in between a Palm and a Newton in capability. It runs the EPOC OS.

Python

Python is an interpreted, object-oriented language popular for Internet applications. It is extremely portable with free versions existing for virtually every platform.

queue

A queue is a waiting list of things to be processed. Many computers provide printing queues, for example. If something is being printed and the user requests that another item be printed, the second item will sit in the printer queue until the first item finishes printing at which point it will be removed from the queue and get printed itself.

QuickDraw

A high-level 3D graphics library with an emphasis on quick development time created by Apple.

RAM

Random access memory is the short-term memory of a computer. Any information stored in RAM will be lost if power goes out, but the computer can read from RAM far more quickly than from a drive.

random access

Also called "dynamic access" this indicates that data can be selected without having to skip over earlier data first. This is the way that a CD, record, laserdisc, or DVD will behave -- it is easy to selectively play a particular track without having to fast forward through earlier tracks. The other common behavior is called sequential access.

RDF

The Resource Description Framework is built upon an XML base and provides a more modern means of accessing data from Internet resources. It can provide metadata (including annotations) for web pages making (among other things) searching more capable. It is also being used to refashion some existing formats like RSS and iCalendar; in the former case it is already in place (at least for newer RSS versions), but it is still experimental in the latter case.

real-time

Something that happens in real-time will keep up with the events around it and never give any sort of "please wait" message.

Rexx

The Restructured Extended Executor is an interpreted language designed primarily to be embedded in other applications in order to make them consistently programmable, but also to be easy to learn and understand.

RISC

Reduced instruction set computing is one of the two main types of processor design in use today, the other being CISC. The fastest processors in the world today are all RISC designs. There are several popular RISC processors, including Alphas, ARMs, PA-RISCs, PowerPCs, and SPARCs.

robot

A robot (or 'bot for short) in the computer sense is a program designed to automate some task, often just sending messages or collecting information. A spider is a type of robot designed to traverse the web performing some task (usually collecting data).

robust

The adjective robust is used to describe programs that are better designed, have fewer bugs, and are less likely to crash.

ROM

Read-only memory is similar to RAM only cannot be altered and does not lose its contents when power is removed.

RSS

RSS stands for either **R**ich **S**ite **S**ummary, **R**eally **S**imple **S**yndication, or **R**DF **S**ite **S**ummary, depending upon whom you ask. The general idea is that it can provide brief summaries of articles that appear in full on a web site. It is well-formed XML, and newer versions are even more specifically well-formed RDF.

Ruby

Ruby is an interpreted, object-oriented language. Ruby was fairly heavily influenced by Perl, so people familiar with that language can typically transition to Ruby easily.

scanner

A scanner is a piece of hardware that will examine a picture and produce a computer file that represents what it sees. A digital camera is a related device. Each has its own limitations.

Scheme

Scheme is a typically interpreted computer language. It was created in 1975 in an attempt to make Lisp simpler and more consistent. Scheme is a fairly portable language, but is not particularly fast.

script

A script is a series of OS commands. The term "batch file" means much the same thing, but is a bit dated. Typically the same sort of situations in which one would say DOS instead of OS, it would also be appropriate to say batch file instead of script. Scripts can be run like programs, but tend to perform simpler tasks. When a script is run, it is always interpreted.

SCSI

Loosely speaking, a disk format sometimes used by MS-Windows, Mac OS, AmigaOS, and (almost always) UNIX. Generally SCSI is superior (but more expensive) to IDE, but it varies somewhat with system load and the individual SCSI and IDE components themselves. The quick rundown is that: SCSI-I and SCSI-II will almost always outperform IDE; EIDE will almost always outperform SCSI-I and SCSI-II; SCSI-III and UltraSCSI will almost always outperform EIDE; and heavy system loads give an advantage to SCSI. Note that although loosely speaking it is just a format difference, it is deep down a hardware difference.

sequential access

This indicates that data cannot be selected without having to skip over earlier data first. This is the way that a cassette or video tape will behave. The other common behavior is called random access.

serial

Loosely speaking, serial implies something that has to be done linearly, one at a time, like people being served in a single check-out line. Serial connections are by their nature less expensive than parallel connections (including things like SCSI) but are typically slower.

server

A server is a computer designed to provide various services for an entire network. It is typically either a workstation or a mainframe because it will usually be expected to handle far greater loads than ordinary desktop systems. The load placed on servers also necessitates that they utilize robust OSes, as a crash on a system that is currently being used by many people is far worse than a crash on a system that is only being used by one person.

SGML

The **S**tandard **G**eneralized **M**ark-up **L**anguage provides an extremely generalized level of mark-up. More common mark-up languages like HTML and XML are actually just popular subsets of SGML.

shareware

Shareware is software made for profit that allows a trial period before purchase. Typically shareware can be freely downloaded, used for a period of weeks (or sometimes even months), and either purchased or discarded after it has been learned whether or not it will satisfy the user's needs.

shell

A CLI designed to simplify complex OS commands. Some OSes (like AmigaOS, the Hurd, and UNIX) have built-in support to make the concurrent use of multiple shells easy. Common shells include the Korn Shell (ksh), the Bourne Shell (sh or bsh), the Bourne-Again Shell, (bash or bsh), the C-Shell (csh), etc.

SIMM

A physical component used to add RAM to a computer. Similar to, but incompatible with, DIMMs.

Smalltalk

Smalltalk is an efficient language for writing computer programs. Historically it is one of the first object-oriented languages, and is not only used today in its pure form but shows its influence in other languages like Objective-C.

Solaris

Solaris is the commercial variant of UNIX currently produced by Sun. It is an industrial strength, nigh bulletproof, powerful multitasking OS that will run on SPARC, x86, and PowerPC based machines.

spam

Generally spam is unwanted, unrequested e-mail or Usenet news. It is typically sent out in bulk to huge address lists that were automatically generated by various robots endlessly searching the Internet and newsgroups for things that resemble e-mail addresses. The legality of spam is a topic of much debate; it is at best only borderline legal, and spammers have been successfully persecuted in some states.

SPARC

The SPARC is a RISC processor developed by Sun. The design was more or less released to the world, and it is currently produced by around a dozen different companies too numerous to even bother mentioning. It is worth noting that even computers made by Sun typically sport SPARCs made by other companies. A couple different OSes run on SPARC based machines, including Solaris, SunOS, and Linux. Some of the newer SPARC models are called UltraSPARCs.

sprite

The term sprite originally referred to a small MOB, usually implemented in hardware. Lately it is also being used to refer to a single image used piecemeal within a Web site in order to avoid incurring the time penalty of downloading multiple files.

SQL

SQL (pronounced **Sequel**) is an interpreted language specially designed for database access. It is supported by virtually every major modern database system.

Sugar

The window manager used by the OLPC XO. It is made to run on top of Linux.

SunOS

SunOS is the commercial variant of UNIX formerly produced (but still supported) by Sun.

SVG

Scalable Vector Graphics data is an XML file that is used to hold graphical data that can be resized without loss of quality. SVG data can be kept in its own file, or even embedded within a web page (although not all browsers are capable of displaying such data).

Tcl/Tk

The Tool Command Language is a portable interpreted computer language designed to be easy to use. Tk is a GUI toolkit for Tcl. Tcl is a fairly popular language for both integrating existing applications and for creating Web applets (note that applets written in Tcl are often called Tcklets). Tcl/Tk is available for free for most platforms, and plug-ins are available to enable many browsers to play Tcklets.

TCP/IP

TCP/IP is a protocol for computer networks. The Internet is largely built on top of TCP/IP (it is the more reliable of the two primary Internet Protocols -- TCP stands for Transmission Control Protocol).

terminator

A terminator is a dedicated device used to mark the end of a device chain (as is most typically found with SCSI devices). If such a chain is not properly terminated, weird results can occur.

TEX

TEX (pronounced "tek") is a freely available, industrial strength typesetting program that can be run on many different platforms. These qualities make it exceptionally popular in schools, and frequently software developed at a university will have its documentation in TEX format. TEX is not limited to educational use, though; many professional books were typeset with TEX. TEX's primary drawback is that it can be quite difficult to set up initially.

THz & terahertz

One terahertz is equivalent to 1000 gigahertz.

TrackBack

TrackBacks essentially provide a means whereby different web sites can post messages to one another not just to inform each other about citations, but also to alert one another of related resources. Typically, a blog may display quotations from another blog through the use of TrackBacks.

UDP/IP

UDP/IP is a protocol for computer networks. It is the faster of the two primary Internet Protocols. UDP stands for User Datagram Protocol.

Unicode

The Unicode character set is a superset of the ASCII character set with provisions made for handling international symbols and characters from other languages. Unicode is sixteen bit, so takes up roughly twice the space as simple ASCII, but is correspondingly more flexible.

UNIX

UNIX is a family of OSes, each being made by a different company or organization but all offering a very similar look and feel. It can not quite be considered non-proprietary, however, as the differences between different vendor's versions can be significant (it is still generally possible to switch from one vendor's UNIX to another without too much effort; today the differences between different UNIXes are similar to the differences between the different MS-Windows; historically there were two different UNIX camps, Berkeley / BSD and AT&T / System V, but the assorted vendors have worked together to minimalize the differences). The free variant Linux is one of the closest things to a current, non-proprietary OS; its development is controlled by a non-profit organization and its distribution is provided by several companies. UNIX is powerful; it is fully multitasking and can do pretty much anything that any OS can do (look to the Hurd if you need a more powerful OS). With power comes complexity, however, and

UNIX tends not to be overly friendly to beginners (although those who think UNIX is difficult or cryptic apparently have not used CP/M). Window managers are available for UNIX (running under X-Windows) and once properly configured common operations will be almost as simple on a UNIX machine as on a Mac. Out of all the OSes in current use, UNIX has the greatest range of hardware support. It will run on machines built around many different processors. Lightweight versions of UNIX have been made to run on PDAs, and in the other direction, full featured versions make full advantage of all the resources on large, multi-processor machines. Some different UNIX versions include Solaris, Linux, IRIX, AIX, SunOS, FreeBSD, Digital UNIX, HP-UX, NetBSD, OpenBSD, etc.

upload

To upload a file is to copy it from your computer to a remote computer. The opposite is download.

UPS

An uninterrupted power supply uses heavy duty batteries to help smooth out its input power source.

URI

A Uniform Resource Identifier is basically just a unique address for almost any type of resource. It is similar to but more general than a URL; in fact, it may also be a URN.

URL

A Uniform Resource Locator is basically just an address for a file that can be given to a browser. It starts with a protocol type (such as http, ftp, or gopher) and is followed by a colon, machine name, and file name in UNIX style. Optionally an octothorpe character "#" and and arguments will follow the file name; this can be used to further define position within a page and perform a few other tricks. Similar to but less general than a URI.

URN

A Uniform Resource Name is basically just a unique address for almost any type of resource unlike a URL it will probably not resolve with a browser.

USB

A really fast type of serial port that offers many of the best features of SCSI without the price. Faster than many types of parallel port, a single USB port is capable of chaining many devices without the need of a terminator. USB is much slower (but somewhat less expensive) than FireWire.

uucode

The point of uucode is to allow 8-bit binary data to be transferred through the more common 7-bit ASCII channels (most especially e-mail). The facilities for dealing with uucoded files exist for many different machine types, and the most common programs are called "uuencode" for encoding the original binary file into a 7-bit file and "uudecode" for restoring the original binary file from the encoded one. Sometimes different uuencode and uudecode programs will work in subtly different manners causing annoying compatibility problems. Bcode was invented to provide the same service as uucode but to maintain a tighter standard.

variable width

As applied to a font, variable width means that different characters will have different widths as appropriate. For example, an "i" will take up much less space than an "m". The opposite of variable width is fixed width. The terms "proportional width" and "proportionally spaced" mean the same thing as variable width. Some common variable width fonts include Times, Helvetica, and Bookman.

VAX

The VAX is a computer platform developed by Digital. Its plural is VAXen. VAXen are large expensive machines that were once quite popular in large businesses; today modern UNIX workstations have all the capability of VAXen but take up much less space. Their OS is called VMS.

vector

This term has two common meanings. The first is in the geometric sense: a vector defines a direction and magnitude. The second concerns the formatting of fonts and images. If a font is a vector font or an image is a vector image, it is defined as lines of relative size and direction rather than as collections of pixels (the method used in bitmapped fonts and images). This makes it easier to change the size of the font or image, but puts a bigger load on the device that has to display the font or image. The term "outline font" means the same thing as vector font.

Veronica & Veronica2

Although traditionally written as a proper name, Veronica is actually an acronym for "**v**ery **e**asy **r**odent-**o**riented **n**etwide **i**ndex to **c**omputerized **a**rchives", where the "rodent" refers to gopher. The acronym was obviously a little forced to go along with the pre-existing (and now largely unused) Archie, in order to have a little fun with a comic book reference. Regardless, Veronica (or these days more likely Veronica2) is essentially a search engine for gopher resources.

VIC-20

The Commodore VIC-20 computer sold millions of units and is generally considered to have been the first affordable home computer. It features a ROM-based BASIC and uses it as a default "OS". It is based on the 65xx family of processors. VIC (in case you are wondering) can stand for either **v**ideo **i**nterface **c** or **v**ideo **i**nterface **c**omputer. The VIC-20 is the precursor to the C64/128.

virtual machine

A virtual machine is a machine completely defined and implemented in software rather than hardware. It is often referred to as a "runtime environment"; code compiled for such a machine is typically called bytecode.

virtual memory

This is a scheme by which disk space is made to substitute for the more expensive RAM space. Using it will often enable a comptuer to do things it could not do without it, but it will also often result in an overall slowing down of the system. The concept of swap space is very similar.

virtual reality

Virtual reality (often called VR for short) is generally speaking an attempt to provide more natural, human interfaces to software. It can be as simple as a pseudo 3D interface or as elaborate as an isolated room in which the computer can control the user's senses of vision, hearing, and even smell and touch.

virus

A virus is a program that will seek to duplicate itself in memory and on disks, but in a subtle way that will not immediately be noticed. A computer on the same network as an infected computer or that uses an infected disk (even a floppy) or that downloads and runs an infected program can itself become infected. A virus can only spread to computers of the same platform. For example, on a network consisting of a WinTel box, a Mac, and a Linux box, if one machine acquires a virus the other two will probably still be safe. Note also that different platforms have different general levels of resistance; UNIX machines are almost immune, Win '95 / '98 / ME / XP is quite vulnerable, and most others lie somewhere in between.

VMS

The industrial strength OS that runs on VAXen.

VoIP

VoIP means "Voice over IP" and it is quite simply a way of utilizing the Internet (or even in some cases intranets) for telephone conversations. The primary motivations for doing so are cost and convenience as VoIP is significantly less expensive than typical telephone long distance packages, plus one high speed Internet connection can serve for multiple phone lines.

VRML

A **V**irtual **R**eality **M**odeling **L**anguage file is used to represent VR objects. It has essentially been superceded by X3D.

W3C

The World Wide Web Consortium (usually abbreviated W3C) is a non-profit, advisory body that makes suggestions on the future direction of the World Wide Web, HTML, CSS, and browsers.

Waba

An extremely lightweight subset of Java optimized for use on PDAs.

WebDAV

WebDAV stands for Web-based Distributed Authoring and Versioning, and is designed to provide a way of editing Web-based resources in place. It serves as a more modern (and often more secure) replacement for FTP in many cases.

WebTV

A WebTV box hooks up to an ordinary television set and displays web pages. It will not display them as well as a dedicated computer.

window manager

A window manager is a program that acts as a graphical go-between for a user and an OS. It provides a GUI for the OS. Some OSes incorporate the window manager into their own internal code, but many do not for reasons of efficiency. Some OSes partially make the division. Some common true window managers include CDE (Common Desktop Environment), GNOME, KDE, Aqua, OpenWindows, Motif, FVWM, Sugar, and Enlightenment. Some common hybrid window managers with OS extensions include Windows ME, Windows 98, Windows 95, Windows 3.1, OS/2 and GEOS.

Windows '95

Windows '95 is currently the second most popular variant of MS-Windows. It was designed to be the replacement Windows 3.1 but has not yet done so completely partly because of suspected security problems but even more because it is not as lightweight and will not work on all the machines that Windows 3.1 will. It is more capable than Windows 3.1 though and now has excellent driver support and more games available for it than any other platform. It is made to run on top of MS-DOS and will not do much of anything if MS-DOS is not on the system. It is thus not strictly an OS per se, but nor is it a true window manager either; rather the combination of MS-DOS and Windows '95 result in a full OS with GUI. It is partially multitasking but has a much greater chance of crashing than Windows NT does (or probably even Mac OS) if faced with a buggy program. Windows '95 runs only on x86 based machines. Currently Windows '95 has several Y2K issues, some of which have patches that can be downloaded for free, and some of which do not yet have fixes at all.

Windows '98

Windows '98 is quite possibly the second most popular form of MS-Windows, in spite of the fact that its official release is currently a point of legal debate with at least nineteen states, the federal government, and a handful of foreign countries as it has a few questionable features that might restrict the novice computer user and/or unfairly compete with other computer companies. It also has some specific issues with the version of Java that comes prepackaged with it that has never been adequately fixed, and it still has several Y2K issues, most of which have patches that can be downloaded for free (in fact, Microsoft guarantees that it will work properly through 2000 with the proper patches), but some of which do not yet have fixes at all (it won't work properly through 2001 at this point). In any case, it was designed to replace Windows '95.

Windows 2000

Windows 2000 was the intended replacement for Windows NT and in that capacity received relatively lukewarm support. Being based on Windows NT, it inherits some of its driver support problems. Originally it was also supposed to replace Windows '98, but Windows ME was made to do that instead, and the merger between Windows NT and Windows '98 was postponed until Windows XP.

Windows 3.1

Windows 3.1 remains a surprisingly popular variant of MS-Windows. It is lighter weight than either Windows '95 or Windows NT (but not lighter weight than GEOS) but less capable than the other two. It is made to run on top of MS-DOS and will not do much of anything if MS-DOS is not on the system. It is thus not strictly an OS per se, but nor is it a true window manager, either; rather the combination of MS-DOS and Windows 3.1 result in a full OS with GUI. Its driver support is good, but its game selection is limited. Windows 3.1 runs only on x86 based machines. It has some severe Y2K issues that may or may not be fixed.

Windows CE

Windows CE is the lightweight variant of MS-Windows. It offers the general look and feel of Windows '95 but is targetted primarily for hand-held devices, PDAs, NCs, and embedded devices. It does not have all the features of either Windows '95 or Windows NT and is very different from Windows 3.1. In particular, it will not run any software made for any of the other versions of MS-Windows. Special versions of each program must be made. Furthermore, there are actually a few slightly different variants of Windows CE, and no variant is guaranteed to be able to run software made specifically for another one. Driver support is also fairly poor for all types, and few games are made for it. Windows CE will run on a few different processor types, including the x86 and several different processors dedicated to PDAs, embedded systems, and hand-held devices.

Windows ME

Windows ME is yet another flavor of MS-Windows (specifically the planned replacement for Windows '98). Windows ME currently runs only on the x86 processor.

Windows NT

Windows NT is the industrial-strength variant of MS-Windows. Current revisions offer the look and feel of Windows '95 and older revisions offer the look and feel of Windows 3.1. It is the most robust flavor of MS-Windows and is fully multitasking. It is also by far the most expensive flavor of MS-Windows and has far less software available for it than Windows '95 or '98. In particular, do not expect to play many games on a Windows NT machine, and expect some difficulty in obtaining good drivers. Windows NT will run on a few different processor types, including the x86, the Alpha, and the PowerPC. Plans are in place to port Windows NT to the Merced when it becomes available.

Windows Vista

Windows Vista is the newest flavor of MS-Windows (specifically the planned replacement for Windows XP). Windows Vista (originally known as Longhorn) currently only runs on x86 processors.

Windows XP

Windows XP is yet another flavor of MS-Windows (specifically the planned replacement for both Windows ME and Windows 2000). Windows XP currently only runs on the x86 processors. Windows XP is currently the most popular form of MS-Windows.

WinTel

An x86 based system running some flavor of MS-Windows.

workstation

Depending upon whom you ask, a workstation is either an industrial strength desktop computer or its own category above the desktops. Workstations typically have some flavor of UNIX for their OS, but there has been a recent trend to call high-end Windows NT and Windows 2000 machines workstations, too.

WYSIWYG

What you see is what you get; an adjective applied to a program that attempts to exactly represent printed output on the screen. Related to WYSIWYM but quite different.

WYSIWYM

What you see is what you mean; an adjective applied to a program that does not attempt to exactly represent printed output on the screen, but rather defines how things are used and so will adapt to different paper sizes, etc. Related to WYSIWYG but quite different.

X-Face

X-Faces are small monochrome images embedded in headers for both provides a e-mail and news messages. Better mail and news applications will display them (sometimes automatically, sometimes only per request).

X-Windows

X-Windows provides a GUI for most UNIX systems, but can also be found as an add-on library for other computers. Numerous window managers run on top of it. It is often just called "X".

X3D

Extensible 3D Graphics data is an XML file that is used to hold three-dimensional graphical data. It is the successor to VRML.

x86

The x86 series of processors includes the Pentium, Pentium Pro, Pentium II, Pentium III, Celeron, and Athlon as well as the 786, 686, 586, 486, 386, 286, 8086, 8088, etc. It is an exceptionally popular design (by far the most popular CISC series) in spite of the fact that even its fastest model is significantly slower than the assorted RISC processors. Many different OSes run on machines built around x86 processors, including MS-DOS, Windows 3.1, Windows '95, Windows '98, Windows ME, Windows NT, Windows 2000, Windows CE, Windows XP, GEOS, Linux, Solaris, OpenBSD, NetBSD, FreeBSD, Mac OS X, OS/2, BeOS, CP/M, etc. A couple different companies produce x86 processors, but the bulk of them are produced by Intel. It is expected that this processor will eventually be completely replaced by the Merced, but the Merced development schedule is somewhat behind. Also, it should be noted that the Pentium III processor has stirred some controversy by including a "fingerprint" that will enable individual computer usage of web pages etc. to be accurately tracked.

XBL

An XML Binding Language document is used to associate executable content with an XML tag. It is itself an XML file, and is used most frequently (although not exclusively) in conjunction with XUL.

XHTML

The Extensible Hypertext Mark-up Language is essentially a cleaner, stricter version of HTML. It is a proper subset of XML.

XML

The Extensible Mark-up Language is a subset of SGML and a superset of XHTML. It is used for numerous things including (among many others) RSS and RDF.

XML-RPC

XML-RPC provides a fairly lightweight means by which one computer can execute a program on a co-operating machine across a network like the Internet. It is based on XML and is used for everything from fetching stock quotes to checking weather forcasts.

XO

The energy-efficient, kid-friendly laptop produced by the OLPC project. It runs Sugar for its window manager and Linux for its OS. It sports numerous built-in features like wireless networking, a video camera & microphone, a few USB ports, and audio in/out jacks. It comes with several educational applications (which it refers to as "Activities"), most of which are written in Python.

XSL

The Extensible Stylesheet Language is like CSS for XML. It provides a means of describing how an XML resource should be displayed.

XSLT

XSL Transformations are used to transform one type of XML into another. It is a component of XSL that can be (and often is) used independently.

XUL

An XML User-Interface Language document is used to define a user interface for an application using XML to specify the individual controls as well as the overall layout.

Y2K

The general class of problems resulting from the wrapping of computers' internal date timers is given this label in honor of the most obvious occurrence -- when the year changes from 1999 to 2000 (abbreviated in some programs as 99 to 00 indicating a backwards time movement). Contrary to popular belief, these problems will not all manifest themselves on the first day of 2000, but will in fact happen over a range of dates extending out beyond 2075. A computer that does not have problems prior to the beginning of 2001 is considered "Y2K compliant", and a computer that does not have problems within the next ten years or so is considered for all practical purposes to be "Y2K clean". Whether or not a given computer is "clean" depends upon both its OS and its applications (and in some unfortunate cases, its hardware). The quick rundown on common home / small business machines (roughly from best to worst) is that:

All Mac OS systems are okay until at least the year 2040. By that time a patch should be available.

All BeOS systems are okay until the year 2040 (2038?). By that time a patch should be available.

Most UNIX versions are either okay or currently have free fixes available (and typically would not have major problems until 2038 or later in any case).

NewtonOS has a problem with the year 2010, but has a free fix available.

Newer AmigaOS systems are okay; older ones have a problem with the year 2000 but have a free fix available. They also have a year 2077 problem that does not yet have a free fix.

Some OS/2 systems have a year 2000 problem, but free fixes are available.

All CP/M versions have a year 2000 problem, but free fixes are available.

PC-DOS has a year 2000 problem, but a free fix is available.

DR-DOS has a year 2000 problem, but a free fix is available.

Different versions of GEOS have different problems ranging from minor year 2000 problems (with fixes in the works) to larger year 2080 problems (that do not have fixes yet). The only problem that may not have a fix in time is the year 2000 problem on the Apple][version of GEOS; not only was that version discontinued, unlike the other GEOS versions it no longer has a parent company to take care of it.

All MS-Windows versions (except possibly Windows 2000 and Windows ME) have multiple problems with the year 2000 and/or 2001, most of which have free fixes but some of which still lack free fixes as of this writing. Even new machines off the shelf that are labelled "Y2K Compliant" usually are not unless additional software is purchased and installed. Basically WinNT and WinCE can be properly patched, Windows '98 can be patched to work properly through 2000 (possibly not 2001), Windows '95 can be at least partially patched for 2000 (but not 2001) but is not being guaranteed by Microsoft, and Windows 3.1 cannot be fully patched.

MS-DOS has problems with at least the year 2000 (and probably more). None of its problems have been addressed as of this writing. Possible fixes are to change over to either PC-DOS or DR-DOS.

Results vary wildly for common applications, so it is better to be safe than sorry and check out the ones that you use. It should also be noted that some of the biggest expected Y2K problems will be at the two ends of the computer spectrum with older legacy mainframes (such as power some large banks) and some of the various tiny embedded computers (such as power most burglar alarms and many assorted appliances). Finally, it should also be mentioned that some older WinTel boxes and Amigas may have Y2K problems in their hardware requiring a card addition or replacement.

Z-Machine

A virtual machine optimized for running interactive fiction, interactive tutorials, and other interactive things of a primarily textual nature. Z-Machines have been ported to almost every platform in use today. Z-machine bytecode is usually called Z-code. The Glulx virtual machine is of the same idea but somewhat more modern in concept.

Z80

The Z80 series of processors is a CISC design and is not being used in too many new stand-alone computer systems, but can still be occasionally found in embedded systems. It is the most popular processor for CP/M machines.

Zaurus

The Zaurus is a brand of PDA. It is generally in between a Palm and a Newton in capability.

zip

There are three common zips in the computer world that are completely different from one another. One is a type of removable removable disk slightly larger (physically) and vastly larger (capacity) than a floppy. The second is a group of programs used for running interactive fiction. The third is a group of programs used for compression.

Zoomer

The Zoomer is a type of PDA. Zoomers all use GEOS for their OS and are / were produced by numerous different companies and are thus found under numerous different names. The "classic" Zoomers are known as the Z-7000, the Z-PDA, and the GRiDpad and were made by Casio, Tandy, and AST respectively. Newer Zoomers include HP's OmniGo models, Hyundai's Gulliver (which may not have actually been released to the general public), and Nokia's Communicator line of PDA / cell phone hybrids.

———